PERSECUTED FROM WITHIN

Joshua Charles and Alec Torres

PERSECUTED FROM WITHIN

How the Saints Endured Crises in the Church

SOPHIA INSTITUTE PRESS
Manchester, New Hampshire

To Our Lady

Contents

PERSECUTED FROM WITHIN

Introduction: When Shepherds Turn on the Flock

JESUS CHRIST PROMISES US persecution.

"There is no one who has left house or brothers or sisters or mother or father or children or lands, for my sake and for the gospel, who will not receive a hundredfold ... houses and brothers and sisters and mothers and children and lands, with persecutions — and in the age to come eternal life" (Mark 10:29–30).

All of the apostles except for St. John were martyred, and St. John only survived an attempted martyrdom miraculously. Nearly every Catholic in the New Testament ended up a martyr, as did every pope for the first 250 years of Catholicism. Baptism in the early Church was not only "baptism into the death of Christ" but also into one's own death (Rom. 6:3). But none of this should surprise us. Time and again, Scripture warns us that "a servant is not greater than his master" (e.g., John 13:16). Following Christ means suffering the same rejection He suffered and imitating Him who had "nowhere to lay his head" (Matt. 8:20).

If we have forgotten these truths, it is because recent generations have been able to live off the hard-won victories of previous ages. Even more likely, Catholics in the modern West neglect these truths because of the furtive creep of decadent comfort or the perennial temptation of lukewarmness.

Yet even if we recognize that trials are a necessary part of the Christian life, the most disturbing are not those imposed from outside the Church. The worst come from within. The lash of the ignorant and wicked centurion could not sting nearly so much as the kiss of Judas the Apostle. "Even my bosom friend in whom I trusted, who ate of my bread, has lifted his heel against me" (Ps. 41:9).

Committed Catholics may prepare themselves psychologically and spiritually to suffer at the hands of the state or in a rapidly secularizing culture. We are familiar with the stories of past martyrs who died under tyrants from Diocletian to Stalin. But is our faith strong enough to endure Judas?

Perhaps we are surprised to find Judas among the Twelve, sitting close enough to Christ that they can dip a morsel in the same dish. His presence provokes uncomfortable questions.

What are Christians to do when those who lead the Church are unwise, imprudent, or even downright wicked? Is the Church really the spotless Bride of Christ, when her miters are stained by sin, error, and division? How does Christ protect His sheep when shepherds appointed over them are sometimes the very ones leading their flocks astray? Perhaps most importantly for the Church Militant here on earth, how can we become the saints God has called us to be when bishops, cardinals, and even the pope seem to question the Magisterium or persecute faithful, orthodox Catholics precisely for their faithfulness and orthodoxy?

These are far from academic questions. Today, faithful Catholics who affirm and try to live by the hard teachings of Our Lord Jesus Christ frequently feel abandoned in the spiritual field of battle.

Worse, as the assaults of the world become more painful and severe, we see many of the leaders who were ordained to defend us instead turn and attack their own flock.

When the world shut down in the face of a global pandemic, faithful Catholics turned toward the light of the Church and the consolation of the sacraments. Many found their sanctuary doors locked. Even last rites — on which a soul's eternal salvation might well depend — were often denied to the dying out of fear of illness. While some brave priests did continue to feed their lambs, they often risked censure and punishment — not from the state, but from their very own bishops.

Such disregard for the value of spiritual things precedes the pandemic. Many Church leaders have long been more inclined to focus on political posturing and bureaucratic management than on boldly proclaiming the gospel. These finely coiffed and curated executives of a religiously themed NGO have overseen financial scandals, sexual impropriety, pedophilia, liturgical abuse, and cover-ups that have shaken the faith of Catholics across the globe.

The hierarchy's most prominent personalities generate confusion on fundamental doctrines related to issues like marriage, adultery, grace, and the worthy reception of Communion. In a Church beset with declining Mass attendance, disturbingly low levels of belief in the Real Presence of Christ in the Eucharist, and widespread apathy among Catholics living in open rejection of the Church's moral teaching — not to mention entire national churches on the verge of open schism — Rome nonetheless often treats those who are faithful to the full, historic Magisterium of the Church with the greatest harshness.

This has been a long-advancing crisis. In 1972, Paul VI decried the "autodemolition" of the Church, saying "the smoke of Satan has entered the sanctuary."[1] A year later, Our Lady of Akita warned Sr. Agnes Sasagawa in Japan that "the work of the devil will infiltrate even into the Church in such a way that one will see cardinals opposing cardinals, and bishops against other bishops."[2]

Our Lord Himself warned us in Scripture about wolves "in sheep's clothing" (Matt. 7:15) and of weeds among the wheat (Matt. 13:24–30). In fact, the reason we have most of the books of the New Testament is because apostles such as Sts. Paul, John, and Jude were sounding the alarm about widespread heresy, even among the clergy. As early as A.D. 51, St. Paul wrote about heretics in the Church, saying, "The mystery of lawlessness is already at work" (2 Thess. 2:7).

If we see the prophesies of Jesus Christ and the words of His apostles coming true, that is no reason to lose faith in Him. Rather, that should only increase our joy at the opportunity to be even more united with Christ in His suffering. "But rejoice in so far as you share Christ's sufferings, that you may also rejoice and be glad when his glory is revealed" (1 Pet. 4:13).

We do not suffer unexpectedly. Sin and persecution occur in all ages. That our suffering sometimes comes at the hands of our own spiritual fathers hurts most of all, but it should not shake our faith. And if the scale of apostasy and immorality seem great to us now, remember that it was in this hour that God chose us to live and work out our salvation (Jer. 1:5).

Even as we are comforted by the words of Christ, Peter, and Paul, we must still respond to the crisis within the Church. Yet no sooner do we resolve to confront this crisis than we face two temptations. The first is to leave the Church the way Protestants have. When the clergy are corrupt or wrong, give up hope that God can mend what is broken and reform what is wayward — and throw them off. Hang a shingle, start your own church, or join someone else's. Free yourself from the burden of unity and obedience that Christ demanded of His people.

But no true Catholic could even contemplate going this route. Ecclesiastical freelancing is completely unheard of in Sacred Scripture, both Old Testament and New. In fact, the only time it is mentioned, it is condemned: in the book of Numbers, God kills Korah and all his followers for attempting to start a new Israel. If we go into schism, we should expect our souls to meet the same fate. As faithful Catholics, we are neither schismatics nor Donatists — those who believe that the clergy must be without fault in order to be legitimate. We recognize that our clergy will never be perfect, and that their imperfections are never an excuse to break from the Church.

If our faith is shaken by bad Christians, then our faith is not in Christ but in men. We are not Catholics because we follow priests but because we follow Christ, who founded the Church and promised to be with her until the end of time. Heretical homilies, liturgical abuse, effeminacy among priests, weak leadership, financial and sexual sins, and even doctrinal error on the part of clergy must never be allowed to shake our faith. Instead, they are crosses for us to bear with Christ, challenges for us to confront as we fulfill our true identity as children of God.

Confronted by the temptation to abandon the Barque of Peter, we must keep firmly in mind that Jesus in His final priestly prayer before His Passion asked His Holy Father for unity: "Keep them in thy name, which thou hast given me; that they may be one, even as we are one" (John 17:11).

Just as there is but one Christ, there can only be one Body of Christ: one Church, having one faith, one Baptism, and one Lord.

Schism is clearly forbidden. But there is also a second and more insidious temptation in our times: to make no protest at all, silently submitting to the abuses of the hierarchy. By preying upon false notions of meekness and obedience, the enemy undermines the strength of the Church.

The *regula fidei* is Tradition and Scripture, which itself was born out of Tradition. Doctrine can develop, the way an acorn grows into an oak tree. But Tradition and Scripture never change. "Jesus Christ is the same yesterday and today and forever" (Heb. 13:8). We are to follow the bishops and popes, but never to sin and never to follow falsehood. True obedience is not blind.

Therefore, clergy are to be followed to the extent that they adhere to Sacred Tradition. When they lead us astray, it is not merely our right but our Catholic obligation to contradict, to resist, and to correct.

In fact, St. Thomas Aquinas taught that the faithful should shun wicked priests.[3] Our Lord Himself was betrayed by the very religious leaders whom He had appointed. His three-year ministry frequently involved contentions against priests, scholars of the law, and rabbis, the most devout of the day. His Passion was precipitated by the betrayal of an apostle.

Counter to the twin temptations of proud protest and false meekness, we have only one path to take. We must strive to become saints.

This book will tell the stories of some of the Church's greatest saints, particularly saints who were persecuted by the clergy. We will examine the lives of priests, bishops, laywomen, and two nuns, as well as Our Lord Himself, spanning two millennia and six continents. They are all exemplars of the words of Our Lord that we too must remember: "In the world you have tribulation; but be of good cheer, I have overcome the world" (John 16:33).

Only one holy soul in these pages has not been canonized (save Our Lord, of course), though the cause of his beatification is still advancing: Ven. Archbishop Fulton Sheen. When reflecting ever-so-briefly in his autobiography on his own suffering at the hands of a member of the hierarchy, Archbishop Sheen issued a word of warning those who would dwell on strife inside the Church:

> The curious would like me to open healed wounds; the media, in particular, would relish a chapter which would pass judgment on others.... As Euripides observed: "Silence is wisdom's first reply." Silence is recommended because any discussion of conflicts within the Church diminishes the content of the Christ — love within the Mystical Body — as the hand excessively rubbing the eye diminishes vision.[4]

Perhaps Archbishop Sheen would be skeptical of the very book you hold in your hands. It has been written, after all, to discuss conflicts within the Church. Yet the motives behind his silence and this book's stories are the same: to help souls to see Christ. Proudly nursing a grudge in his autobiography would have served nobody. On the other hand, refusing to acknowledge and understand internal conflicts with charitable and dispassionate eyes — particularly the predation of the hierarchy on those beneath them — can allow scandals to take root, bitterness to fester, and, in some cases, people to lose their faith. Furthermore, as conflicts in the Church are regularly described in the secular media from a secular and anti-Catholic perspective, it is important that Catholics explain the trials within our own Church from an orthodox and supernatural perspective.

This book was not written to reopen long closed wounds. Nor should any discourse on past transgressions be read as a condemnation of particular persons or authorities in our own times. Concerning those who are in error or have abused their authority, we look to the saints in these pages as our guides, praying as many of them did that those who harm us would be reconciled to God and welcomed into Heaven. Our purpose is not to judge, but to illuminate.

To that end, let us turn like the saints with everlasting faith and confidence to our Father in heaven and to our mother, the Blessed Virgin Mary. Through their protection and mercy, the Church will be purified.

We know already that Christ will be victorious. He has given us His promise. The question is: Will we be with Him when His final victory comes? Only we can decide the answer.

CHAPTER 1

Our Lord Jesus Christ — The King of Betrayed Saints

OUR LORD JESUS CHRIST is never referred to as a "saint." Rather, He is the King of saints. In Him, the saints who have been "persecuted from within" find their highest example: the suffering servant, the crucified Messiah, the Son of the Father rejected by His own who He came to save.

Jesus was the victim of history's greatest betrayals — by Judas, as well as by many of His own beloved people — and at their hands He endured unimaginable torment and suffering. But all the while, He prayed through blood-soaked sweat in the Garden of Gethsemane, "Father, if thou art willing, remove this cup from me; nevertheless not my will, but thine, be done" (Luke 22:42).

What makes Christ's example all the more compelling to those persecuted from within is that His entire purpose was to come and suffer at the hands of those He came to save. This had long ago been prophesied by the saints of the Old Testament.

"The stone which the builders rejected has become the head of the corner. This is the Lord's doing; it is marvelous in our eyes," declared the Psalms (118:22–23), words Jesus would repeat in reference to Himself.

Likewise, in Isaiah's famous prophecy, the suffering Messiah is subjected to injustice for the sake of achieving His salvific mission:

> He was oppressed, and he was afflicted,
> yet he opened not his mouth;
> like a lamb that is led to the slaughter,
> and like a sheep that before its shearers is dumb,
> so he opened not his mouth. (Isa. 53:7–9)

The book of Wisdom[i] also contains a similar prophecy of the "righteous man" who would be hated, opposed, and eventually killed by his enemies:

> Let us lie in wait for the righteous man,
> because he is inconvenient to us and opposes our actions;
> he reproaches us for sins against the law,
> and accuses us of sins against our training.
> He professes to have knowledge of God,
> and calls himself a child of the Lord.
> He became to us a reproof of our thoughts;
> the very sight of him is a burden to us,
> because his manner of life is unlike that of others,
> and his ways are strange.
> We are considered by him as something base,
> and he avoids our ways as unclean;
> he calls the last end of the righteous happy,
> and boasts that God is his father.
> Let us see if his words are true,
> and let us test what will happen at the end of his life;

---

[i]   Ironically, the book of Wisdom is rejected by Protestants, who had themselves rejected the Church.

> for if the righteous man is God's son, he will help him,
> and will deliver him from the hand of his adversaries.
> Let us test him with insult and torture,
> that we may find out how gentle he is,
> and make trial of his forbearance.
> Let us condemn him to a shameful death,
> for, according to what he says, he will be protected.
> (Wisd. 2:12–20)

From almost the beginning of His public ministry, Jesus suffered attacks from Jewish leaders, especially as the true nature of His claim to be God's Son — and thus God Himself — became clear. Jesus likewise warned His disciples many times that He would be betrayed and killed. Countless pages have been written on every aspect of Christ's Passion. But for our purposes, we shall focus on three fundamental features of Christ's suffering that can guide all those who likewise suffer persecution from within: the eucharistic element of Christ's betrayal; His willing endurance of the greatest miscarriage of justice in history; and the seemingly foolish ("to those who are perishing") but salvific nature of His decision to endure it.

The Eucharistic Nature of Betrayal

Christ's "persecution from within" began with the Eucharist, when Jesus explained to His disciples that His flesh was true food and His blood true drink. It was at this moment that St. John specifically identified Judas as His betrayer:

> Many of his disciples, when they heard it, said, "This is a hard saying; who can listen to it?" But Jesus, knowing in himself that his disciples murmured at it, said to them, "Do you take offense at this? Then what if you were to see the Son of man ascending where he was before? It is the spirit that gives life, the flesh is of no avail; the words that I have spoken to you are spirit and life. But there are some of you

that do not believe." For Jesus knew from the first who those were that did not believe, and who it was that should betray him. And he said, "This is why I told you that no one can come to me unless it is granted him by the Father."

After this many of his disciples drew back and no longer went about with him. Jesus said to the twelve, "Will you also go away?" Simon Peter answered him, "Lord, to whom shall we go? You have the words of eternal life; and we have believed, and have come to know, that you are the Holy One of God." Jesus answered them, "Did I not choose you, the twelve, and one of you is a devil?" He spoke of Judas the son of Simon Iscariot, for he, one of the twelve, was to betray him. (John 6:60–71)

Indeed, at His final Passover at which He instituted the sacrifice of the Holy Eucharist, Jesus quietly informed St. John of how He would identify His betrayer — by the Eucharist:

When Jesus had thus spoken, he was troubled in spirit, and testified, "Truly, truly, I say to you, one of you will betray me." The disciples looked at one another, uncertain of whom he spoke. One of his disciples, whom Jesus loved, was lying close to the breast of Jesus; so Simon Peter beckoned to him and said, "Tell us who it is of whom he speaks." So lying thus, close to the breast of Jesus, he said to him, "Lord, who is it?" Jesus answered, "It is he to whom I shall give this morsel when I have dipped it." So when he had dipped the morsel, he gave it to Judas, the son of Simon Iscariot. Then after the morsel, Satan entered into him. Jesus said to him, "What you are going to do, do quickly." (John 13:27)

By his unworthy reception of the Holy Eucharist, in which he did not believe, Judas sealed his fate. "For anyone who eats and drinks without discerning the body," warned St. Paul, "eats and drinks judgment upon himself" (1 Cor. 11:29). Judas's judgment was God allowing him to be possessed by Satan. By his treachery, Judas transformed Our Lord's greatest gift to His people into the instrument of his own destruction. But he would maintain the façade until the end, identifying Jesus to the soldiers who came to arrest Him in the Garden of Gethsemane with a kiss, a sign of friendship.

Likewise, every betrayal from within in some sense involves the Eucharist — either preventing one's own worthy reception of it, or its worthy reception by others. It always ends in sacrilege, the crucifying of Christ among His own people, or the apostasy of former followers, as Christ Himself experienced after delivering the teaching on His Real Presence in the Eucharist: "After this many of his disciples drew back and no longer went about with him" (John 6:66, in a seemingly providential chapter and verse number).

False brethren within the Church always attempt to destroy the Eucharist, the liturgy that ornaments it, and the souls it was meant to feed and nourish. One's posture toward the Eucharist is, as was the case with Judas, the ultimate window into one's soul. Since the Eucharist is the "source and summit" of the Church's life, to be persecuted from within has, from the beginning, always been eucharistic in its implications and consequences. But as Christ warned, "Temptations to sin are sure to come; but woe to him by whom they come! It would be better for him if a millstone were hung round his neck and he were cast into the sea, than that he should cause one of these little ones to sin" (Luke 17:1–2).

A Miscarriage of Justice

The Pharisees and their allies were prepared to go to great lengths to achieve their goal of killing Jesus — even violating the very Torah by which they claimed to condemn Him. Early on, they sought to seize Him without any judicial procedure whatsoever, though Nicodemus rebuked them saying, "Does our law judge a man without first giving him a hearing and learning what he does?" (John 7:51).

When the time came to arrest Jesus in Gethsemane, there was still no testimony against Him. But even then, Christ acknowledged that this was their hour to do what they willed:

> Then Jesus said to the chief priests and captains of the temple and elders, who had come out against him, "Have you come out as against a robber, with swords and clubs? When I was with you day after day in the temple, you did not lay hands on me. But this is your hour, and the power of darkness." (Luke 22:52–53)

Christ would then suffer the greatest miscarriage of justice in history, at the hands of both the spiritual (the Sanhedrin) and temporal (the Romans) powers of His day. When Jesus was brought before the Sanhedrin, those seeking to condemn Him still lacked evidence; indeed, they were still attempting to procure false testimony. Nevertheless, Jesus remained silent in the face of their efforts — though when the time came, He clearly identified Himself as the Messiah prophesied by Daniel, and he chose to suffer contempt, slander, and mocking as a result:

> Now the chief priests and the whole council sought false testimony against Jesus that they might put him to death, but they found none, though many false witnesses came forward. At last two came forward and said, "This fellow said, 'I am able to destroy the temple of God, and to build it in three days.'" And the high priest stood up and said, "Have you no answer to make? What is it that these men testify against you?" But Jesus was silent. And the high priest said to him, "I adjure you by the living God, tell us if you are the Christ, the Son of God." Jesus said to him, "You have said so. But I tell you, hereafter you will see the Son of man seated at the right hand of Power, and coming on the clouds of heaven." Then the high priest tore his robes, and said, "He has uttered blasphemy. Why do we still need witnesses? You have now heard his blasphemy. What is your judgment?" They answered,

> "He deserves death." Then they spat in his face, and struck
> him; and some slapped him, saying, "Prophesy to us, you
> Christ! Who is it that struck you?" (Matt. 26:59–68)

When Jesus was sent to Herod, He chose again to remain silent; and
He remained silent again when he was finally before Pontius Pilate,
the man who actually possessed the power to execute Him — except
when it came to Pilate questioning Him about His being a king:

> Pilate said to him, "So you are a king?" Jesus answered,
> "You say that I am a king. For this I was born, and for this
> I have come into the world, to bear witness to the truth.
> Everyone who is of the truth hears my voice." Pilate said
> to him, "What is truth?" (John 18:37–38)

Pilate, like the Jews, was convinced that the power of the situation
was in his own hands. But Christ reminded him that his authority
over Christ's life had been given to him by God Himself:

> When Pilate heard these words, he was the more afraid; he
> entered the praetorium again and said to Jesus, "Where are
> you from?" But Jesus gave no answer. Pilate therefore said
> to him, "You will not speak to me? Do you not know that I
> have power to release you, and power to crucify you?" Jesus
> answered him, "You would have no power over me unless it
> had been given you from above; therefore he who delivered
> me to you has the greater sin." (John 19:8–11)

Christ's actions in front of the chief priests, Herod, and Pilate evince an
otherworldly meekness. He did not flinch from telling the truth. But neither
did He engage in a loquacious defense, insisting on His innocence or
decrying His predicament. He could have saved Himself, but He refused
and chose to be nailed to a cross between two criminals and suffer the
mockery of His own people. And yet, fully aware of what they intended
and would indeed succeed at doing, this same quiet Lamb had commanded

His disciples to submit to their lawful authority: "Then said Jesus to the crowds and to his disciples, 'The scribes and the Pharisees sit on Moses' seat; so practice and observe whatever they tell you, but not what they do; for they preach, but do not practice'" (Matt. 23:1–3).

The Foolishness of God to Be Persecuted from Within

Christ chose to permit His persecution from within. He allowed Himself to be betrayed by one of His own apostles, tormented by the machinations of His own people, condemned by the cowardice of those temporal rulers God Himself allowed to crucify Him — precisely because it hurt most of all. The Passion of Our Lord, the very means by which God saved the world, was in fact an inside job. It was the greatest betrayal, the greatest crime in history, made into the means of our salvation.

Christ warned the apostles that they would endure a similar persecution as He: "Remember the word that I said to you, 'A servant is not greater than his master.' If they persecuted me, they will persecute you; if they kept my word, they will keep yours also" (John 15:20).

In fact, the Scriptures are replete with warnings from both Jesus and the apostles that wolves in sheep's clothing would constantly bedevil the Church. The Church consists of both wheat and chaff, of sheep and goats, of lambs and wolves, of clean and unclean. As St. Augustine warned new converts received at Easter Vigil nearly two millennia ago:

> Therefore, because you have become members of Christ, I warn you; I fear for you, not so much from the pagans, nor so much from the Jews, nor so much from the heretics, as from the bad Catholics. Choose for yourselves those whom you may imitate among the people of God. For, if you wish to imitate the crowd, you will not tread the narrow path in the company of the few.[5]

But what is to be done? We are to follow God's will and endure the sufferings in a manner that glorifies Him. As Our Lord Himself rhetorically asked as He approached the cusp of His Passion, "Now is my soul troubled. And what shall I say? 'Father, save me from this hour'? No, for this purpose I have come to this hour. Father, glorify thy name" (John 12:27–28).

After all, when St. Peter raised his sword to defend Christ against His persecutors, Our Lord scolded him: "Then Jesus said to him, 'Put your sword back into its place; for all who take the sword will perish by the sword. Do you think that I cannot appeal to my Father, and he will at once send me more than twelve legions of angels? But how then should the scriptures be fulfilled, that it must be so?'" (Matt. 26:52–54).

The sovereign God, in whose hands rest all things, who retained the power to save Himself from suffering, from persecution by His own, and yet refused to do so.

Thus, every would-be saint being persecuted from within has always borne a similar disposition as Christ Himself — an unflinching devotion to truth, combined with an abandonment of self-will, even in the face of injustice. Like Our Lord, they bear their sufferings, refusing to inflict injustice in exchange for injustice. They live St. Peter's admonition: "Do not return evil for evil or reviling for reviling; but on the contrary bless, for to this you have been called, that you may obtain a blessing" (1 Pet. 3:9). They commend themselves to Divine Providence, always confident that "no eye has seen, nor ear heard, nor the heart of man conceived, what God has prepared for those who love him" (1 Cor. 2:9).

In doing so, each persecuted saint willingly accepts what St. Paul calls the "mystery" of the Passion. This mystery, the Apostle says, appears as foolishness to the outside world — but this apparent "foolishness of God" is in fact the highest and greatest wisdom:

Where is the wise man? Where is the scribe? Where is the debater of this age? Has not God made foolish the wisdom of the world? For since, in the wisdom of God, the world did not know God through wisdom, it pleased God through the folly of what we preach to save those who believe. For Jews demand signs and Greeks seek wisdom, but we preach Christ crucified, a stumbling block to Jews and folly to Gentiles, but to those who are called, both Jews and Greeks, Christ the power of God and the wisdom of God. For the foolishness of God is wiser than men, and the weakness of God is stronger than men. (1 Cor. 1:20–25)

No doubt those who have experienced persecution within the Church and choose to remain likewise appear foolish in the eyes of many. What earthly explanation can there be for such a choice?

The answer is simple: none. As Christ's decision to come and die on behalf of His beloved can be explained by no earthly rationale, likewise the aspiring saint who refuses to abandon His Church when faced by similar persecution from within must maintain a supernatural perspective. It is only foolishness "to those who are perishing" (1 Cor. 1:18). To those who are conformed to Christ, it is a source of awe, as it is even to the angels. Choosing to live out this mystery is, as the character of St. Thomas More observed in the play *A Man for All Seasons*, ultimately "a matter of love," a choice made while "we see in a mirror dimly" (1 Cor. 13:12), confident nonetheless that "when the perfect comes, the imperfect will pass away" (1 Cor. 13:10).

Such saints, and those who aspire to be like them, mortify their own wills, and with Christ embrace the foolishness of God.

CHAPTER 2

St. Paul the Persecutor
and Persecuted

FROM THE WORLD'S PERSPECTIVE, Saul of Tarsus seems an especially unlikely champion of Our Lord's gospel. He was a man who, by his own admission, blasphemed, persecuted, and insulted Jesus (1 Tim. 1:13), a man who consented to the murder of the first martyr of the Church, St. Stephen (Acts 8:1), and a man who dragged Christian men and women out of their homes and threw them into prison (Acts 8:3). The Acts of the Apostles reveal that Saul "made havoc" or "laid waste" to the Church (the original Greek denotes the act of an animal ravaging a field or a king authorizing terrible cruelties).[6]

Early Christians feared him, and with good reason. He was intelligent, merciless, passionate, and effective. But as Saul pursued the followers of Christ, chasing them down to Damascus so he could bring them back bound to Jerusalem (Acts 9:2), God was waiting for him. The story of his conversion is no less remarkable because it is well known. On the road, there was a flash of light. Saul fell to the ground, and Jesus, identifying Himself as one with every faithful

Christian who suffers abuse and evil for His name's sake, said, "Saul, Saul, why do you persecute me?... I am Jesus whom you are persecuting" (Acts 9:4–5) Saul's rage against the Church cut to the heart of God Himself, and from that wound mercy poured out — a mercy so profound that Saul was elevated from persecutor to apostle.

Saul arose from his vision blind but changed. His outward sight was lost, but his spiritual sight was finally awakened. For three days he fasted without food or drink. Saul had undoubtedly heard the apostles speak in Jerusalem before chasing them down to Damascus. He knew who followers of Christ were and what they preached, or else he would not have been so enraged by it. He had time to be convinced. Yet, until that encounter with Jesus, nothing changed his mind.

Thus, Saul was not won over by logic or commitment to a moral system. It wasn't preaching or kindness or ecumenism that finally turned him from the vain traditions of his fathers. As with all converted sinners, it was only a personal encounter with Christ Himself that could soften Saul's heart and bring him to repentance. Saul's conversation with Jesus was more tangible and awe-inspiring than most conversion stories. But the miracle of grace worked in his heart was the same as that which inspires any person to let go of his hatred, his self-love, and his tepidity, and fasten on the yoke of Christ.

From that moment on, Paul's life (he had changed his name to *Paulos*, that is, "little" or "of no importance") was a continual testament to the power of Christ to transform enemies into brothers. Grace is made perfect in weakness, and the foolishness of God is wiser than the wisdom of men. It was precisely the unlikelihood of Paul's conversion that made it all the more fitting. Jesus had preached that we were to love our enemies and pray for those who persecute us. When He had ascended and was not there to verbally remind his disciples of His teachings, they must have felt the temptation to anger and vengeance as they watched Paul strip away from them their friends, family members, and fellow disciples, condemning them to suffer in prison or even to face death.

Loving in fact — in those circumstances — is much harder to bear than loving one's enemy in theory. God chose Paul not only to be an instrument of His will, but also to be a sign to all generations of the power of His mercy, mercy that His disciples must imitate. That is why even the worst evildoer on earth should not be hated, because God has the power to turn a persecutor into a brother. As Paul would later write to the Corinthians, "Do not pronounce judgment before the time, before the Lord comes, who will bring to light the things now hidden in darkness and will disclose the purposes of the heart" (1 Cor. 4:5). Judging an enemy too quickly may serve only to condemn a future friend.

Paul's conversion marked a nearly immediate role reversal. Humbled and sightless, the man who led the charge against the early Church had to be led by his companions to Damascus by hand. At first, friend and foe alike were shocked. When Ananias, a Christian in Damascus, was told by Jesus in a vision to lay his hands on Paul to help Paul regain his sight, he didn't say no. Yet he spoke almost as if he wanted to be sure that Our Lord was talking about the right person. "Lord, I have heard from many about this man," Ananias said, "how much evil he has done to thy saints at Jerusalem; and here he has authority from the chief priests to bind all who call upon thy name" (Acts 9:13–14).

Jesus answered that He had conquered Paul's past. Responding to Ananias, He said, "Go, for he is a chosen instrument of mine to carry my name before the Gentiles and kings and the sons of Israel; for I will show him how much he must suffer for the sake of my name" (Acts 9:15–16). Ananias obeyed the Lord, laid his hands upon Paul, and the scales fell from his eyes (Acts 9:18) like the removal of the blindness of Tobit (Tob. 11:13–15).

Paul then underwent a profound inversion of roles: he who had made others suffer was marked for suffering himself. Within days Paul exhibited his new identity in Christ by proclaiming Jesus in the synagogue in Damascus. Soon after, the Jews in that city plotted to kill him (Acts 9:20–23). It was a scene that would be repeated again and again across the Roman Empire. Like Christ, Paul was targeted by his own nation. Five times he received thirty-nine lashes. He was beaten with rods, stoned, and was shipwrecked three times. Hungry, thirsty, cold, naked, imprisoned (2 Cor. 11:24–27), Paul was a living refutation of the lies of the "prosperity gospel," which promises a life of peace and wealth free from hardship.

Paul felt the pain of rejection — especially by Jews — profoundly. He wrote and spoke frequently about how his mission was to preach first to the Jews, the Chosen People of God, before converting the Gentiles (Acts 13:46). However, despite Paul's illumination of the law and the prophets along with the testimony of his life of sacrifice for Christ, relatively few of his fellow Hebrews responded to his call. The Jews who rejected Christ remained Paul's most ardent adversaries throughout his missions. His reception among the Gentiles was sometimes warmer, yet many Gentiles were likewise repulsed by his presence. He was beaten and imprisoned by Gentiles in Philippi (Acts 16:19–24), faced a riot of pagans in Ephesus (Acts 19:21–41), and languished in prison for years under the Romans (Acts 24:27).

Like so many of us, Paul frequently found in the Church a place of refuge. He had brothers and companions at his side, such as Timothy and Barnabas, and fledgling churches from Asia Minor to Greece and Macedonia to the Italian peninsula looked to him as a spiritual father. He was respected, beloved, and held in the highest esteem. But Heaven does not exist on earth: even within the Church, a cross was waiting for him.

A Cross for Paul, Carved by James

Many idealize the early Church as a time of profound spiritual gifts, rapid growth, and godly charity. After Pentecost, the Spirit reveals that the disciples of Jesus sold all their possessions, holding all things in common and distributing to all who had need while gathering in fellowship and the breaking of bread (Acts 2:44–47). It is true that the early Church was blessed with an abundance of healings, miracles, and wholehearted devotion to the teachings of Christ among many followers of the Way. But there is also evidence of gross immorality, such as when Paul excommunicated a man in the Corinthian church who committed incest (1 Cor. 5:1–2), as well as heresy, a subject that Paul discussed extensively, such as when he wrote that "the mystery of lawlessness is already at work" (2 Thess. 2:7).

Baptism wipes away Original Sin (John 3:5), but it does not erase concupiscence, man's proclivity to sin. Salvation is not completed at initial conversion. It requires perseverance in sanctification through the consistent application of our will and exercise of our works to correspond to God's grace. Until our death, when our final decision for good or evil is irrevocably made, we remain free to fall away from grace. The grace of Baptism and Confirmation, and the continual working of the Holy Spirit, give every Christian the strength to choose good. But the choice is ours to make. Thus, it was inevitable that Paul would face trials at the hands not just of Jews and pagans, but from his fellow Christians as well.

Paul's trials within the Church stemmed from a fierce internal debate over whether or not Christians must follow the Jewish law. A faction called the Judaizers claimed that in order to be saved, followers of Jesus should adhere to the Jewish law and be circumcised according to the customs of Moses (Acts 15:5). Paul — though he was educated as a Pharisee and had observed the Jewish law in the strictest fashion all of his life (Acts 22:3) — vehemently disagreed.

This wasn't some technical debate over customs or devotional practices. At its root, the disagreement struck at the heart of the nature of salvation and Christ's infinite sacrifice on the Cross. As Paul wrote in his Letter to the Galatians, "I testify again to every man who receives circumcision that he is bound to keep the whole law. You are severed from Christ, you who would be justified by the law; you have fallen away from grace.... For in Christ Jesus neither circumcision nor uncircumcision is of any avail, but faith working through love" (Gal. 5:3–4, 6). Or, as he wrote to the Romans, "Real circumcision is a matter of the heart, spiritual and not literal" (Rom. 2:29). The law without Christ yields death, and Christ did not need the law to bring life.

That is not to say the law is worthless or rejected. Rather, Jesus fulfilled the law by leading us to the law's true goal: love of God and love of neighbor as ourselves. The minutiae of the Jewish law had their time and purpose, and these had been fulfilled. As Paul wrote to the Galatians, "Now before faith came, we were confined under the law, kept under restraint until faith should be revealed. So that the law was our custodian until Christ came, that we might be justified by faith. But now that faith has come, we are no longer under a custodian" (Gal. 3:23–25). The law was like a tutor to the infantile human race, slowly preparing us through the chosen Jewish people for the fullness of the truth in Christ. In a way, the Judaizer's love of the law was understandable. The law had been fitting before Christ, and Christ Himself perfectly followed every precept of the law. But after Jesus' sacrifice on Calvary, everything changed.

Now that the fullness of the truth has come, we are free to live out the true purpose of the law in faith, hope, and charity. But by continuing to demand adherence to the 613 commandments of the Jewish law, the Judaizers ultimately rejected the power of Christ's sacrifice. They attempt to gain salvation through the works of the law, but "man is not justified by works of the law but through faith in Jesus Christ," as Paul wrote (Gal. 2:16). Those who preached justification through the law missed the point of Jesus' agony, death, and Resurrection — and they steered others away from the truth of the gospel, putting souls at risk.

To resolve this contention, the apostles convened the first council in Church history, the Council of Jerusalem (Acts 15:6). After heated debate, Peter himself, chief of the apostles and the first pope, rose up to settle the matter. "Why do you make trial of God by putting a yoke upon the neck of the disciples," Peter said to the Judaizers, "which neither our fathers nor we have been able to bear? But we believe that we shall be saved through the grace of the Lord Jesus, just as they will" (Acts 15:10–11). The pronouncement seemed definitive. Word was sent out to the churches to address some of the concerns of the Judaizers while making it clear that Gentiles did not have to follow the Jewish law.

The letter sent out after the council by the leaders of the Church not only confirmed moral absolutes but also offered more prudential, pastoral decrees to manage ethnic tensions. For example, the decree on chastity concerning the moral law applies to all people at all times. But the decrees on food — refraining from eating meat from animals sacrificed to idols — were more prudential, helping Christians to avoid the scandal of appearing to accept idol worship.[i] Nevertheless, the leaders of the Church definitively decided that the Gentiles did not have to obey the Jewish ceremonial law.

Like the Church's most recent council, major provisions in the Council of Jerusalem[ii] were not dogmatic and were designed to address pastoral concerns of divided ministers and laity. Yet, also like the Church's most recent council, long after the official documents were issued by ecclesial authorities dissension remained. When Paul returned to Jerusalem at the end of his third missionary journey, Church authorities attempted to manage the dissension in a way that put Paul at grave risk.[7]

When Paul arrived in the city, he was welcomed by James the Greater, one of the original twelve apostles and the bishop of Jerusalem. While the leaders in Jerusalem rejoiced at the abundant success Paul and his companions had had among the Gentiles of Antioch,

---

[i]   The Council of Florence in 1422 made clear that the food restrictions were meant for this particular ethnic division in the early Church.

[ii] Note that while the Council of Jerusalem was the first gathering of the bishops of the Church, it was not the first ecumenical council. That distinction belongs to the Council of Nicaea in 325.

Ephesus, Philippi, Thessalonica, Corinth, and elsewhere throughout the Greek-speaking world (Acts 21:19–20), the concerns of the Judaizers remained at the top of their minds.

In fact, immediately after glorifying God for Paul's work, James and the elders changed their tone: "You see, brother, how many thousands there are among the Jews of those have believed; they are all zealous for the law," they told Paul. "And they have been told about you that you teach all the Jews who are among the Gentiles to forsake Moses, telling them not to circumcise their children or observe the customs" (Acts 21:20–21). Apparently the Judaizers had accepted that the Gentiles need not follow Jewish customs in order to be saved, but they persisted in demanding that those of Jewish lineage follow the law, which was allowed at this time but not required.[iii]

The Judaizers' concerns over rumors that Paul was preaching salvation without circumcision could have served as a teaching moment, a time for the Church leadership in Jerusalem to assert the universal power of Christ's redemptive sacrifice. Instead, St. James and the elders were perhaps understandably worried about keeping peace within their community and the risk of enraging Jewish Christians. They wondered what they should do with Paul, since the Judaizers would certainly learn that he had arrived in Jerusalem and cause an uproar (Acts 21:22–23).

"Do therefore what we tell you," they said to Paul. "We have four men who are under a vow; take these men and purify yourself along with them and pay their expenses, so that they may shave their heads. Thus all will know that there is nothing in what they have been told about you but that you yourself live in observance of the law" (Acts 21:23–24). In effect, they used their position of authority to pressure

---

[iii] While it is true that the letter sent out from the Council of Jerusalem was addressed to the Gentiles, the theological principles expounded by Paul applied to Jewish and Gentile Christians alike. No matter our backgrounds, we are saved by our faith in Jesus and our response to the grace of God — not by the works of the law.

Paul to pay for four men to take a Nazarite vow and ritually purify themselves in the Temple, demonstrating their fidelity to the Jewish law.[iv]

This was no minor request to quell the fears of an easily enraged minority, as it would very likely expose Paul in the Temple and put him at grave risk. Jews across the Roman Empire had threatened Paul; they had chased him out of Antioch (Acts 9:23), attempted to kill him in Jerusalem (Acts 9:26–31), incited persecution against him in Antioch of Pisidia (Acts 13:50), and attempted to stone him in Iconium (Acts 14:5). Before he had departed for Jerusalem, while he was still in Ephesus, Paul told the Christians there that "I am going to Jerusalem, bound in the Spirit, not knowing what shall befall me there; except that the Holy Spirit testifies to me in every city that imprisonment and afflictions await me" (Acts 20:22–23).

His fears were soon confirmed when, shortly before arriving in the Holy City, a prophet named Agabus took Paul's belt and tied up his feet and hands to symbolize that the Jews in Jerusalem would bind Paul and deliver him to the Gentiles, just as they had done to Christ (Acts 21:10–11).

When St. James and the elders of the Jerusalem church instructed Paul to go to the Temple, they were setting the stage for this prophesy to be fulfilled. St. James must have known that he was putting Paul's life in danger. But even if he was unaware, Paul knew that fulfilling the charge of one of Jesus' twelve closest companions in His earthly life would yield persecution, pain, and imprisonment. Paul faced a grave choice: Resist or obey?

He obeyed. The words of the Acts of the Apostles are matter of fact. James and the elders finished speaking, "then Paul took the men, and the next day he purified himself with them and went into the temple" (Acts 21:26). Acts reports that Paul issued no warnings, no expressions of fear, and no prudential concerns about how the

---

[iv] The vow is described in Numbers 6:1–21.

Jews might respond to the preeminent traitor to their cause appearing publicly in Jerusalem once again.

Paul's Submission to the Hierarchy

This was not the first time that Paul had submitted to the authority of his fellow apostles. During one of Paul's visits to Jerusalem, he presented the gospel he was preaching to the senior apostles in the city, "lest somehow I should be running or had run in vain" (Gal. 2:2). While Paul had received instruction in the Faith directly from Jesus Himself (Gal. 1:12), he recognized that the Holy Trinity operates through the means of the Church, the hierarchy that Jesus Himself had erected.[v] Likewise, when Paul and Barnabas contested with Judaizers in Antioch over circumcision, Paul didn't assert authority because of his private revelation from Jesus or his superior interpretation of the Scriptures;[vi] rather the local church deferred to the apostles and Church leadership in Jerusalem to decide on the matter (Acts 15:1–2).

Just as Paul submitted his revelation of the gospel to the apostles, now in Jerusalem again, Paul sacrificed his safety to fulfill what James and the elders asked of him. He ritually purified himself, paid for the men to fulfill their vow, and appeared in the Temple. When the seven days of the Nazarite vow were coming to a close, "the Jews from Asia,

---

[v] Christ chose that His gospel would be spread and mediated through men. When He ascended into Heaven, He commissioned His disciples to bring His earthly work to completion. As such, even Paul's reception of a direct revelation from Jesus did not supersede the authority of the apostles, for before Paul ever penned his letters or the four evangelists ever wrote their Gospels, there was the Church. As Paul wrote to the Ephesians, it was the divine plan "that *through the church* the manifold wisdom of God might now be made known to the principalities and powers in the heavenly places" (3:9–10, emphasis added) — the Church that Paul elsewhere declared is "the pillar and bulwark of the truth" (1 Tim. 3:15).

[vi] Of course, what we call the Bible didn't exist as a single, agreed-upon collection of books until the Catholic Church promulgated the seventy-three-book canon at the Council of Rome in 382.

who had seen [Paul] in the temple, stirred up all the crowd, and laid hands on him" (Acts 21:27).

The uproar was immediate and deafening. People grabbed hold of Paul and dragged him out of the Temple. They began to beat him, intending to kill him, until the Roman authorities swiftly marched in, pushed through the mob, and took Paul into custody, binding him in chains (Acts 21:30–33). The Roman tribune then kept Paul in custody while he attempted to discover what had caused the commotion (22:22 and following). Paul was so vehemently hated and the outcry against him was so violent that the tribune sent Paul to Caesarea, escorted by an astonishing two hundred soldiers, two hundred spearmen, and seventy horsemen (23:23). Ultimately, Paul spent over two years in prison in Caesarea before enduring a harrowing journey, as a captive, to Rome (24:27; 27 — 28).

Withstanding the Pope to His Face

What lesson does Paul teach us? Are we to blindly submit to every troubling decision made by the leaders of our Church? Is the answer always to simply obey? After all, Paul did write, "Let every person be subject to the governing authorities. For there is no authority except from God, and those that exist have been instituted by God. Therefore he who resists the authorities resists what God has appointed, and those who resist will incur judgment" (Rom. 13:1–2).

Paul seemed to confirm a literal reading of this verse with his actions. He silently exposed himself to violence and persecution to fulfill the will of James and the elders in Jerusalem — even as their instructions were calculated to mollify a group that had been Paul's biggest adversaries within the Church. Furthermore, Paul showed no bitterness toward his opponents despite circumstances fraught with peril.

Nevertheless, Paul was no blind follower, and his Letter to the Romans cannot be read in isolation but must be seen in light of his other words and actions. In another circumstance, Paul boldly opposed his superiors when it was necessary to uphold correct doctrine: he rebuked the chief of the apostles, St. Peter himself, publicly and to his face — the clearest proof in Scripture that even the highest ecclesial authority is not above contradiction or criticism and that obedience to earthly authorities is always subject to obedience to a higher authority in Heaven.

The controversy between Peter and Paul concerned the same issue that incensed the Judaizers. During the Council of Jerusalem, Peter had proclaimed that there was "no distinction" between Jewish or Gentile believers and condemned the idea of imposing the Jewish law upon the Gentiles (Acts 15:9–10). Yet sometime later, Peter undermined his words with his actions and gave the impression of endorsing the doctrines of the Judaizers: when Judaizers aligned with James confronted Peter about his habit of eating with Gentiles — an act that violated Jewish customs that condemned social contact and shared meals between Jews and non-Jews[8] — Peter backed down (Gal. 2:12). He separated himself from the Gentiles and treated them like second-class citizens.

Not only was this deeply insulting to members of the Church, but it also implied that the pope himself still believed that the Law had some saving power beyond Christ's sacrifice. Such public confusion risked steering people away from the truth of the gospel, and thus from eternal life. The stakes of Peter's fainthearted refusal to eat with his Gentile brothers couldn't have been higher.

Paul reacted with righteous anger, and, as he wrote in his Letter to the Galatians, withstood Peter to his face in the form of a question, or a *dubium* (2:11). "If you, though a Jew, live like a Gentile and not like a Jew, how can you compel the Gentiles to live like a Jew?" (2:14). Paul's question noted that Peter had already dropped many Jewish customs while living out his Christian Faith. Peter knew the truth that we are justified by faith in Christ, not by works of the Law. His public betrayal of the Council of Jerusalem required a public correction. That the Holy Spirit ensured this scene was recorded in the Scriptures proves that God desired all to know that even the pope is not above correction.

However, we should not read into Paul's rebuke any bitterness, disrespect, or pride. Paul makes it clear in an epistle that the servant of the Lord must be "kindly to every one … forbearing, correcting his opponents with gentleness. God may perhaps grant that they will repent and come to know the truth" (2 Tim. 2:24–25). The goal is not just to proclaim the truth, but to do so in a way that helps those who are wrong so that "they may escape from the snare of the devil, after being captured by him to do his will" (2 Tim. 2:26). Despite his challenge to Peter, Paul still fulfilled what he wrote to the church in Ephesus: "Let no evil talk come out of your mouths, but only such as is good for edifying, as fits the occasion, that it may impart grace to those who hear" (Eph. 4:29). Sometimes grace is delivered by telling others that they are wrong.

Internal Consistency

Yet even so, Paul's responses can seem contradictory and provoke the question, Why did he submit to James but rebuke Peter? The confusion is compounded when we read of other events in Paul's ministry. For example, he frequently preached against the power of circumcision, yet when Paul first met his close companion Timothy, the son of a Gentile father and a Jewish mother, he took Timothy to be circumcised in order to avoid conflict with the Jews (Acts 16:3). Or again, Paul was willing to rebuke the Christian pope, but when he stood before the Jewish council after being arrested in the Temple while helping the four men take their Nazarite vow, he effectively apologized for criticizing the Jewish high priest: "I did not know, brethren, that he was the high priest," Paul said in defense, "for it is written, 'You shall not speak evil of a ruler of your people'" (Acts 23:5).

Perhaps the tension can be resolved by remembering that Paul was human and may have acted inconsistently.

But perhaps there was a deeper logic that explains Paul's actions. When souls and the integrity of Catholic doctrine were at stake, Paul stood boldly. But in matters not concerning true doctrine, Paul was willing to submit himself with humility.[vii] As St. John Chrysostom wrote, "Where there was no imposition of the law as necessary to salvation, Paul in no way antagonized it, but rather trusted to the free working of the principles of the gospel to gradually accomplish the abolition of its rites and forms."[9] During this period of transition, Jews could still keep the Law, even though it was not necessary.

James's instruction for Paul to go to the Temple did not contradict the clear rulings of the council, it did not impose a grave burden on the Gentiles, and it did not change the teaching that works of the Law cannot save. It may well have been imprudent, but the imprudence only put Paul at risk of suffering, and so Paul obeyed. Likewise, Paul's decision to have Timothy circumcised can be understood in an orthodox way. Timothy was Jewish by virtue of his mother and was most likely instructed by Paul that circumcision had no salvific power. Paul thus chose to have Timothy circumcised as a prudential matter to allow acceptance with the Jews for the purpose of spreading the gospel, not because it was required.[viii] Just as he did not want

---

[vii] As we will see in later chapters, correction of the pope is necessary when the integrity of Catholic doctrine and the good of souls are at stake. That was not the case when Paul criticized the chief priest, but it was when he rebuked Peter, whose public refusal to eat with the Gentiles risked leading others astray. Similarly, when James instructed Paul to go to the Temple, it was not to please heretics who were contradicting the Council of Jerusalem, but rather fellow Christians with divergent pastoral judgments. While the cultural laws of circumcision and of Moses were to be set aside eventually, the Council of Jerusalem had not outlawed Jewish ceremonial practices.

[viii] As noted, St. John Chrysostom did not fault St. Paul for having "accommodated himself to Jewish requirements, as in shaving his head at Cenchrea and circumcising Timothy." However, in the Council of Florence in the fifteenth century, the Church condemned such actions: "[The Church] commands all who glory in the name of Christian, at whatever time, before or after baptism, to cease entirely from circumcision." Yet, even if Paul erred with Timothy, that does not negate the truth of his divinely inspired teachings against the power of circumcision, nor does it tarnish the example he set in his justified rebuke of Peter — it would merely demonstrate that even great men do not always act with perfect wisdom and consistency.

to impose a lifeless burden on the Gentiles, he also did not want to needlessly scandalize the Jews.[10]

As Paul acknowledged, "I have become all things to all men, that I might by all means save some" (1 Cor. 9:22). He preached the same gospel in season and out of season (1 Tim. 4:2), and to do so he ingratiated himself to all people for the sake of the gospel, in any way that did not violate God's commandments.

> To the Jews I became as a Jew, in order to win Jews; to those under the law I became as one under the law — though not being myself under the law — that I might win those under the law. To those outside the law I became as one outside the law — not being without law toward God but under the law of Christ — that I might win those outside the law. To the weak I became weak, that I might win the weak.... I do it all for the sake of the gospel. (1 Cor. 9:20–23)

The Law of Love

Whether correcting or submitting, rebuking or coaxing, praising or criticizing, fulfilling the Law of Moses or setting it aside, Paul was ruled by his desire to share the gospel. Paul was ruled by love — and only by viewing Paul's actions through the lens of this ultimate goal is the inner consistency revealed. Paul never condoned doing evil so that good may come (Rom 3:8). Yet in the vast middle ground of actions that are neither morally mandated nor ethically prohibited, he did whatever it took to draw people to the Supreme Good. He acted with heroic virtue beyond what was merely necessary to avoid sin, all to gather more souls for Christ.

That his decisions — like his choice to submit to James — commonly led to hardship was not a defect of his actions or planning. True love cannot be separated from the Cross. The Jews wanted signs from God and the Greeks wanted the delights of worldly wisdom, but Paul preached and lived Christ crucified, "a stumbling block to Jews and folly to Gentiles" (1 Cor. 1:23). It is no different in our times. We want God to save us with great wonders. We want to rationalize our way out of pain and into meaning and purpose. And all the while Christ remains on the Cross saying, "Follow me."

Christ never promised riches or human peace or avoidance of trials. But He did promise suffering. "For it has been granted to you that for the sake of Christ, you should not only believe in him," Paul wrote, "but also suffer for his sake" (Phil. 1:29). Suffering is not merely a possibility but a guarantee, for "all who desire to live a godly life in Christ Jesus will be persecuted" (2 Tim. 3:12).

This is the great paradox of human happiness and the Christian Faith. We cannot live until we die to ourselves (1 Cor. 15:36). We cannot be happy until we neglect our own happiness and live for others. To embrace God's will, sometimes we must also embrace injustice done to ourselves. Yet God does not want merely the outward submission of our actions to His will. He wants the assent of our hearts as well.

Suffering persecution is not a contest to determine who can be the least happy. Through God's grace, we can embrace trials without bitterness, anger, or malice (Eph. 4:31). For God promises not only victory, but joy. From Paul: "We are afflicted in every way, but not crushed; perplexed, but not driven to despair; persecuted, but not forsaken; struck down, but not destroyed; always carrying in the body the death of Jesus, so that the life of Jesus may also be manifested in our bodies" (2 Cor. 4:8–10).

The life of Christ is the key. Our hope, like St. Paul's, is grounded in the Resurrection of Christ. Persecution and tribulations and trials are worthless save for the Resurrection of Christ. The triumph of Jesus over death is what gives everything meaning. That is why Paul could endure. That is why Paul could submit. That is why Paul could stand boldly. He clung not only to the truth of Christ crucified, but also to the promise of Christ resurrected. That promise remains un-shakable if we keep the Faith. For, as Paul wrote, "I am sure that nei-ther death, nor life, nor angels, nor principalities, nor things present, nor things to come, nor powers, nor height, nor depth, nor anything else in all creation, will be able to separate us from the love of God in Christ Jesus our Lord" (Rom. 8:38–39).

CHAPTER 3

The Persecution and Exiles
of St. Athanasius

ONLY A FEW OF the throng of saints recognized by the Church have ever been described as "the Great." St. Athanasius is one of them. In an age of mass apostasy among the clergy, he stood like a rock for the Catholic Faith. For his steadfast orthodoxy, he has been recognized as a Doctor of the Church.

Born around 296 in Alexandria, Egypt, Athanasius grew up in a region that was famous for its theological and philosophical school. Perhaps the most controversial of its teachers had been Origen, whose ideas about the pre-existence of souls, the possibility that even Satan could repent, and other matters had aroused decades of controversy before Athanasius was born.

Athanasius was trained in the Alexandrian school from a young age before becoming a priest. His enemies later accused him of having been ordained without having reached the canonical age, perhaps because he was so intellectually precocious. In any event, he became a close confidant, and then deacon, of Bishop Alexander of Alexandria, who himself would become a saint.

In 313, the Roman Emperor Constantine defeated the pagan Maxentius at the Battle of Milvian Bridge and the Catholic Church entered into a brief period of unprecedented liberty. Constantine was now emperor of the western Roman Empire. Around the same time, his colleague in the army, Licinius, became emperor of the eastern Roman Empire, and the two enjoyed an uneasy peace for a decade. While Constantine openly espoused Christianity, his co-emperor Licinius was a pagan and somewhat cooler toward the new religion. But he also granted liberty to the Christians and returned confiscated property to the Church.

It was during this *pax ecclesia* that one of the most dangerous heresies ever to infect the Church arose in Athanasius's own backyard: Arianism.

The author of this poisonous doctrine was an Alexandrian clergyman, a priest named Arius. Around 319, he had accused Bishop Alexander of teaching a previously condemned heresy, Sabellianism, which essentially collapsed the distinction between the Father and the Son within the Trinity. While there is no evidence that Bishop Alexander was teaching Sabellianism, in his condemnation of his bishop Arius himself spawned a new, more poisonous heresy, which would later bear his name. According to the ecclesiastical historian Socrates, Arius articulated his new doctrine this way: "If ... the Father begat the Son, he that was begotten had a beginning of existence: and from this it is evident, that there was a time when the Son was not. It therefore necessarily follows, that he had his substance from nothing."[11]

In making this assertion, Arius denied Christ His very divinity. According to Arius, there was a time when the second Person of the Trinity was *not*. But if that was true, then the Son was not, like the Father, God, since God must exist from all eternity. If this was true, then the basis of Christian salvation was destroyed, as we'll see.

For teaching this novel doctrine, Arius was excommunicated by Bishop Alexander, who wrote a letter to all his fellow Catholic bishops throughout the world. "Know therefore," he warned them, "that there have recently arisen in our diocese lawless and anti-Christian men, teaching apostasy such as one may justly consider and denominate the forerunner of Antichrist." He specifically named Arius and several of his cohorts, as well as their chief episcopal supporter, Eusebius of Nicomedia (in modern-day Turkey), whom Alexander called "the head of these apostates."[12]

But despite Bishop Alexander's actions, the Arian ranks grew rapidly through word of mouth, as well as the open episcopal support of serpents such as Eusebius.

The Great Council

In 324, Constantine defeated Licinius at the Battle of Adrianople (ironically, the very site where Licinius himself had won the battle that had secured his claim as emperor of the eastern empire). With his supremacy over the whole Roman Empire now secured, Constantine sought to quell the growing disunity within the Catholic Church. So in 325, he summoned a council of bishops to meet at Nicaea (in modern-day Turkey) to settle the crisis of faith with an authoritative determination on Christian doctrine.

Bishop Alexander obeyed the emperor's summons and brought Athanasius with him as a theological advisor. After much discussion, the council produced a synodal letter that was addressed to the churches in Alexandria and other eastern provinces. It declared its condemnation of Arius and his doctrine in no uncertain terms:

> Investigation was made of matters concerning the impiety and transgression of Arius and his adherents; and it was unanimously decreed that he and his impious opinion should be anathematized, together with the blasphemous words and speculations in which he indulged, blaspheming the Son of God, and saying that he is from things that

are not, and that before he was begotten he was not, and that there was a time when he was not, and that the Son of God is by his free will capable of vice and virtue; saying also that he is a creature. All these things the holy Synod has anathematized, not even enduring to hear his impious doctrine and madness and blasphemous words.[13]

Furthermore, in response to the Arian heresy, the council promulgated its famous Creed, which is an integral part of Catholic liturgies to this day. It declared that the Father and the Son were of the "same substance" — *homoousion* ("ὁμοούσιον") in Greek:

> We believe in one God, the Father Almighty, maker of all things visible and invisible; and in one Lord Jesus Christ, the Son of God, the only-begotten of his Father, of the substance of the Father, God of God, Light of Light, very God of very God, begotten, not made, being of one substance with the Father. By whom all things were made, both which be in heaven and in earth.[14]

Over the ensuring decades, various Arian and quasi-Arian formulations would weaponize the term *homoiousian* — which was almost the same as the Catholic *homoousion* but actually meant "similar substance" rather than "same substance" — to describe the relationship between the Father and the Son. The similarity of the terms often lured otherwise orthodox bishops into accepting heretical creeds. The Arians were masters of weaponized ambiguity. But on the slight difference stood the divinity of the Son, and thus the entire economy of salvation. One letter was enough to deny the only Faith that saves and to profess another faith altogether. Such is the ease with which heresy can, and so frequently has, been adopted when Catholic authority has been repudiated.

Three years after the Council of Nicaea, Bishop Alexander died, and Athanasius succeeded him on the apostolic throne of Alexandria in 328. But despite the council's condemnation of Arius and his doctrines and despite the fact that the Church had authoritatively defined its teaching, the Arians had the support of the imperial authority and the elites who sought favor at court. The troubles of the Church and of Athanasius were just beginning. In fact, Athanasius was exiled from his see in Alexandria at least five times.

First Exile (February 336 to November 337)

Athanasius's first exile stemmed from false accusations by brother bishops, who used the accusations as cover to attack him for his orthodoxy. They accused him of not having been old enough to be a priest at the time of his consecration; of imposing a tax upon various provinces; of having subordinates who profaned the sacraments; and finally of having arranged the execution of a man named Arenius and dismembered his body for the sake of performing magic rituals.

Athanasius eventually agreed to address the charges by appearing before a synod of bishops in Tyre (modern-day Lebanon) in 335. Although fifty men testified to his innocence, the council condemned Athanasius. He refused to recognize its authority and escaped by ship to Byzantium to take his case directly to the emperor. While he managed to get to the emperor, Athanasius was condemned by him to exile in Treves (modern-day Trier, Germany) without any formal trial. His journey west began in February of 336, and upon arriving he was welcomed by the local bishop and Constantine, the emperor's eldest son.

In 336, the heresiarch, Arius himself, died suddenly. (Later historians claimed Arius died while in the restroom due to a hemorrhage of his bowels, but there is no contemporaneous evidence of this.) Sudden death was taken to be a sign of disfavor with God. Then, on May 22, 337, Constantine himself died. His third son, who became Emperor Constantius II in the east, invited Athanasius back to his see, where he was re-installed as bishop in November 337. This initial sign of imperial favor, however, would prove ephemeral.

Second Exile (338 to 346)

Even with the death of its heresiarch, the Arian faction was relentlessly tenacious, driven by that dark energy of the enemy, convinced of his ability to snuff out the Faith. They began to influence the mind of the young Constantius II. Within a few years, the old charges were revived, except this time they included even weightier ecclesiastical accusations, namely that Athanasius had ignored the verdict of the synod in Tyre and had returned to his bishopric without being summoned by ecclesiastical authority, having relied only on the instructions of the new emperor.

This was deeply ironic given the Eusebian faction's constant attempts to co-opt the emperor for their own purposes. They would do so again, and the emperor turned on Athanasius. In 340, Gregory of Cappadocia was forcibly installed on the apostolic throne of Alexandria, and Athanasius once again had to go into hiding.

Several weeks later, he fled to Pope Julius in Rome to make his case. The pope was a firm and steadfast supporter of Athanasius as the champion of orthodoxy, and later chided the eastern bishops for proceeding against Athanasius contrary to the custom of the Church. Meanwhile, Athanasius wrote to faithful Catholics in Egypt, exhorting them to suffer the Arian scourge well, in keeping with the example of Christ:

> It does not become us to be agitated because of the trials which befall us. It is not right to fear if the gang that contended with Christ should conspire against godliness; but we should the more please God through these things and should consider such matters as the probation and exercise of a virtuous life. For how shall patience be looked for, if there be not previously labors and sorrows? Or how can fortitude be tested with no assault from enemies? Or how shall magnanimity be exhibited, unless after contumely and injustice? Or how can long-suffering be proved unless there has first been the calumny of Antichrist? And

finally, how can a man behold virtue with his eyes unless the iniquity of the very wicked has previously appeared?

Thus even our Lord and Savior Jesus Christ comes before us, when He should show men how to suffer. Who when He was smitten bore it patiently, being reviled He reviled not again, when He suffered He threatened not, but He gave His back to the smiters, and His cheeks to buffetings, and turned not His face from spitting; and at last, was willingly led to death, that we might behold in Him the image of all that is virtuous and immortal, and that we, conducting ourselves after these examples, might truly tread on serpents and scorpions, and on all the power of the enemy.[15]

With the Anti-Church of his day possessing many of the buildings and physical infrastructure of the Church, Athanasius's flock was desperately in need of encouragement. Writing to the faithful Catholic bishops of the world in 339, Athanasius lamented: "Thus, those persons who were excommunicated by us for their impiety, now glory in the plunder of our churches; while the people of God, and the Clergy of the Catholic Church are compelled either to have communion with the impiety of the Arian heretics, or else to forbear entering into them."[16]

In 343, Athanasius was in Gaul to consult with the holy bishop, Hosius of Cordoba, who had presided over the ecumenical Council of Nicaea. Hosius would likewise preside over the Council of Sardica, which had been summoned by the pope. Athanasius was tried once again, and his innocence was again affirmed. Letters were written by both the pope and the council to eastern bishops in Egypt and Libya making clear that Athanasius was to be re-established in his see. However, the Eusebian faction once again anathematized Athanasius, and they manipulated Constantius into once more persecuting him and those who supported the orthodox cause. In fact, the emperor even condemned Athanasius to death if he should return to Alexandria.

Athanasius was given a friendly summons to the Italian city of Aquileia by the Emperor Constans, Constantine's youngest son. From this exile, Athanasius wrote to the faithful Catholic remnant in Alexandria, comparing the actions of the Arian Anti-Church with those of the fratricidal Cain:

> They followed the example of Cain and fled like him; in that they greatly wandered, for they imitated his flight, and so have received his condemnation.... All the Bishops know how they have sinned, and how many things they have done against our Churches and others; and accordingly they have expelled these men from the Churches like Cain.[17]

The following year, Gregory of Cappadocia, who had usurped Athanasius's see, died, and Constantius reconsidered his condemnation of Athanasius — likely because of a growing Persian military threat on his eastern borders and his desire to have a united empire. However, despite three letters from Constantius, Athanasius was hesitant to return. From Aquileia, he traveled to Treves, then back to Rome, then Adrianople, and finally to Antioch, where he met Constantius in person. The imperial interview was gracious, and Athanasius was once again returned to his bishopric in 346.

Upon returning from his second exile, he sat on the apostolic throne of Alexandria undisturbed for a decade. During this period he wrote his famous *Apology Against the Arians*, which defended the Catholic doctrine of the Incarnation and the Nicene Creed.

Third Exile (356 to 362)

With the death of Pope Julius in 352, the intrigues of the Arians began once again. Pope Liberius succeeded to the throne of Peter. Although he, like his predecessors, stoutly defended Athanasius, the Arians were once again on the march. In 353, Constantius II attained imperial supremacy over the entire empire, after brutally killing a number of relatives whom he saw as a threat to his power. In 355, a council was held in Milan that once again condemned Athanasius, forcing him into yet another exile.

It began in 356 in very dramatic fashion:

> It was now night, and some of the people were keeping a vigil preparatory to a communion on the morrow, when the General Syrianus suddenly came upon us with more than five thousand soldiers, having arms and drawn swords, bows, spears, and clubs, as I have related above. With these he surrounded the Church, stationing his soldiers near at hand, in order that no one might be able to leave the Church and pass by them. Now I considered that it would be unreasonable in me to desert the people during such a disturbance, and not to endanger myself in their behalf; therefore I sat down upon my throne, and desired the Deacon to read a Psalm, and the people to answer, "For His mercy endures forever," and then all to withdraw and depart home.
>
> But the General having now made a forcible entry, and the soldiers having surrounded the sanctuary for the purpose of apprehending us, the Clergy and those of the laity, who were still there, cried out, and demanded that we too should withdraw. But I refused, declaring that I would not do so, until they had retired one and all.
>
> Accordingly I stood up, and having bidden prayer, I then made my request of them, that all should depart before me, saying that it was better that my safety should be endangered, than that any of them should receive hurt. So when the greater part had gone forth, and the rest were following, the monks who were there with us and certain of the Clergy came up and dragged us away.
>
> And thus (Truth is my witness), while some of the soldiers stood about the sanctuary, and others were going round the Church, we passed through, under the Lord's guidance, and with His protection withdrew without observation, greatly glorifying God that we had not betrayed

the people, but had first sent them away, and then had been able to save ourselves, and to escape the hands of them which sought after us.[18]

Athanasius remained in Egypt, fleeing to the monks who lived in the desert, where he remained for six years. Soon after this period of exile began, he wrote to the Catholic bishops of Egypt and Libya, describing to them how the Arian heretics had managed to take over the physical structures of the Church:

> They have caused the Churches to be snatched out of our hands, they have banished as they pleased, the Bishops and Presbyters who refused to communicate with them; and the people who withdrew from them they have excluded from the Churches, which they have given up into the hands of the Arians who were condemned so long ago, so that with the assistance of the hypocrisy of the Meletians they can without fear pour forth in them their impious language, and make ready, as they think, the way of deceit for Antichrist, who sowed among them the seeds of this heresy.[19]

Meanwhile, Pope Liberius had also been exiled by the emperor for his failure to condemn Athanasius. This exile would come to an end in 357 when Liberius was compelled under duress from the emperor to approve a heretical creed proposed by the Council of Sirmium, as well as condemn Athanasius. This apostate convocation repudiated not only the Nicene Creed's language of "one substance" to describe the relationship between the Father and the Son but even the quasi-Arian language of "similar substance." This "Blasphemy of Sirmium" justified its departure from orthodoxy by appealing to the fact that neither term was found in Scripture.

Athanasius defended Pope Liberius's orthodoxy, noting that his apparent change of heart had occurred under duress:

> But Liberius after he had been in banishment two years gave way, and from fear of threatened death subscribed. Yet even this only shows their violent conduct, and the hatred of Liberius against the heresy, and his support of Athanasius, so long as he was suffered to exercise a free choice. For that which men are forced by torture to do contrary to their first judgment, ought not to be considered the willing deed of those who are in fear, but rather of their tormentors. They however attempted everything in support of their heresy, while the people in every Church, preserving the faith which they had learned, waited for the return of their teachers, and condemned the Antichristian heresy, and all avoid it, as they would a serpent.[20]

But with the apparent capitulation of the pope — who would later vindicate his orthodoxy by annulling the decrees of the Arian councils of Ariminum and Seleucia — Athanasius was surrounded on all sides. The holy bishop Hosius, who had presided over the proceedings at Nicaea, was in exile. The orthodox bishops who had withstood the Arians alongside Athanasius were scattered. Meanwhile, the Arian faction once again succeeded in having one of their own — George of Cappadocia — installed as the bishop of Alexandria.

Despite the darkness of the hour, this third exile was one of the most prolific of Athanasius's entire career, with many of his most famous and influential works being written, including the *Apology to Constantius*, the *Apology for His Flight* (explaining why he fled), his *Letter to the Monks*, *Four Orations Against the Arians* (also known as the *Discourses*), and his memoirs, *History of the Arians*. Athanasius did not despair — he prepared for the long fight ahead.

In the *History*, Athanasius had no qualms about asserting that George of Cappadocia was a precursor of the antichrist. "He has," he observed, "thought to change laws, by transgressing the ordinance of the Lord given us through His Apostles, by altering the customs of the Church, and inventing a new kind of appointments."[21] Athanasius compared George's sitting on the apostolic throne of Alexandria and the takeover of much of the visible Church by heretical and apostate "bishops" to the "abomination of desolation" prophesied by Daniel:

> Terrible indeed, and worse than terrible are such proceedings; yet conduct suitable to him who assumes the character of Antichrist. Who that beheld him [George] taking the lead of his pretended Bishops, and presiding in Ecclesiastical causes, would not justly exclaim that this was "the Abomination of Desolation" [Dan. 9:27] spoken of by Daniel? For having put on the profession of Christianity, and entering into the holy places, and standing therein, he lays waste the Churches, transgressing their Canons, and enforcing the observance of his own decrees. Will anyone now venture to say that this is a peaceful time with Christians, and not a time of persecution? A persecution indeed, such as never arose before, and such as no one perhaps will again stir up, except "the son of lawlessness," [2 Thess. 2:8] do these enemies of Christ exhibit, who already present a picture of him in their own persons.[22]

The stalwart bishop in exile declared that this persecution from both within and without the Church was a precursor of the persecution of the antichrist, even taking direct aim at Emperor Constantius: "For behold, he [the emperor] has now again thrown into disorder all the Churches of Alexandria and of Egypt and Libya, and has publicly given orders, that the Bishops of the Catholic Church and faith be cast out of their churches, and that they be all given up to the professors of the Arian doctrines."[23]

Likewise, he stated with approval that "the people, perceiving the iniquitous proceedings of the heretics, would not allow them to enter the Churches, and *withdrew themselves far from them*."[24] The exiled bishop also offered open support for faithful Catholics "going out" from the Arian Anti-Church that had taken over in their particular parishes or dioceses:

It will be well to content ourselves with the divine Scripture, and that we all obey the precept which it has given us both in regard to other heresies, and especially respecting this. That precept is as follows; "Depart, depart, go out from thence, touch no unclean thing; go out of the midst of them, and be separate, that bear the vessels of the Lord" [Isa. 52:11]. This may suffice to instruct us all, so that if anyone has been deceived by them, he may go out from them, as out of Sodom, and not return again unto them, lest he suffer the fate of Lot's wife.[25]

In his first *Discourse Against the Arians*, Athanasius flatly contradicts many modern myths about the supposed "later development" of Christian belief in the Trinity, chastising the Arians for admitting themselves that their doctrines were novel and had never before been heard among Catholics:

But if they themselves [the Arians] own that they have heard it [their heresy] now for the first time, how can they deny that this heresy is foreign, and not from our fathers? But what is not from our fathers, but has come to light in this day, how can it be but that of which the blessed Paul has foretold, that "in the latter times some shall depart from the sound faith, giving heed to seducing spirits and doctrines of devils, in the hypocrisy of liars; cauterized in their own conscience, and turning from the truth" [1 Tim. 4:1]?[26]

In 359, the Arians conspired with Constantius II to convene two councils — in Ariminum in the West, and in Seleucia in the East — that repudiated the language of Nicaea, substituting in its place quasi-Arian formulations of the Creed. It was of these events that St. Jerome later famously observed, "The whole world groaned, and was astonished to find itself Arian."[27] From a human perspective, the situation looked hopeless. Despair would have been the "rational" option.

Athanasius chastised both councils for despising the teaching of the Fathers as authoritatively defined at Nicaea. He also noted that while the Arians had temporarily succeeded in hoodwinking the bishops at these councils, their own doctrinal formulations had continually changed — a telltale sign of all heresies — whereas the Catholic Creed of Nicaea had remained clear and sufficient. He grounded the Catholic veneration of patristic tradition in biblical injunctions, charging the Arians with disagreeing not only with the Catholic Church but also among themselves:

> The blessed Apostle approves of the Corinthians because, he says, "you remember me in all things, and keep the traditions as I delivered them to you" [1 Cor. 11:2]. But they [heretics], as entertaining such views of their predecessors, will have the daring to say just the reverse to their flocks: "We praise you not for remembering your fathers, but rather we make much of you when you hold not their traditions."[28]

But both Constantius and George would die in 361 — and Athanasius was once again able to return to his see on February 22, 362.

Fourth Exile (362 to 363)

Upon his return, Athanasius exemplified that charitable heart so often exhibited by the saints by forgiving his enemies. He summoned the Synod of Alexandria in 362, which decided that clergy who had previously succumbed to Arian pressure could be readmitted to communion, so long as they themselves had never subscribed to an Arian creed. The synod also reaffirmed Catholic teaching on the Trinity, further elucidating the distinctions between substance and persons, and affirming that both the Son and the Holy Spirit were consubstantial with the Father while remaining separate divine Persons.

However, once again his return would prove to be short-lived: the accession to the imperial throne of Julian the Apostate, who had been raised a Catholic and even took minor orders as a lector but later began to dabble in pagan and occult practices, precipitated one of the worst persecutions of the Church up to that point, and the anti-Christian emperor even attempted to rebuild the Jewish Temple in Jerusalem. The project was miraculously prevented, however, by the appearance of a cross in the sky and fiery explosions in the ground that workers were digging in preparation for rebuilding the Temple.[i]

Julian the Apostate also ordered Athanasius to leave Alexandria almost as soon as he had returned, and so again the saintly bishop fled to the Egyptian wilderness, where he lived until Julian's death in 363.

Fifth and Final Exile (365)

Julian was succeeded by the emperor Valens, who favored the Arian party. Predictably, Athanasius was ordered into exile in October 364, during which time some said he remained in the tombs of his ancestors on the outskirts of the city.[29] However, after about four months the emperor was persuaded to reconsider his decision. Athanasius returned for the final time, reigning in his see for eight more years before dying peacefully in 373.

St. Athanasius: Pillar of the Church

"Let what was confessed by the Fathers of Nicaea prevail." So wrote Athanasius to a philosopher in his final years.

Even to this day, Catholics recite the Nicene-Constantinopolitan Creed at every Mass. We take for granted what St. Athanasius sacrificed so much to defend. It would serve us well to consider why he defended it, and how.

---

[i]   Among the sources that report this story are the emperor, Julian the Apostate himself, in a letter to the Jews; the pagan historian Ammianus Marcellinus; St. Ambrose of Milan; St. Gregory Nazianzen; St. John Chrysostom; and the ecclesiastical historians Socrates Scholasticus, Theodoret, and Sozomen.

In short, if the Son was not fully God and fully man, then man could not be saved. The essence of Christian salvation, as Athanasius well knew, was humanity's partaking in the divine nature, as St. Peter had written (2 Pet. 1:4), and as the priest prays at every Mass: "May we share in the divinity of Christ, who humbled Himself to share in our humanity." But if the divine had not fully assumed human nature, then human nature could no longer partake of the divine. Athanasius explained why this was so vital to the Catholic Faith: "Man had not been deified, unless the Word who became flesh had been by nature from the Father and true and proper to Him. For therefore the union was of this kind, that He might unite what is man by nature to Him who is in the nature of the Godhead, and his salvation and deification might be sure.[30]

And yet, standing up for this most basic and essential truth of the Catholic Faith came at great cost — particularly at the hands of his fellow bishops. All other dogmas depended upon this one. In defending it, St. Athanasius presents Catholics with a model of steadfastness under persecution. He stood by the Council of Nicaea at every turn, never bending to the supposed authoritative statements of other bishops and councils that contradicted its dogmas, even when they presumed to declare him guilty of crimes he did not commit and slandered his reputation. He was anathematized by many, for which he fled to Rome and the papacy for support. While Popes Julius and Liberius ultimately stood by him, there was a point at which even the papacy seemed to founder when Liberius — under duress — subscribed to an Arian creed. Athanasius knew the pope to be orthodox and consistently defended him. But the point is that for a brief time, all the world knew is that the pope had supposedly compromised the Faith. But even then, Athanasius stood firm.

Not only did Athanasius stand firm, the great saint often and explicitly encouraged laymen to do the same. He encouraged them to disobey heretical bishops. He encouraged them to withdraw from parishes taken over by heretical priests. He encouraged them to stand by the Faith of Nicaea as steadfastly as he did.

And yet, Athanasius never saw his actions as opposed to the Catholic Church and her discipline. Quite the opposite. Arianism was a heretical novelty. Thus, anyone presuming to rule, govern, or punish in its name was in fact outside the Church and in opposition to the true Catholic Church. Furthermore, the Church had authoritatively spoken at Nicaea, and so to reject its teaching was heresy — and heretics could have no authority in the Church, and indeed heresy necessarily entailed the loss of office in the Church. As he wrote to the bishops of Egypt and Libya, "Thus Judas was degraded from the Apostolical office, not because he sacrificed to idols, but because he proved a traitor."[31] And as we saw earlier, he explicitly compared apostolic thrones being physically possessed by heretics to the abomination of desolation prophesied by Daniel. Nicaea had removed all doubt about the Church's teaching on the second Person of the Trinity, Jesus Christ. To be moved from its determination was to fall from the Faith.

St. Gregory Nazianzen described Athanasius as "the pillar of the Church," in a time when "the truth of our faith [had] been torn asunder, confused, and parceled out into various opinions and portions by many."[32] He compared his actions to that of Christ cleansing the Temple:

> He cleansed the temple of those who made merchandise of God, and trafficked in the things of Christ, imitating Christ in this also ... He restored too the teaching which had been overthrown: the Trinity was once more boldly spoken of, and set upon the lampstand, flashing with the brilliant light of the One Godhead into the souls of all.[33]

In our own days, when so many have challenged so many teachings of the Church — even members of the hierarchy — we are faced with a similar challenge as Athanasius, whose spectacular example of steadfastness serves as a model for all Catholics. May we, as St. Gregory Nazianzen recommended, call upon the prayers of this great saint to "cast upon us from above a propitious glance, and conduct this people in its perfect worship of the perfect Trinity, which, as Father, Son, Holy Ghost, we contemplate and adore."[34]

CHAPTER 4

The Persecution of St. Bruno

His Times and Early Life

St. Bruno of Segni was born to a noble family in Piedmont (modern-day Italy) in 1045.[35] He studied the humanities in his hometown at the Benedictine monastery of St. Perpetuus, a holy bishop whose image in the monastery it is said the young Bruno contemplated with devotion. At about age seventeen, Bruno moved to Bologna to continue his Benedictine education.[36] Following the holy example of his teachers, Bruno joined the order and set off for Monte Cassino, a journey of some five hundred miles.

About halfway there, at Siena, Bruno fell ill and had to remain in the city. As he had recently been ordained a priest, the local bishop, Rudolphus, made him a canon of the cathedral. It was there that St. Bruno began to author biblical commentaries, as he would for the rest of his life. His writings quickly earned him renown for his knowledge of Scripture and his personal holiness — a reputation that would lead him to long, and often troubled, relationships with the popes of his day.

A Church in Crisis

As a young priest, Bruno entered a clergy that was still struggling to recover from almost unprecedented disaster. After the collapse of the Frankish Empire at the end of the ninth century, Western Europe had fallen into chaos. Vikings raided the coasts from Norway to Sicily. Trade routes and lines of communication broke down. Muslims overran Catholic Iberia and the ancient Catholic communities of the Middle East, in a pincer movement that would squeeze Europe for the next millennium. In St. Bruno's lifetime, Muslims would overrun Asia Minor and threaten Europe from the east.

In practice, the West's descent into chaos led to extreme localization in matters of both Church and state. While in many places bishops had long been appointed by the pope, by local clergy, or even by popular acclamation, it became more and more common for kings and nobles to appoint the local bishops — which opened wide the door to corruption. Buying a bishopric was often a sound investment: the new bishop would come into possession of a great deal of Church property, and he could use it however he wanted. As a result, the Western clergy increasingly succumbed to this temptation, spiraling deeper and deeper into immorality. The shepherds of souls became hirelings, and their sheep became helpless before the wolves.

Worse, the corruption spread all the way up to the papacy. Indeed, Cardinal Baronius famously named the tenth century *saeculum obscurum,* the Dark Century, a low point in the history of the Church that saw an unprecedented level of corruption among the popes. From about 882 to 964, popes were surrounded and even largely controlled by prostitutes, giving the papacy during this period its historical designation: "the pornocracy," the rule of prostitutes. In 897, Stephen VI dug up the bones of his predecessor, purported to put him on trial, and then threw the body into the Tiber River. In 964, Pope John XII was allegedly killed *in flagrante delicto* with a married woman. In 1045, the year of St. Bruno's birth, Benedict IX became the only pope to sell the papacy.

Bruno would later write of the age he was born into:

> The whole world was placed in wickedness, sanctity had failed, justice had perished, and truth lay buried. Iniquity was king, avarice was lord, Simon magus held the Church, bishops and priests were given over to pleasure and fornication. Priests were not ashamed to take wives, they held their weddings openly, they contracted nefarious marriages, and endowed with laws those with whom, according to the laws, they should not live in the same house.... But what is even worse than all this — hardly anyone was found who either was not a simoniac or had not been ordained by simoniacs. As a result, to this very day, there are some people who ... contend that starting from that time the priesthood failed in the Church. For they say: "If all were like this, i.e. if all either were simoniacs or had been ordained by simoniacs, you who are now [priests], how did you come to be here? Through whom did you pass, if not through them? There was no other way. Hence, those who ordained you received their orders from none other than those who either were simoniacs or had been ordained by simoniacs...." Such was the Church, such were the bishops and priests, such were even the Roman pontiffs, who should illuminate all the others."[37]

Bruno served as a priest in a time when the priesthood was corrupted and weak — and civil powers, while weaker than they had been before, were stronger than the Church. This created a long-running friction between civil and ecclesial authority, a friction that would spark a conflagration after the election of Pope St. Gregory VII in 1073, around the same time Bruno was ordained.

The new pope took immediate action against simony and in favor of the Church's requirement of clerical celibacy. He excommunicated any bishop who had been appointed by a layman.[38] In 1074, Gregory held a synod in Rome that again decreed the removal of simoniacs and sexually incontinent clergy (including married clergy) from office. St. Gregory implored the laity to avoid married or simoniacal priests.[39]

Gregory sent out legates across the West and gave them authority to depose simoniacal and incontinent clergy, even bishops. In 1075 he held a synod at Rome that excommunicated "any person, *even if he were emperor or king,* who should confer an investiture in connection with any ecclesiastical office." He then explicitly deposed the simoniacal bishops who had been appointed by King Henry IV of Germany, the future Holy Roman Emperor.[40]

These claims did not come out of thin air or from the mind of Gregory VII, of course. They reiterated traditional Catholic doctrine, with precedent as early as the magisterium of Pope St. Gelasius I in 494 and exemplified by St. Ambrose's excommunication of Theodosius the Great in 390. It was a precept of reason that, just as in the human person the spirit is greater than the body, so also among groups of people the spiritual part necessarily predominates over the physical part. Pope Gregory and his reforming bishops could also cite revelation in their favor, for the Lord had said not to "fear those who kill the body but cannot kill the soul; rather fear him who can destroy both soul and body in hell" (Matt. 10:28).

But all that aside, the specific conflict with Henry revolved around the power to depose and appoint bishops. Henry believed that if his father could appoint four popes, then he could certainly appoint bishops in his own lands.

In 1076, Gregory summoned Henry to give an account of himself before a council at Rome. Henry refused. Instead, Henry called his own council (or *diet*) at Worms, composed entirely of his ecclesiastical supporters. The diet made hysterical accusations of immorality and tyranny against the pope and purported to depose him. Two groups of bishops in Lombardy (most of them appointed by Henry) quickly declared their assent and their belief that the Chair of Peter was vacant.

In response, Gregory excommunicated Henry and every bishop who supported him. He even released the subjects of the empire from their oaths of allegiance to Henry.[41] Gregory's rebuke had the intended effect, which was Henry's personal repentance. The king secretly fled into Italy to seek reconciliation with the pope — his now-legendary "Walk to Canossa." Gregory forced the king to wait in the winter cold for three days of fasting and would only speak to him if he were barefoot and dressed as a penitent. Finally, on the third day, the pope granted an audience to the king and ordered him to go before the nobles at Augsburg. The nobles declared Henry deposed and elected Rudolph of Swabia as a new emperor.

Refuting the Heretic Berengarius

The balance of power was shifting between the Church and secular authority. It was in these fraught times that, in 1079, Bishop Rudolphus sent Bruno to Rome, where he stayed with Rudolphus's friend and fellow Benedictine, Cardinal Pietro, a fierce opponent of the simoniacs and a staunch defender of the rights of the papacy. Bruno's long years close to the papacy would be defined by the battle between the power of kings and that of the papacy. But his first experience with the papal court involved a different matter. When St. Gregory called a synod to promulgate the Church's doctrine of the Real Presence — in response to the denials of French theologian Berengarius — Cardinal Pietro brought Bruno with him.

Unlike simony and clerical sexual activity, the denial of the Real Presence had not yet become a widespread problem in either the East or West. In fact, Berengarius was the first major heresiarch to reject the Real Presence in the Eucharist.[42] (It was not until the explosion of Protestantism nearly five hundred years later that this belief became widespread.)[i]

---

[i]   The only evidence of anyone holding this belief before a single monk in the ninth century is its vehement condemnation by St. Ignatius of Antioch in his *Epistle to the Smyrneans*, ca. A.D. 107.

Berengarius's opinion had already been condemned at a synod in Rome nearly thirty years earlier in 1050, and in 1055, Berengarius had signed a document repudiating his heresy and repenting of resisting correction from the Church.[43] Nevertheless, Berengarius relapsed into heresy in 1059, and the controversy dragged on.

At the synod in 1079, Berengarius once again defended his opinion at the Lateran Palace in front of now-pope Gregory VII. But St. Bruno's reputation for knowledge and holiness had preceded him, so the pope asked him to speak.[44] St. Bruno rose up and defended the Church's constant teaching that the Eucharist is the same Body and the same Blood that were born of the Virgin Mary, the same Body and the same Blood that were spilt on Calvary, the same that were resurrected on Easter Sunday.[45] St. Bruno emphasized the necessity of faith and love of God to overcome the limits of human knowledge and understanding. He explained that it is not necessary to know *how* God does something in order to know *that* He does it, especially when He has revealed it in at least five passages of the Holy Scriptures as well as prefigured it repeatedly throughout both the Old and New Testaments. To believe that God is incapable of turning bread into His Body is to believe that God cannot do miracles — which is to believe that God is not God.

St. Bruno's speech persuaded Berengarius, who once again repented of his heresy and of his stubbornness in resisting correction. It also impressed the pope: the young Bruno was brought into the Roman Curia, where he would remain for the next three decades and the next three pontificates. (In fact, Bruno's simple formulation of eucharistic doctrine remained widely in use even after the more precise definitions made by St. Thomas Aquinas more than a century later.)

In 1079, at the direction of the pope, the canons of Segni elected Bruno their bishop. Bruno vehemently refused election; it is said that he ran away from Segni. Bruno had left home at seventeen to be a Benedictine, not a bishop or a papal advisor. But Gregory VII ordered Bruno to accept his election under obedience. One source claims that

St. Bruno saw a vision in the middle of the night that chastised him for running from the Bride of Christ, reminiscent of the famous *Quo Vadis* tradition, in which Christ appeared to St. Peter as he fled persecution in Rome.[46] St. Bruno returned to Segni and accepted his election as the will of God, and the pope personally consecrated him as bishop.

Bishop and Prisoner

Meanwhile, the struggle between Church and state had only intensified. After the Battle of Flarcheim in 1080, where Rudolph of Swabia had defeated Henry and seemed on the cusp of seizing the throne, Gregory VII finally threw in with Rudolph, excommunicated Henry again, and reiterated that the king was deposed. In response, Henry had thirty bishops declare Gregory deposed and instructed them to elect the arch-bishop of Ravenna — a simoniac bishop named Guibert — as antipope Clement III. But then Rudolph fell in battle. Henry turned his forces against the pope and invaded Italy. As his army got closer, thirteen cardinals switched their allegiance from Gregory to Henry.[47]

On March 21, 1084, Henry finally made it inside the city of Rome, and the pope fled to Castel Sant'Angelo, with Bruno alongside him. Guibert was proclaimed Clement III, and he promptly gave Henry a papal coronation.

Gregory had allied with the Normans, and they marched on the city. Henry fled, and the Normans escorted the pope from Castel Sant'Angelo to the Lateran Palace. But the Roman people rioted at the presence of yet more foreign invaders, and in response the Norman troops burned and looted the city and Gregory VII fled to Monte Cassino. (And we think our times are turbulent.)

Bruno's relationship with St. Gregory grew even stronger during their time at Castel Sant'Angelo, and the pope wanted to increase Bruno's responsibilities even more. By 1086, Gregory wanted to make Bruno a cardinal, but again the saint resisted elevation to higher office. Sources conflict as to whether Bruno technically became a cardinal,

but all agree that he was a cardinal in practice, and indeed he participated in the papal election of 1088. The new Benedictine pope Victor
III named Bruno the official librarian and chancellor of the Roman
Church. As librarian, Bruno was in charge of managing papal documents, and he often appears as a witness on papal documents from
1086 until his falling out with the pope in 1111.

In 1088, Pope Urban II was elected and kept Bruno as librarian,
chancellor, and close advisor.

Urban II spent half of his pontificate in exile, and Bruno seemingly
was inseparable from him. He traveled with him to numerous synods,
consecrations, and missions in southern France and Italy, including the
Council of Clermont in 1095, where Urban called the First Crusade.[48]
Two weeks after Jerusalem fell to the crusaders in 1099, Urban II died,
and the cardinals unanimously elected Urban's designated successor,
who took the name of Paschal II. While Bruno did not participate in
this election, Paschal II was a fellow Benedictine and had served in the
Curia alongside him under Gregory VII. There can be no doubt that
he already knew Bruno well, and he retained St. Bruno as a close advisor as Bruno remained the pope's constant companion, traveling with
him to southern Italy, Tuscany, and France.[49] Thus for roughly two
decades Bruno had been a closer advisor to three separate popes. By all
appearances, Bruno's life to that point was one continuous ascent, receiving not persecution but honors from the Church.

Bishop and Monk

These honors continued in 1103. By then, Bruno had been freed of his
obligations in Rome, and after an illness he finally finished the journey to
Monte Cassino he had started when he was seventeen. For thirty years
his life had been swept up in the biggest controversies of the day. At last
he had decided to live the life he had chosen, but with a big perk: Bruno
became a monk without resigning his office as bishop.[50] This was a highly
unusual arrangement, and it provoked an uproar among the laity of Segni,

who complained directly to the pope about losing their bishop.[51] Nevertheless, the abbot and several cardinals persuaded the pope to allow it.[52] Paschal II himself had attempted to resist his own election to the papacy — on grounds that his monastic background made him unqualified to be pope — so it is likely he was sympathetic to Bruno's longing for the monastic vocation. Nevertheless, Paschal II stipulated that Bruno could enter Monte Cassino only if he continued to ensure the spiritual welfare of his diocese and continue to participate in the Roman Curia for at least forty days a year. It was not exactly the ideal of the monastic life, but it showed how much the pope trusted his abilities. Bruno accepted.

In just five years as a monk, St. Bruno found himself elected abbot of Monte Cassino, the most prestigious monastic role in the world.[53]

Privilege and Punishment

Meanwhile the struggle with the Emperors Henry continued. In August 1106, Henry IV died after being taken captive and deposed by his son, Henry V. The younger Henry had seen the pope as a potential ally in his quest for the throne; but having attained it, he took an even harder line in favor of lay investiture than had his father. Henry V demanded the right to appoint bishops, as well as a papal coronation, both of which had been enjoyed by his forebears dating back to Otto the Great. Paschal II was amenable to a coronation, but he reaffirmed the Gregorian magisterium.[54]

In 1110, Henry V invaded Italy and pressed his case by force of arms, knowing that he had the support of much of the Lombard nobility. Paschal II entered into negotiations with him, and they reached a compromise. Under the agreement, the emperor would renounce the right to investiture and the bishops would renounce the privileges and benefits they had received from the civil power. Paschal II agreed to an imperial coronation at old St. Peter's Basilica in February 1111.[55]

This compromise had something for everyone to hate: the nobles rejected the renunciation of investiture; the bishops refused to give up their benefits from the emperor and the nobles; and the Roman people were opposed to a coronation in Rome and rose up in protest to the compromise. The treaty looked like it would be impossible to carry out. But in response, Henry simply kidnapped the pope and the cardinals and took them prisoner. After two months in prison, and after a failed rescue mission from the Normans, the pope despaired of release. On April 11, 1111, Paschal II signed the Concordat of Ponte Mammolo, not a compromise but a complete surrender to Henry's demands. The pope conceded to Henry V the right to appoint the bishops in his lands, agreed to an imperial coronation, and promised under oath not to punish him for kidnapping the pope and the cardinals. He got nothing in return but his release from prison, and two days later, Paschal II crowned Henry V at old St. Peter's Basilica in Rome.[56]

To Bruno, this agreement was not merely a surrender, but a denial of the Catholic Faith, since it contradicted the constant teaching of the Magisterium.[ii] Indeed, it was contrary to both reason and revelation to make ecclesiastical authority dependent upon the laity, who had no ecclesiastical authority at all.

Bruno had been one of the pope's closest advisors and one of the strongest defenders of the rights of the papacy for decades. Because he believed so steadfastly in the papacy, he put all his influence on the line and became the pope's loudest and most vigorous critic.

St. Bruno thundered against the agreement, and called the pope's grant to Henry not a *privilegium* but a *pravilegium*, a perversion. Bruno effectively started a movement of resistance to the pope, first among the bishops and then among the clergy and even the laity. He confronted cardinals who had signed their names to the

---

[ii]   It should also be noted that the word *heresy* at the time was often used in a broader sense to mean "factional" or schismatic. Nevertheless, Bruno accused Paschal II of directly violating Catholic doctrine as laid out in the 1075 *Dictatus* of Gregory VII.

agreement while in prison. He wrote to one of them, "My dearest friend," who had apparently been a former ally in the reform movement, "we have heard that some of our brethren not only do not condemn what has just been done against the church, but also try to defend it imprudently. It is heretical. No one can say that this is not heresy, because the holy and apostolic church in many councils has named it a heresy, and excommunicated it."[57]

Bruno's public condemnation of the pope and the cardinals quickly earned him enemies up and down the hierarchy. His subsequent letters make pains to show that he bore no ill will toward those he criticized. He wrote an open letter to the cardinals and bishops that is much more moderate in tone and concedes that their culpability was lessened by their duress in prison. He went out of his way to make clear that his real enemy was not Paschal and the cardinals but rather Guibert and Henry. "Whoever says that Guibert was not a heretic denies that we are Catholics," he wrote. "They are [true] Catholics who praise and defend the faith and doctrine of the Catholic Church. Those who obstinately contradict the faith and doctrine of the Catholic Church are heretics."[58]

St. Bruno's argument distinguished between those who participated in lay investiture and those who praised or defended the Ponte Mammolo agreement. The former were sinners; it is the latter who were heretics, since they willingly and openly dissented from irreformable doctrine. Bruno wrote that he was alarmed that "there were few [captive cardinals] who said, 'what we preached before, we preach now; what we condemned before, we condemn now.'"[59] The rest were heretics. He signed the letter, *Bruno Peccator-Episcopus, Servus Benedicti*, "Bruno the sinner-bishop and slave of St. Benedict." Even while criticizing the pope and the cardinals, he remained charitable and humble.

Bruno wrote to the pope to assure him of his obedience and filial love and to give a longer explanation of his position.

My enemies say that I do not love thee, and that I am speaking badly of thee behind thy back, but they are lying. I indeed, love thee, as I must love a Father and lord. To thee living, I do not desire another Pontiff, as I promised thee along with many others. Nevertheless, I obey Our Savior Who says to me: "Whoever loves father and mother more than me, is not worthy of me."... I must love thee, but greater yet must I love Him who made thee and me.... But that treaty, so abominable, so violent, having come about with such treason, so opposed to piety and religion, I do not approve, but neither do you, as I have heard.... that contract in which the faith is violated, the church loses its liberty, the priesthood abolished, the one and only door of the church is closed, and against it many other doors are opened through which only thieves can enter. We have the Constitutions of Holy Fathers from the times of the Apostles up to you. One must walk on the royal road and not deviate from it.... Condemn this heresy, which you yourself often called heresy, with apostolic authority, and immediately the whole Church will be reconciled with you, soon all will stream to you to gather at your feet as their Father and Lord with great joy and obedience.

Have mercy on the Church of God. Have mercy on the bride of Christ, and through your prudence may they regain the freedom they have lost through you.[60]

He again humbly signed the letter as "Bruno the sinner-bishop and slave of St. Benedict."

Bruno did not lash out in pride. If he had, it would have drowned out his doctrinal message. Yet Bruno's humility showed that he was acting in good faith, and it moved his fellow bishops to support him.

It was obvious even to St. Bruno that the pope had signed the treaty out of weakness and fear, and that he did not intend to change the doctrine of the Catholic Church. In his heart the pope had always held the same position as Bruno, as shown by the fact that he had publicly taught it before imprisonment.

Once the agreement was signed and the cardinals were free, they quickly gathered in Rome, repudiated the agreement, and declared Henry excommunicated and deposed. But Paschal felt bound by what he had signed, even though it was obviously signed under duress. He resisted punishing Henry for his crimes.

Yet he eventually admitted that he had been at fault and had only signed to free the Curia and the Roman people.[61] By October, the pope had confirmed the judgment of the cardinals and bishops that Henry was deposed and excommunicated.

Paschal nonetheless became indignant at the terms with which Bishop Bruno criticized him for succumbing in a moment of weakness. Bishop Bruno called him a heretic. Thus the pope punished Bruno by ending his own *privilegium*: his ability to serve as both bishop and abbot of Monte Cassino. The pope pointed out how extraordinary the arrangement had been, and said that it violated the recent Council of Clermont.[62] "The Apostolic See can no longer tolerate a bishop in charge of such a famous monastery."[63]

The pope ordered Bruno away from his prestigious post, back to Segni to watch after his tiny diocese. Bruno obeyed and accepted his punishment, leaving behind, according to tradition, his abbatial crozier on the altar at Monte Cassino as an offering to God.

In the ecclesiastical world, Bruno's fidelity to the Faith had cost him dearly. When a group of monks wrote to him at Segni asking for his opinion on the crisis, for the first time in three decades he could no longer offer any insights into the pope's state of mind: "You should know first of all that the pope does not love me or my counsel.... I indeed say what I have said, and I remain most firmly in the opinion (*sententia*) of Gregory and Urban. I hope for the mercy of Almighty God, because I will continue in this *sententia* even to the end."[64] No longer an abbot, Bruno stopped signing his name as *Benedicti Servus*.

On March 23, 1112, during a synod at the Lateran Palace, Pope Paschal II formally repudiated the agreement with Henry. Bruno was conspicuously absent from the relevant session.[65] But his theological position had prevailed.

In 1116, Bruno participated in a Lateran synod where Paschal II again condemned the agreement and the principles behind it, admitting that he had only signed it under compulsion. He condemned the treaty and asked that the bishops do the same. The bishops did so with a shout, and Bishop Bruno cried out, "Thank God we have heard the pope condemn with his own mouth that privilege that contained perversity and heresy!" But to this he added, "If that privilege contained heresy, then the exhibitor of it is a heretic."[66]

The papal chancellor — and future Pope Gelasius II — rose to rebuke Bruno for daring to call the pope a heretic. After several other bishops began to speak, the pope himself arose and gave a lengthy defense, saying that the Roman Church had never been defiled by heresy and had always vanquished heresy.[67] By the end of the synod, it was evident that the pope was even more displeased with Bruno, even if he agreed with him in principle.

The pope never reinstated Bruno at Monte Cassino. Bruno never regained the role in the Curia that he had held for a quarter of a century. The truth was vindicated, but the speaker of that truth still had to suffer. All Bruno had ever wanted was to be a monk of Monte Cassino, and this was the one dignity denied him.

Strictly speaking, the pope was correct that he had not fallen into formal heresy. During the Gregorian reforms it was common to elide the distinction between heresy and schism in theological debate, and the definition of these terms was less precise than they became over the course of subsequent centuries. (They ultimately received their formal definitions in the Council of Trent.) Indeed, there are many examples of the Gregorian reformers referring to lay investiture as a heresy. It must also be admitted that Bruno was so zealous an opponent of lay investiture that he defended the proposition that a simoniacal priest could not say a valid Mass, which is itself erroneous.[68]

Furthermore, the pope is not infallible with respect to disciplinary matters. Popes can and do err in administrative decisions, and some of these errors cause scandal. But error and heresy are two different things. St. Bruno seemed to acknowledge this by distinguishing between the signing of the agreement and the defense of it after the fact. Bruno did not accuse anyone of heresy for signing the agreement, but accused only those who praised it, made excuses for it, or did not condemn it.

Nevertheless, Bruno's vehemence in defending the truth had helped to preserve the Church — and he paid the price for it.

His Final Years and Glorification

Paschal II died in 1118, amid more rioting in Rome. After the brief reign of Gelasius II, Callixtus II, who had also led opposition to the Ponte Mammolo agreement in France, was elected pope.

The new pope called a synod at Rheims to reiterate the Church's condemnations of lay investiture, simony, and clerical concubinage. Henry had agreed to negotiate with the new pope near Rheims, but he arrived for the negotiations with thirty thousand troops. This was no Walk to Canossa: it seemed more like another Ponte Mammolo. Callixtus refused to negotiate and, outraged by the emperor's efforts to intimidate him, he re-excommunicated Henry in front of the bishops and abbots on October 30, 1119.[69]

Callixtus went to Rome, where anti-pope Clement III remained. Upon his arrival, the Roman people rioted and drove out the false pope, who was then captured by the Normans.

The German nobility pressed Henry for an end to the decades-long struggle with Rome, and in 1122, Pope Callixtus II and Henry V finally reached a settlement in the Concordat of Worms. Under the agreement, the clergy were to nominate bishops and abbots, but the emperor could settle contested elections. Further, bishops were to do homage to the emperor with regard to their temporal powers, such as their authority over land, while emperors were to confer spiritual homage on the pope for his spiritual authority, symbolized by the staff and the ring.

The following year, Callixtus convened the First Lateran Council, which confirmed the concordat, decreed the removal of simoniacs from office, and reiterated the Nicaean ban on priests living with women who were not relatives. The council forbade any layman to take possession or dispense of a church property.

Bruno's principles were affirmed, but he himself did not participate in the council, and he died less than a year later.

In 1139, Pope Innocent II called the Second Lateran Council to condemn a heretic who denied the pope's temporal authority. Among other things, the council set forth clearer definitions of what constituted simony. Yet again, the council's teachings were in line with those St. Bruno had articulated forty years earlier. Disregarded by the papacy at the end of his life, Bruno was nonetheless vindicated after his death. Just over forty years after the Second Lateran Council, in 1183, Bruno was canonized.

CHAPTER 5

The Persecution, Excommunication, and Execution of St. Joan of Arc

ST. JOAN OF ARC — *La Pucelle d'Orleans,* the Maid of Orléans — is perhaps the only female saint martyred as a direct result of the actions of the Catholic hierarchy.

Born around 1412 in Domrémy, France (now known as Domrémy-la-Pucelle, in her honor), to two tenant farmers, Joan came into a world torn by schism and war. The Great Western Schism, which began in 1378 and continued unresolved until five years after the Maid's birth, had divided the Catholic Church between, at one point, three putative popes. Meanwhile, France was fighting the Hundred Years' War with England; and she was internally divided between the Valois and the Burgundians, the latter of which were allied with the English. (The conflict is traditionally considered to have begun in 1337, and finally ended in 1475 with a victory of the Valois dynasty, which would rule France until the end of Henry III's reign in 1589.)

The *Pucelle,* born slightly past the midpoint of this great civil war, would play a crucial role in shifting the fortunes of war in favor of her homeland, and the eventual expulsion of the English from the continent.

Growing up, Joan was known to be deeply pious. She frequented the sacraments, was faithful in her recitation of the prayers of the Church her parents had taught her, and loved the poor. She was also, in many ways, a normal girl who often joined her friends in playing near what was known as the "Fairy Tree" — a fact that her future inquisitors would attempt to use to imply she had been engaged in witchcraft or other superstitious practices.

Around the age of thirteen, Joan began hearing voices. Though at first she was uncertain as to whose they were, soon enough she discerned that they were St. Michael the Archangel (and often other angels as well), as well as Sts. Katherine of Alexandria, and Margaret of Antioch (both ancient martyrs). The voices were often accompanied by a blazing light — and in time, they gave her a mission upon which the life and destiny of France would depend.

The Return of the King

In 1427, the war had already been raging for nearly a century. On one side were the English and their Burgundian allies fighting for King Henry VI, who claimed the throne of France through his mother, Catherine of Valois, the daughter of Charles VI. But under Salic law, the ancient French code, the throne could not be inherited through a woman. On the other side was the Valois. Their dynasty had ruled the kingdom of France since 1328, but now it seemed on the brink of defeat. The Valois king, Charles VI, had died in 1522. But five years after his death, his son Charles VII remained uncrowned. Since the fifth century Baptism of the Frankish king Clovis by the bishop of Reims, St. Remigius, Reims had served as the traditional site of the French coronation, where the new king would be recognized as the rightful ruler of the kingdom. But Reims was deep in enemy territory in 1427, threatening Charles's claim to the throne.

In the midst of what seemed a hopeless situation, the Maid's voices told her to go to the *dauphin*, or heir-in-waiting. In May 1428, at sixteen years old and without parental permission, she traveled to Vaucouleurs, the closest stronghold loyal to Charles. When she asked its garrison captain, Robert de Baudricourt, to take her to the *dauphin*, he dismissed her as a silly girl. However, she approached him again in January 1429, and this time her persistence and piety impressed him. Captain Baudricourt gave his blessing for her to travel to the *dauphin* at Chinon with six men-at-arms and wearing men's clothing. The journey took eleven days.

Upon arriving in Chinon, Charles's advisors were divided on whether or not to give her an audience. But the future king decided to grant one to her several days later, with a catch: as a test, he did not identify himself among all his courtiers. Joan was able to identify him immediately, despite never having seen him before. Charles was impressed, though he instructed his ecclesiastical advisors and theologians to question Joan to ensure that she was not a witch or a heretic.

It was during this religious examination that the Maid declared that the city of Orléans would witness a turning point that would validate her mission. On the advice of his advisors, Charles accepted her offer of assistance and provided her with a military cohort. It was at this time that Joan began using her famous white linen battle standard with a field of lilies, two angels on the sides, and the names of Jesus and Mary, whose names she always included in her letters.

The Turning Point at Orléans

With a military household and army provided by Charles, Joan set out for Orléans. On May 5, 1429, two days prior to the French counterattack, the *Pucelle* delivered an ultimatum to the English:

> You men of England, you have no right in this kingdom of
> France, the King of Heaven orders and commands you

through me, Joan the Pucelle, to abandon your strong-
holds and go back to your own country. If not, I will make
a war cry that will be remembered forever. And I am writing this to you for the third and final time; I will not write
anything further.
Jesus Maria.
Joan the Pucelle.[70]

Joan's prophecy that Orléans would be a turning point proved to be
true. The city had been under siege since October 12, 1428. On May
7, 1429, it was finally liberated, under the Maid's leadership. She was
injured during the battle. But her presence at multiple points had rallied the troops.

On the evening of May 9, 1429, Charles VII wrote a letter to
various towns celebrating the victory. Initially, he made no mention
of Joan. But after the arrival of messengers who informed him of her
decisive role in the battle, he added postscripts the following day in
which he called on the French to "honor the virtuous deeds and
wondrous things that this herald, who was present, has reported to
us, and the others too, regarding the Pucelle [Joan], who has always
been present at the accomplishment of all these deeds."

The King's Coronation

While some of his more conservative advisors counseled Charles to
proceed to the conquest of Normandy, Joan urged him to proceed
immediately to Reims to be crowned. Her advice won the day, though
there were still English positions to be cleared from a number of towns
along the Loire River. The English army was soundly defeated by Joan
at Patay on June 18, 1429. But Charles continued to vacillate on the
need to proceed to Reims. Yet, prodded by Joan, he once again as-
sented to her counsel and proceeded to Reims.

A month later, on July 17, 1429, Charles VII was crowned king
of France. Joan was present and stood near the altar with her battle

standard. She knelt before the finally consecrated monarch, and for the first time called him her king. That same day, she penned a letter to the Duke of Burgundy, who had hitherto been allied with the English, and urged him to make peace with the new king of France:

> Joan the Pucelle calls upon you by the King of Heaven, my rightful and sovereign Lord, that the King of France and you make a firm and lasting peace, pardoning each other with a sincere heart, as faithful Christians should do.... And I would have you know, by the King of Heaven, my rightful and sovereign Lord, for your good, for your honor and upon your life, that you will not win any battle against loyal Frenchmen, and that all those who wage war against the holy kingdom of France, wage war against King Jesus, King of Heaven and of all the world, my rightful and sovereign Lord.

Despite the extraordinary turn of events, Paris — the French capital — remained in the hands of the English and their Burgundian allies.

Joan's Capture

In the meantime, Joan's fame had spread across France. Now considered a living saint, in the following months she engaged in several military actions against the enemy. In the last of these, near Compiègne, she was outflanked and captured by the English. Charles VII made no attempt to rescue or bargain for her return.

News of her capture reached Paris — still under the control of the English-Burgundian alliance — on May 25, 1430. The faculty of the University of Paris — the most prestigious theological school in all Christendom — demanded that she be delivered either to the chief inquisitor or to Pierre Cauchon, the bishop of the Diocese of Beauvais, where she had been captured. The university was firmly on the English side and would be instrumental in Joan's eventual condemnation as a heretic and a witch.

On January 3, 1431, Joan was delivered to Bishop Cauchon, who had requested her on behalf of the English king, Henry VI. Her trial would take place in Rouen in February and March at the behest of a bishop and a theological faculty largely controlled by the English, and thus engaged in a political confrontation under the guise of religion. If Joan could be condemned as a heretic and a witch, then Charles VII's claim to the throne of France would once again be undermined.

The Maid on Trial

The *Pucelle*'s trial began with a public examination on February 21, 1431. The inquisition had several theories by which it attempted to condemn her. First, it sought to delegitimize her visions by arguing that they were actually demonic spirits. Second, they claimed she was impious for leaving her hometown without parental permission and for wearing male clothes. Third, they attempted to undermine her assertion that she had received God's command to fight the English, her denial that they had any claims on the kingdom of France, and her support of Charles VII. Finally, they maintained that she was unwilling to submit to the authority of the Church, despite the facts that she had consistently and explicitly stated that she would, and that she had appealed — as was her right — to the pope. In a blatant miscarriage of justice (which ultimately led to her rehabilitation by the pope) this appeal was denied, revealing the ugly, political nature of the trial.

Joan was repeatedly enjoined to take an oath swearing to answer any and every question she was asked by the tribunal. She repeatedly refused, declaring "she would willingly swear with regard to what concerned her father and her mother and what she had done after she had taken the road to France." But as for her revelations, she said:

> She had never told or revealed them to anyone except only to Charles [VII], who, she said, was her King, and she would not reveal them even if her head should be cut

off, because she would not reveal to anyone what she knew from her visions or her secret counsel; and within the following eight days, she would know for sure whether she ought to reveal these things.

The judges admonished the Maid to swear an oath that she would speak the truth "regarding those things which concerned our faith." She did so, on a missal. Bishop Cauchon forbade Joan from leaving the prison, under penalty of being convicted of the crime of heresy. "But she replied," says the trial record, "that she did not accept this injunction, adding that if she escaped, no one could blame her for having broken or violated her oath because she had never given her oath to anyone."

Her second public examination took place the following day, on February 22, 1431. The Maid recalled that at the age of thirteen she began hearing a voice from God that was often accompanied by a "great light." She later discerned that it was the voice of an angel, "that this voice had always protected her well and that she understood this voice clearly." This angel, she said, guided her to Charles and taught her how to recognize him, despite the fact that she did not know what he looked like.

Her third public examination took place two days later, on February 24, 1431. She was again asked to swear an oath, but she again refused, asserting her right not to answer certain questions, especially those related to her revelations, as they had contained information she believed was confidential. Although just a young girl in what must have been a terrifying situation, the saint showed an otherworldly boldness that came from absolute confidence in God. After she requested God's counsel, "the voice told her that she would answer boldly, and that God would help her." She then said the following directly to the bishop: "You say that you are my judge; take care what you are doing because, in truth, I have been sent by God and you put yourself in great danger."

She was asked whether the voice forbade her from answering certain questions, to which she responded: "I will not answer you about that. And I have revelations concerning the King [Charles VII] which I will not tell you."

"She firmly believed — as firmly as she believed in the Christian faith and that God redeemed us from the pains of hell — that this voice came from God and by His command," the trial minutes record.

"This voice comes from God," said the Maid, "and I believe that I am not telling you clearly what I know, and I am much more afraid of failing them by saying something that may displease these voices than I am of answering you.... The voices told me to say certain things to the King and not to you."

The judges consistently tried to trap her in theological error in order to convict her of heresy. For example, when asked whether she was in a state of grace, Joan said, "If I am not, may God put me there, and if I am, may God keep me there. I would be the saddest person in the world if I knew that I was not in the grace of God."

Her fourth public examination took place on February 27, 1431. She once again said that the voices had told her in the intervening period to answer her judges boldly, and that Sts. Katherine of Alexandria and Margaret of Antioch, who had not spoken to her in seven years, were among them, having named themselves to her. St. Michael, she said, had also comforted her. She told the court she would reveal anything she had permission from the Lord to reveal, "but with regard to the revelations concerning the King of France, she would not say this without the permission of her voice."

At this examination she was directly confronted on the issue of wearing male clothing:

> Asked if [God] ordered her to wear the clothing of a man, she answered that the clothing was such a small matter, the least thing; and she did not take male clothing on the advice of any man of this world; and she did not take this outfit, or do anything, except by the command of God and the angels.

Asked if it seemed to her that the command for her to take up male clothing was lawful, she replied: "Everything I have done is by the command of the Lord; and if He had ordered me to take up a different outfit, I would have done it, because this would have been done by the command of God."...

Asked if she believed that she had done well in taking male clothing, she replied that everything that she had done by the command of the Lord, she believed had been done well and she expected a good guarantor and aid for it.

The court also asked her if she had ever put her sword on an altar, as this would have been considered a desecration of it. She said she had not. She also said she herself carried a standard into battle in order to avoid killing anyone, which she declared she had never done.

Her fifth public examination took place several days later, on March 1, 1431. "Everything that I truly know to relate to the trial, I will gladly tell," Joan once again declared. Again, "Joan held and believed that we should obey our lord the pope who was at Rome." During this examination, the Maid also delivered a prophecy of an even greater English defeat within seven years:

She said that before seven years were past, the English would lose a greater prize than they did before Orleans, and that they would lose everything in France. She added that the English would suffer a greater loss than they had ever had in France, and that this would be a great victory that God would send to the French.

Asked how she knew this, she answered: "I know this for sure by revelation that has been made to me, and that this will happen within seven years...." She also said that she knew this by revelation, just as well as she knew that we were then in front of her.

Asked when it would happen, she replied that she did not know either the day or the hour....

> She also said that she knew for certain her King
> would win the kingdom of France.

She also claimed that Sts. Katherine and Margaret "told her that her King would be restored in his kingdom, whether his enemies wished it or not. She also said that they promised to lead this Joan to heaven and so she asked it of them."

Once again, the court attempted to get Joan to claim she was certain of her soul's state, which would have violated Catholic doctrine. They also continued their attempt to extract from her what she had told Charles VII, clearly revealing their political agenda: "Asked what sign she gave to her King that she came from God, she replied: 'I have always answered that you will not drag that from my mouth. Go and ask him.'"

They pressed again:

> Asked if she did not know the sign that she gave to the
> King, she replied: "You will not learn it from me."
> Then, because it was said to her that this concerned
> the trial, she answered: "I will not tell you anything about
> that which I have promised to keep most secret." And she
> also said: "I have promised this in such a place that I could
> not tell you without perjury."

Her sixth public examination came on March 3, 1431. She was once again challenged on her wearing of male clothing: "Asked if she believed that she would have been delinquent or in mortal sin for taking a woman's dress, she replied that she did better to obey and to serve her sovereign Lord, that is to say God."

Given the lack of progress, the bishop and his clerics concluded they must approach Joan privately in her prison cell. The first such examination took place on March 10, 1431. Nothing significant came of this or many of the other private examinations. She consistently refused to perjure herself, by either violating the oaths she had already taken or assuming new oaths she did not in conscience believe she could take given what her voices had told her.

Her eighth private examination took place on March 17, 1431. Once again, she was asked whether she would accept the Church's verdict:

> Asked if she would submit her words and deeds to the verdict of the Church, she replied: "I submit myself to God who sent me, to the Blessed Mary and to all the saints of heaven. And it seems to me that God and the Church are one, and no difficulty should be made about this. Why do you make difficulties about this?"

She was once again challenged on her wearing of male clothing, to which she responded with more detail:

> Asked whether it would please God that she had said that she would take the clothing of a woman if they would allow her to go [free], she answered that if she were given permission to go in woman's dress she would immediately put on male clothing and do what was commanded of her by the Lord. And she had formerly answered this, and nothing whatsoever would induce her to take an oath not to arm herself or to wear male clothing, but she would accomplish the command of the Lord.

When asked if Sts. Katherine and Margaret hated the English (a question that was obviously political, having nothing to do with the Catholic Faith), Joan replied in a way reminiscent of Christ's response to the duplicitous Pharisees: "They love what God loves and they hate what God hates."

They pressed her again:

> Asked if God hated the English, she answered that she knew nothing of the love or hatred that God had for the English or of what he would do to their souls, but she was certain that they would be driven out of France, with the

exception of those who died there, and that God would
send victory to the French against the English.

Her inquisitors asked her whether God had been against the English
when they had been prospering in France: "She replied that she did
not know whether God hated the French, but she believed that he
wished to allow them to be beaten for their sins, if they were in sin."

Once again, she was challenged on her male clothing: "Asked
what warrant and what help she expected from the Lord because she
wore male clothing, she answered that she awaited no other reward
than the salvation of her soul both for the clothing and for the other
things that she had done."

Her ninth and final private examination took place later the
same day. She was questioned whether her military victories were
due to her or to the Lord: "Asked if the hope of victory was founded
upon this standard or upon herself, she answered that it was founded
on the Lord and on no one else."

The *Pucelle* once again appealed to the pope:

> Asked if it did not seem to her that she was bound to an-
> swer truthfully to our lord the pope, the vicar of God, on
> all that she might be asked regarding the faith and the
> matter of her conscience more fully than she had replied
> to us, she answered that she demanded to be led before
> our lord the pope, and then she would answer before him
> all that she should answer.

With that, her examinations came to an end. A few days later, on Palm
Sunday, March 25, 1431, Joan asked to attend Mass in male clothing.
She had always claimed that the issue of whether or not she could
wear female clothing was not in her power but rather in that of the
voices she had heard, namely the angels and saints: "Joan replied to
this that as far as this depended upon her, she would not receive the

Eucharist [*viaticum*] by changing her costume for that of a woman; and she begged to be allowed to hear mass in the clothing of a man, saying that this outfit would not change her soul, and that to wear it was not against the Church."

A final interrogation was inflicted on the Maid on Easter Sunday, March 31, 1431. She was once more asked if she would submit to the authority of the Church:

> She answered that she submitted to the Church militant regarding that which was sought from her, provided that it did not command her to do anything impossible. And she held it [to be] impossible that she revoke what she had done or said, as declared to the trial, on the subject of her visions and the revelations that she said that she had had from God; and she would not revoke them for anything. She would not stop doing what God made, commanded and would command her to do for any man alive. And it would be impossible for her to revoke these [visions and revelations]; and if the Church wished to make her do anything else contrary to the command that she said had been given by God, she would not do it for anything.
>
> Asked if she would submit to the Church, if the Church militant told her that her revelations were illusions or diabolical things, she replied that she would always submit to God whose command she would always obey; and she certainly knew that what was written in her trial came from the command of God, and it would have been impossible for her to do contrary to what she claimed at the trial to have done at the command of God. And if the Church commanded her to do the contrary, she would not rely upon any man in the world except God, and she would always carry out the just command of God himself.
>
> Asked if she believed herself subject to the Church of God on earth, namely to our lord the pope, the cardinals, archbishops, bishops and other prelates of the Church, she answered yes, God being served first.

In the saint's answer, we hear the simple but powerful articulation of basic Catholic doctrine since the beginning: that no prelate, including the pope, can be followed if his actions are in direct contravention of the Faith.

On April 5, 1431, twelve articles of accusation were read against her. On May 19, 1431, the University of Paris delivered its own opinions of each article.

It claimed of her revelations that "either these are imagined, corrupting and pernicious lies, or that these apparitions and revelations are superstitious, from malign and diabolical spirits such as Belial, Satan, and Behemoth."

They also accused Joan of being a blasphemer, and consecrating herself to Satan:

> The said woman is a blasphemer of God, and a despiser of God in His sacraments, setting aside divine law, sacred doctrine and the laws of the Church; she thinks evilly and strays from the faith, all the while boasting vainly. She must be held to be suspect of idolatry, and of the consecration of herself and of her garments to demons, imitating the rites of pagans.

Her revelations made her, they said, "an idolater, an invoker of demons, and a wanderer from the faith; she utters rash assertions and has made an unlawful oath." Presumably this "unlawful oath" was that by which she promised her voices she would not reveal to the English what she had said to her own king.

With respect to the authority of the Church, they accused her of being "schismatic, holding a reprehensible view on the unity and the authority of the Church, an apostate, and until now strays stubbornly from the faith."

The faculty declared her an apostate on the grounds that "she has had the hair that God gave her for a veil cut off for an evil purpose, and also because, to the same end, she has abandoned the clothing of a woman and is dressed like a man." Likewise, "this woman is a liar and soothsayer when she says that she is sent from God and that she speaks to angels and to saints, whereas she does not demonstrate this by the operation of a miracle or by testimony of the scriptures."

Thus, they recommended that "she must be abandoned to the decision of the secular judge on whether she receives the punishment appropriate to the quality of her crime."

The Maid Blinks

Several days later, on May 24, 1431, a sermon was preached to Joan in which she was corrected for her supposed errors. When it was complete, she was once again asked if she would submit to the judgment of the Church, in response to which she once again appealed to the pope: "Regarding the submission to the Church, I have answered them on this point: let everything that I have said and done be sent to Rome, to our holy lord the pope, upon whom I rely after God. As for my words and deeds, I have done them for God."

She was once more asked if she would revoke *all* her condemned words and deeds. She again responded, "I rely upon God and our lord the pope." Her judges responded that "this would not do, and that it was not possible to go in search of our lord the pope so far away," claiming that the bishops, as ordinaries of their dioceses, were competent to pass final judgment.

This was an abuse, and ecclesiastical corruption of the highest order, as canon law itself preserved the right of appeal to the pope. The ordinaries were assuming to themselves the totality of the Church's authority.

Bishop Cauchon then began to read the final sentence. At this point, Joan "blinked" and declared that she

> wished to abide by all that the Church ordained and that we, the judges wished to say and decree, saying that she would obey our ruling in all things. And she said repeatedly that since the churchmen said that the apparitions and revelations that she said she had seen were not to be upheld or believed,

she did not wish to maintain them; but in all things she would rely upon our holy mother the Church and us, the judges.

She was asked to sign an abjuration, which was read out loud, repeated by her, and signed with her own hand. Despite the abjuration, Joan continued to be subject to solitary penance in prison.

Four days later, on May 28, 1431, the judges visited Joan in her cell, and discovered that she had again put on male clothing. They also asked if she had again heard the voices of Katherine and Margaret. She confirmed she had, and they told her she had committed "treason" by her abjuration. She told the judges that she did not understand herself to have made an oath that she would not wear male clothing. She once again asked to go to Mass, but was denied. She told her accusers: "If she declared that God had not sent her, she would damn herself and that in truth God had sent her."

Thus, at the encouragement of her voices, she recanted the abjuration:

> She said that she had never done anything against God or the faith, whatever they had ordered her to revoke, and she did not understand what was in the schedule of abjuration.... She said that she did not intend to revoke anything unless it pleased God.... She said that if the judges wished, she would resume female clothing; and for the rest, she would not do anything more.

With that, the *Pucelle's* fate was sealed. "We declare you excommunicate by law and a heretic," her panel of judges unanimously proclaimed,

> and since your errors have been condemned in a public sermon, we judge that, as a limb of Satan cut from the Church, infected with the leprosy of heresy, so that you may not equally infect the other limbs of Christ, you must be abandoned to the secular power, and so we abandon

you, beseeching this same power to limit its judgment of you this side of death and the mutilation of your limbs and, if true signs of repentance appear in you, to permit the sacrament of penance to be administered to you.

The Death of the Pucelle

On Monday, May 30, 1431, nineteen-year-old Joan was escorted to the Place du Vieux-Marché in Rouen, where a final sermon was preached to her; then she was escorted to the pyre upon which she would be burned. She asked a Dominican who was present to lift a crucifix so she could see it, and to shout assurances of salvation to her. Nearly all who were present who were later interviewed for her resuscitation trial said they believed she was a faithful Christian. A few days later, King Henry VI of England and the University of Paris announced that she had been executed on the grounds of heresy, witchcraft, and a litany of other false charges.

Joan Resuscitated

After Joan's death, the French and the English agreed that her military campaigns had made a huge impact and had shifted the fortunes of war decisively in France's favor. As the Duke of Bedford, one of Henry VI's senior advisors, observed in an oft-quoted letter to the king:

> Everything prospered there for you until the siege of Orléans, undertaken by God knows whose advice.... It seemed that there fell by the hand of God a great stroke upon your people assembled there, caused in great part, as I think, by lack of proper belief and by unlawful doubt aroused by a disciple and follower of the fiend called the Pucelle, who used false enchantment and sorcery.... [Her] strikes and complete victory not only greatly reduced the number of your people there but also drained the courage of the remnant in marvelous ways and encouraged your adversary's party and enemy to rally at once in great number.

Twenty years later, when Charles VII entered Rouen, he ordered an inquiry into the trial, which was followed by an even more thorough investigation by cardinal legate Guillame d'Estouteville. But Joan's rehabilitation didn't begin in earnest until her family appealed to Pope Calixtus III, who on June 11, 1455, ordered a resuscitation trial to take place.

He said that the testimony of her family and friends was that Joan "had detested all heresy during her life and did not hold any belief, [or make any] affirmation or declaration, that smacked of heresy or was contrary to the Catholic faith and to the traditions of the holy Roman Church." In addition, the pope said, the evidence was such that it appeared bribes had convinced enemies of Joan and her family to accuse her of heresy and other crimes. The pope's conclusions were damning:

> At last, though the inquiry had not been legitimately constituted and it could not establish that this Joan had fallen into heresy or other things contrary to the faith, or had committed abuses or crimes of this type, or had persisted in errors contrary to the faith, because this was neither notorious nor true, and although Joan had asked the Bishop and Jean Le Maistre [the Inquisitor] that if they were claiming to accuse her of having said any words smacking of heresy or against the faith they should submit these questions to the examination of the holy apostolic see, whose judgment she would accept, they did not pay any attention; removing from Joan all means of defending her innocence and rejecting the rules of law, following their sole desire and their private will, proceeding in this matter of inquisition in a manner [that was] invalid and contrary to law, they brought an iniquitous and definitive sentence against Joan, judging her a heretic and guilty of other crimes and abuses of that type. On these grounds, Joan was then led cruelly to the last torture, to the peril of the souls of those who had condemned her; to the ignominy and disgrace, the pain and suffering of her mother, brothers, and relatives.

The pope declared that Joan had been "condemned maliciously, without having committed an error." He ordered the appropriate ecclesiastical ordinaries to convene a nullification trial. Many witnesses from Joan's childhood as well as from the time of her military exploits confirmed she was a woman of great piety and prayer. Far from being a heretic, let alone a witch, she was a faithful Catholic, intent on nothing more than faithfulness to her God-given mission.

The new tribunal, consisting of three French bishops, declared its sentence of nullification on July 7, 1456. "[We] consider that the actions of the deceased [Joan] were more worthy of admiration than condemnation," they said. "We are amazed at the judgment brought against her, which condemned her, by reason of its form and its substance."

With regard to her supposed revelations, the bishops declared they did not know if they were true or not, "so we rely on God in this matter." This is a remarkable admission, for as French bishops, they no doubt had as much of an earthly interest in politicizing Joan's nullification trial as the English-backed clergyman had to politicize her initial trial. But they did not. They were not canonizing her — this would not happen for nearly five hundred years — but simply exonerating her of the grave and ultimate injustice that had been done to her by men who were successors of the apostles and their priesthood.

As to the conduct of her trial itself, they declared that the twelve articles of indictment against her were made in a "malicious, deceitful, slanderous manner with fraud and spitefulness." They continued:

> The truth was passed over in silence, and false assertions were introduced at many essential points, so that the minds of those who were deliberating and judging could be drawn towards another opinion. Numerous aggravating circumstances not contained in the trial record and in the declarations cited above were also added, without due cause, and nothing was said about some circumstances that exonerated and justified her on many points. Finally, the forms of

words were modified, changing the substance. This is why we quash, reject, and annul these articles as false, extracted by slander and deceit, different from the testimony.

They concluded:

> We say and pronounce that we judge that this trial record and sentences that contain deceit, slander, contradiction, and manifest error of law and of fact, as well as the aforesaid abjuration, the execution and all that then ensued, were and are null, invalid, without effect or value.... [W] e justify her [Joan] in this completely.

They ordered that a cross be erected in the square "where Joan died in a cruel and horrible fire," and that a "solemn sermon" be delivered in her memory.

Pope Pius II, who succeeded Calixtus III and was the only medieval pope to write an autobiography, wrote that he believed Joan "was inspired by the Holy Spirit, as her deeds proved." On the issue of her wearing male clothing, he wrote:

> When Joan was questioned about her faith, she replied in conformity with the Christian religion. When examined as to her character, she was found to be chaste and very honest. The examination lasted for many days. They found no deceit, guile, or evil intent in her. The only difficulty was her dress. When asked why she had worn the garments of men that were forbidden to women, she replied that she was a virgin, and either outfit was suitable for a virgin. She had been instructed by God to wear men's dress and to use the arms of men. Having been examined, she was again sent before the dauphin. "I have come to you, son of kings," she said, "at the command of God, not by my own counsel. He commands you to follow me. If you obey, I will restore your throne to you, and very soon, I will place the crown on your head at Reims."

Thus, for the pope, Joan's wearing male clothing was simply part of her God-assigned military mission on behalf of France, whose authenticity was confirmed on numerous occasions, including the fulfillment of various prophecies made by Joan herself.

Pius II also believed that Joan had been sent by God to assist France in its fight against the English to keep it from falling into pride, describing her deeds in glowing terms:

> It might be that now too it [France] was to be defended by a virgin sent by God, and that the task had been committed to the weaker sex so that the French might not trust in their own virtue with pride, as was their habit; in any case a girl whose advice was so full of sense could not be regarded as mad....
>
> It is possible that the English, who had been vanquished by her in so many battles, never regarded themselves as entirely safe with the virgin alive, even though she was a prisoner, and that they feared that she might escape or work some magic and therefore sought an excuse for her death. When the judges learned that the girl had taken the clothing of a man, they condemned her to be burned as a relapse. She bore the flames with unshakeable and undaunted spirit.

"Thus died Joan," wrote Pius II. He commended her as "an astonishing and marvelous virgin, who restored the kingdom of France when it had collapsed and was almost torn asunder, who inflicted so many heavy defeats upon the English, who, having been made a commander of men, kept her purity unstained among companies of soldiers, about whom no breath of scandal was ever heard."

The New Deborah

While she was unjustly condemned, excommunicated, and executed at the behest of the hierarchy itself, the behavior of the local bishop who condemned Joan as a heretic and sorceress does not necessarily implicate the whole Church. Bishop Pierre Cauchon may well have believed the lies about Joan.

Nevertheless, he still denied her the right of appeal to the pope — a right the Church itself had guaranteed in canon law — and according to the conclusion of the nullification trial, the accusations against Joan were extracted by slander, lies, and political intrigue by the English, which required the figure behind their enemy's victories to be a villain.

But Joan was not a villain. She was a new Deborah, the great judge of the Israelites in a time when the men were weak, cowardly, and evil. "And the people of Israel again did what was evil in the sight of the Lord," says Scripture of the time preceding the judgeship of Deborah (Judg. 4:1). She too was raised to guide the nation of Israel alongside a man, Barak, as Joan was raised alongside Charles VII. Deborah and Barak led Israel to victory against its enemies, whom God had sent as a scourge for their sins. Likewise with Joan and Charles against the English.

On May 16, 1920, Pope Benedict XV promulgated the bull *Divine Disponente*, which canonized St. Joan the *Pucelle*. In the bull, the pope called Joan the "Handmaid of God." "But now let the eyes of all Christians be turned to the nineteen-year-old Saint, who, in order to carry out the commandments of God, left her family, abandoned feminine practices, took up arms and led soldiers to fight," he declared. And in perhaps the greatest lesson to be drawn from this saint who was persecuted from within, the pope offered this stirring exhortation to the Church regarding Joan's Christ-like endurance of suffering at the very hands of the hierarchy:

> That justice, which was lacking in the process [of Joan's condemnation] due to unbridled human emotion, did not slow it down, and the Supreme Pontiff was able more quickly to fully restore the reputation of Joan of Arc, whose example should be before the eyes of all who endure unjust evils, so that they can calmly await restoration from a just and eternal Index.[71]

CHAPTER 6

The Persecution and Execution of St. John Fisher and St. Thomas More

SAINTS JOHN FISHER AND Thomas More rose nearly to the pinnacle of their respective orders: Fisher in the sacred order, as a bishop (and just prior to his execution, appointed as a cardinal by the pope), and More in the temporal order, as chancellor of England. Nonetheless, they were willing to surrender all their honors, and indeed their very lives, in order to remain faithful to Christ and His Church by defending the authority of the pope and the holiness of marriage.

A Brewing Storm

In 1501, Catherine of Aragon, the daughter of King Ferdinand and Queen Isabella of Spain, married Prince Arthur, the son of King Henry VII of England and the heir apparent to the English throne. Arthur died several months later.

Catherine would be in limbo for years as the royalty of both countries sought to maintain their alliance. In 1503, the rulers of both countries requested a dispensation from Pope Alexander VI that would allow the English king's new heir apparent, Henry (who would become Henry VIII), to marry Catherine. The law of the Church forbade marriages between a man and a woman who were too closely related by either blood (consanguinity) or marriage (affinity). While Henry and Catherine were not related by blood, they did fall within the Church's proscribed degrees of affinity because of Catherine's marriage to Henry's brother, Arthur. In order to get married, they needed a dispensation from Church law, which could only be obtained from the pope — who, as the chief lawgiver of the Church, had the authority to dispense from Church law on a case-by-case basis.

The dispensation was granted in 1504 by Pope Julius II. However, because of complications relating to the dowry and other issues, Henry and Catherine did not marry until 1509.

Once married, the couple lived a happy life for almost a decade. Naturally, Henry desired a male heir who could inherit the throne upon his death, as a female heir would create problems for dynastic succession. Between 1510 and 1518, Catherine gave birth to six children. Two of these were male. Unfortunately, all of them except Mary (who would later become the queen of England from 1553 to 1558) were stillborn or died in early infancy.

In 1522, a young noblewoman named Anne Boleyn returned to England after spending much of her childhood in France. She caught the eye of the king, who would soon initiate proceedings to end his marriage with Catherine and marry Anne, with the ostensible hope of obtaining a male heir to the throne.

"The King's Great Matter"

Those proceedings — the beginning of "the king's great matter" — began in 1527, when Henry secretly requested an annulment from the pope of his marriage to Catherine.

Henry claimed that the book of Leviticus made his marriage to Catherine contrary to divine law. The verses in question were Leviticus

18:16, and 20:21, which read respectively as follows: "You shall not un-cover the nakedness of your brother's wife; she is your brother's naked-ness"; and "If a man takes his brother's wife, it is impurity; he has uncovered his brother's nakedness, they shall be childless."

Henry interpreted the fact that Catherine had not produced a male heir to be a confirmation of the Levitical curse that "they shall be childless." Of course, having female children contradicted that argument, but Henry plowed forward anyway.

The English king also maintained that the Levitical verses were part of the divine law. The Catholic Church had traditionally divided the ancient Israelite law into three categories: the moral, ritual, and judicial precepts. The ritual and judicial precepts were considered to be specific to the Old Covenant and to have been fulfilled by Christ, and were thus not binding. The moral precepts, however, including the Ten Commandments, re-mained binding as a matter of divine law. Henry claimed that these provi-sions of Leviticus were among those moral precepts and thus binding by divine law. If that was true, then the pope had no authority to issue the original dispensation that allowed Henry and Catherine to marry — and thus Henry was entitled to an annulment, freeing him to marry Anne.

While annulments were often granted to Christian princes as a mat-ter of course, 1527 was not a good year to be applying for annulments to the pope — especially when the spouse in question was the aunt of the Holy Roman Emperor, Charles V. The queen's uncle was not only em-peror but was also holding the pope prisoner in Rome after he had be-sieged the Eternal City that same year (with mostly Lutheran troops).

Political considerations aside, Catherine also had the much stronger argument, which consisted of three points: first, the Leviti-cal verses didn't mean what Henry claimed; second, they belonged to the ritual and judicial precepts that were no longer binding; and third, her marriage to Arthur had not been consummated.

On the first point, it seems obvious that the Levitical verses are concerned about adultery between a brother and his brother's current wife, rather than a blanket prohibition on marrying a woman who had previously been your brother's spouse. This is particularly true in light of Deuteronomy 25:5, which enjoined the very thing that Henry claimed violated divine law: "If brothers dwell together, and one of them dies and has no son, the wife of the dead shall not be married outside the family to a stranger; her husband's brother shall go in to her, and take her as his wife, and perform the duty of a husband's brother to her."

Second, the Levitical verses were almost certainly part of what the Church considered the judicial precepts of the Torah, positive precepts specific to Israel rather than binding on humanity as a whole. Thus, they could not be said to be binding on Christians as a matter of divine law.

Third, Catherine swore under oath that she had still been a virgin when she married Henry, and that Henry was aware of this when he married her. She invited him to testify to the contrary under oath, and he refused. Henry almost certainly knew that her previous marriage to his brother had not been consummated, which made the Levitical verses even less applicable.

Nonetheless, Henry — who had earned the title "Defender of the Faith" for his erudite refutation of Lutheran heresies in his 1521 work *Defense of the Seven Sacraments* — convinced himself (or pretended to convince himself) that he was in a state of mortal sin based on his interpretation of the Levitical verses. His scrupulosity predictably led him down the same path that the scrupulous Martin Luther had trod, and to the same end: a final break with Rome.

The King Consults His Greatest Statesman

Sir Thomas More was brought into the "great matter" when he returned from an embassy to France in the summer of 1527. The king opened the Bible before him, and argued that his marriage to Catherine of Aragon was both void and incestuous, given her prior marriage to Henry's late brother.

Initially, More tried to convince the king that he was not qualified to render judgment on the matter. But Henry would not relent. Eventually, More studied the issue and, with significant patristic support, informed the king that he did not believe he had the winning side of the argument.

Despite More's position, Henry appointed him his Lord Chancellor in 1529. At his investiture in Westminster Hall (the same hall where six years later he would be tried and found guilty of treason against the king), the king specifically ordered that there be a "declaration how much all England was beholden to Sir Thomas More for his good service, and how worthy he was to have the highest room in the realm, and how dearly his Grace loved and trusted him, for which ... he had great cause to rejoice."[72]

Perhaps the greatest irony, among many, was that More was recruited for, and had himself expressed a desire to confront, the various heresies that had lately appeared — under the guise of Martin Luther, William Tyndale, and others. In the end, however, his unwillingness to bend to the will of another eventual heretic — the "Defender of the Faith," his king, and his friend — would result in his own martyrdom.

The King Consults His Holiest Bishop

In addition to More, the king likewise consulted John Fisher on his "great matter." Indeed, Fisher was far more involved day-to-day than More. Henry's holiest bishop was by then the most renowned scholar in England, and he emphatically affirmed both the pope's authority to have granted the original dispensation and the validity of Henry's marriage to Catherine. In fact, Fisher became the queen's chief counselor and supporter, for which he would ultimately experience the full weight of royal wrath.

In an early exchange between Henry and some of the bishops he had consulted on the matter (including Fisher), the archbishop of Canterbury had timidly declared, "That is truth if it pleases your highness. I doubt not but all my brethren here present will affirm the same." Fisher would have none of it. "No, sir, not I," he declared. "Ye have not my consent thereto."[73] This practice of openly contradicting the king, when necessary, would become a consistent pattern for Fisher, who went on to represent Catherine at the papal legate's court in 1529. He was even more frank at this meeting, citing the example of St. John the Baptist's defense of the sanctity of marriage before Herod as an inspiration for his own conduct. The secretary of Cardinal Campeggio, who was handling the matter, recorded the following about the exchange between Fisher and the court:

> Therefore, both in order not to procure the damnation of his soul, and in order not to be unfaithful to the king, or to fail in doing the duty which he owed to the truth, in a matter of such great importance, he [Fisher] presented himself before their reverend lordships to declare, to affirm, and with forcible reasons to demonstrate to them that this marriage of the king and the queen can be dissolved by no power human or divine, and for this opinion he declared he would even lay down his life. He added that the Baptist [John the Baptist] in olden times regarded it as impossible for him to die more gloriously than in the cause of marriage, and that as it was not so holy at that time as it has now become by the shedding of Christ's blood [becoming a sacrament], he could encourage himself more ardently, more effectually, and with greater confidence to dare any great or extreme peril whatever....
>
> This affair of [the bishop of] Rochester was unexpected and unforeseen, and consequently has kept everyone in wonder. What he will do we shall see when the day comes. You already know what sort of man he is, and may imagine what is likely to happen.

Statements from both the king and the queen on their positions were submitted. Fisher submitted six in total, which were as follows:

1. There is no obstacle to marriage between the two parties that cannot be removed by the authority of the pope. [Referring to the original dispensation]

2. Since the pope has this power, there can be no doubt that he exercised it by the dispensation.

3. Once these obstacles had been removed, there was nothing to prevent them from marrying according to established law.

4. The contract of marriage and the marriage itself were celebrated according to the rites and ceremonies of the Church, as many can testify.

5. God, by the sacrament of marriage, gave his assent to this union, and consecrated it by his invisible power; that, no one can question.

6. This sacramental union and connection, by which God formed a bond between these persons, made legitimate by the dispensation, is unbreakable by any power.

In these six points, Fisher clearly laid down the gauntlet that would ultimately cost him his life. Later that summer, in August 1529, Fisher and More appeared before Parliament, which had been summoned by the king. By the time it ended in 1536, relations between Church and state had been revolutionized forever.

Meanwhile, Henry was scouring European universities to gain scholarly support for his position in an effort to cajole Rome in his direction. In 1530, he organized a petition laying out that support and persuaded a number of lords and bishops to sign it. Both Fisher and More refused.

The "Reformation Parliament" almost immediately set to work encroaching on what had previously been well-established ecclesiastical jurisdiction. Fisher was alarmed. His speech, as reconstructed by an earlier biographer, called on the legislators to remember the rightful authority and jurisdiction of the Church, excoriated what he saw as the blatant envy and covetousness for the temporal possessions of the Church, and presciently predicted national apostasy if the parliamentary intrusions were not stopped:

> My lords, I pray you for God's sake, consider what bills are here daily preferred from the Commons. What the same may sound in some of your ears I cannot tell, but in my ears they sound all to this effect, that our holy mother the Church, being left unto us by the great liberality and diligence of our forefathers in most perfect and peaceable freedom, shall now by us be brought into servile thraldom like a bondmaid, or rather by little and little to be clean banished and driven out of our confines and dwelling places.... What strange words be here uttered, not to be heard of any Christian ears and unworthy to be spoken in the hearing of Christian princes? For they say that bishops and their officials, abbots, priests and others of the clergy are covetous, ravenous, insatiable, idle, cruel, and so forth. What? Are all of this sort, or is there any of these abuses that the clergy seek not to extirpate and destroy? Be there not laws already provided by them against such and many more disasters? Are not books full of them to be read of such as list to read them if they were executed? But, my lords, beware of yourselves and your country, nay, beware of the liberty of our mother the Church. Luther, one of the most cruel enemies to the faith that ever was, is at hand, and the common people study for novelties and with good will hear what can be said in favor of heresy....
>
> These men now among us seem to reprove the life and doings of the clergy, but after such a sort as they endeavor to bring them into contempt and hatred of the laity. And so finding fault with other men's manners, whom they have no authority to correct, omit and forget their own, which is far worse and much more out of order than the other. But if the truth were known, ye shall find that they rather hunger and thirst after the riches and possessions of the clergy than after amendment of their faults and abuses.... Except ye

resist manfully by your authorities this violent heap of mis-
chief offered by the Commons, ye shall shortly see all obedience withdrawn first from the clergy and after from
yourself. Whereupon will ensue the utter ruin and danger
of the Christian faith, and in place of it (that which is likely
to follow) the most wicked and tyrannical government of
the Turks. For ye shall find that all these mischiefs among
them riseth only through the lack of faith.

In December 1530, a writ of praemunire was issued against the entire
body of the clergy. *Praemunire* referred to a set of fourteenth-century
laws designed to restrict the exercise of papal authority in England.
The clergy offered more than £100,000 for a pardon. But even this
was not sufficient for Henry. The clergy were informed on February
9, 1531, that they would be granted the royal pardon if they agreed to
the king's title as "Protector and Supreme Head of the English Church
and Clergy," a direct usurpation of papal authority over the Church.

Fisher alone stood against the measure initially, but he persuaded the clergy to reject Henry's proposal. But then Henry's coun-
selors convinced them to capitulate with another promise:

That if they would among them acknowledge and confess
him for supreme head of the Church of England, he
would never by virtue of that grant assume unto himself
any more power, jurisdiction, or authority over them than
all other kings of this realm, his predecessors, had done
before, neither would he promulgate any spiritual law or
exercise, any spiritual jurisdiction, nor yet by any kind of
means inter-meddle himself among them in altering,
changing, ordering, or judging any spiritual business.

If Henry intended nothing different than his predecessors, it raises
the question why there was a need for a new title. But the clergy fell
for it — Fisher alone excepted,

who utterly refused to condescend thereunto, and therefore earnestly required the lords and others of the Convocation to consider and take good heed what mischiefs and
inconveniences would ensue to the whole Church of
Christ by this unreasonable and unseemly grant made to
a temporal prince, which never yet to this day was once so
much as demanded before, neither can it by any means or
reason be in the power or rule of any temporal potentate.

Thanks in large part to Fisher they did include the following qualification: "as much as is permitted by the law of God." But Fisher was
bitterly disappointed, even while he consented to this new "qualified"
title, given the physical threats against him and the clergy.

But the king was far from done.

The following year, Parliament passed a statute forbidding the
payment of tithes to the Holy See, though Henry was permitted to
suspend the operation of the law to facilitate an arrangement with
the pope with respect to his marriage to Catherine. The message was
not subtle: if the pope did not allow Henry's divorce, the Holy See's
income from England would be suspended entirely.

Catherine herself was also urged by "the king's men" to withdraw
her appeal to the pope, an appeal which required the king himself to
appear personally in Rome. She refused.

May of 1532 marked the official beginning of the "submission of
the clergy" to the increasingly tyrannical king and his agenda. At that
time, Henry demanded that no canons (Church laws) be promulgated without his consent, required that canon law be revised by
royal commission, and forbade the clergy from gathering in convocation without the royal consent. In order to further pressure the
clergy, Henry bullied them before the House of Commons:

Well-beloved subjects, we thought that the clergy of our
realm had been our subjects wholly, but now we have well

> perceived that they be but half our subjects, yea, and scarce
> our subjects: for all the prelates at their consecration make an
> oath to the pope clean contrary to the oath that they make to
> us, so that they seem to be his subjects, and not ours.

On May 15, 1532, the English priesthood caved, and surrendered
their own right to convoke themselves for the purpose of legislating
for the English Church without the king's consent. Of all the bishops
in England, Fisher alone refused to partake in this act of cowardice.
The English had been Catholic for a millennium, and England had
already earned the honor of being called "Our Lady's Dowry." But
now, because of the animal lusts, greed, and pride of a tyrant, the
English Catholic hierarchy effectively surrendered to error. The way
had been prepared for the Anglican schism.

Divorces Personal and Ecclesiastical

With the surrender of the clergy, More resigned as Lord Chancellor,
though he remained studiously silent as to his reasons for doing so.
Fisher took a different course and publicly preached against Henry's
divorce. In August of 1532, the archbishop of Canterbury died, which
gave Henry the opportunity to fill the most prestigious see in England
with a political lackey, Thomas Cranmer. A few months later, in January
1533, Henry secretly married Anne Boleyn, whom he had impregnated the previous month, increasing the pressure on Henry to
conclude his "great matter." In March, Cranmer was consecrated archbishop. But before he could grant Henry's annulment, appeals to Rome
(such as Catherine's) needed to be made illegal. Cranmer arranged to
have Parliament pass the Act in Restraint of Appeals. Fisher alone
held out in the House of Lords; but Catherine's attempts to appeal to
the pope were now illegal under English law.

Fisher was arrested, presumably in anticipation of Cranmer's announcement of the annulment. The bishop would no doubt speak out against it, as he had done many times before. The annulment of Henry and Catherine's marriage was announced on May 23, 1533, and the king's marriage to Anne announced on May 28. Anne was crowned queen in Westminster Abbey on June 1. More was invited, but refused to attend, studiously maintaining his silence.

On July 11, 1533, the pope declared the marriage between Henry and Anne to be null and void. But for Henry, there was no going back. The king's divorce and remarriage had all but consummated his divorce from Rome.

In March of 1534, the Act of Succession declared Henry VIII's marriage to Catherine of Aragon void, and his marriage to Anne Boleyn valid. The king in Parliament granted himself what the pope had refused to grant.

On April 13 of that year, both Fisher and More refused to take the oath prescribed by the act. Though silent about their reasons at the time, it would be revealed at their trials that while they accepted Parliament's right to specify the succession of the crown, they did not accept its usurpation of papal authority, which they knew had been done to secure Henry his divorce. The Treason Act of 1534 made such denials treason.

The End of the Great Matter, and the Beginning of the Mopping Up

As a biographer of Fisher observed, "The clergy had surrendered their authority; a subservient archbishop, still *legatus natus*, sat in St. Augustine's chair at Canterbury. The king so dominated affairs that it needed heroic courage to oppose his wishes."

Fisher privately expressed his support for the armed intervention of Holy Roman Emperor, Charles V, rightly believing that the majority of the nation did not approve of Henry's actions. Fisher clung to the medieval idea that, in some sense, the Holy Roman Emperor was Christendom's supreme temporal lord, and therefore had a right to intervene in such matters. In 1517, Henry himself had stood as a candidate for emperor, and lost to Charles.

In January 1534, a bill of attainder — a legislative (rather than judicial) declaration of guilt — was passed by Parliament that included both Sir Thomas More and Bishop John Fisher. Both were charged with aiding and abetting the "Nun of Kent" (Elizabeth Barton), who had prophesied against the king's new "marriage" and declared that if he accomplished his desire to put away Catherine, he "should no longer be king of this realm" and would "die a villain's death."

More had met with her briefly and advised her not to speak on the king's matter. Fisher had also corresponded with her, considering her to be a holy woman; he knew the king himself had interacted with Barton and knew of her prophecies. Her popularity continued to increase, as there was widespread popular support for Queen Catherine. The prophetess was eventually imprisoned in the Tower of London, and was executed in April that year. The bill of attainder required everyone listed to forfeit their entire personal estates and be imprisoned at the king's pleasure. Fisher was also deprived of his bishopric, and thereby lost his seat in the House of Lords.

In March 1534, Parliament passed the Act of Succession, which required those summoned to swear to it that the offspring of Henry and Anne were the legitimate heirs to the throne. Failure to do so would be considered treason. The preamble likewise explicitly repudiated the pope's authority over such matters. "This realm of England is an empire," the statute declared — a statement concocted by Henry over the previous years, justified by an appeal to the supposedly mythical founding of England by Brutus of Troy, a legendary exile of the Trojan War. If indeed England was an empire, Henry reasoned, then he was an emperor and could intervene in papal matters, as Fisher had suggested Emperor Charles V was entitled to do.

On March 31, 1534, the clerical Convocation of Canterbury considered the question "whether the Roman pontiff has any greater jurisdiction bestowed on him by God in the Holy Scriptures in this realm of England than any other foreign bishop." Thirty-four replied no, and only four said yes. The Convocation of York unanimously denied papal supremacy. The apostasy of the clergy was complete.

More was summoned to Lambeth Palace to take the oath required by the Act of Succession. He refused and was imprisoned in the Tower of London on April 18, 1534. Fisher was likewise summoned to Lambeth, refused to take the oath, and joined More in the Tower on April 26. In a letter to Thomas Cromwell, Henry's obsequious "fixer," Fisher (generously) declared: "Not that I condemn any other men's conscience. Their conscience may save them, and mine must save mine."

Queen Catherine was also offered the oath in May of 1534. She bravely stood by the pope's decision not to annul Henry's marriage with her. She was tendered the oath again, this time with threats. She replied, "If one of you has a commission to execute this penalty upon me, I am ready. I ask only that I be allowed to die in the sight of the people." She would die in virtual house arrest at Kimbolton Castle in January 1536, after living a life of penance and fasting, cut off from her own daughter, Mary, and stripped of her jewels by her valid but ungrateful husband.

The final break with Rome came in November that year with the passage of the Act of Supremacy, which announced that Henry VIII was and had always been "Supreme Head of the Church of England." This time, no qualification about the law of God was included. Paired with his claims to be an "emperor" of an "empire," his declaration constituted the most blatant example of caesaropapism in the West since perhaps Justinian.

After months of languishing in the Tower, Fisher's last preserved letter to Thomas Cromwell, dated December 22, 1534, showed how resolute the frail, sickly bishop remained: "For as I will answer before God, I would not in any manner of point offend his grace [Henry], my duty saved unto God, whom I must in everything prefer."

The break was made. But Henry still had scores to settle with men like More and Fisher, who, as two of Christendom's most admired figures, stood as living condemnations of the royal maneuverings — and judgment on the royal conscience.

A Final Betrayal

More and Fisher would remain in the Tower of London for over a year. They were carefully kept apart, though they were occasionally able to pass notes to each other, all of which were later burned. Both continued to correspond with friends and family, despite failing health. But perhaps the greatest fruit of their imprisonment was their reflections on Christ and His Passion in the midst of their own suffering.

More, in his contemplative work *The Sadness of Christ*, no doubt had cause to ponder the betrayal of Christ by His own given his own situation:

> So do they kiss him also [referring to Christ being kissed by Judas] that pretending to be Christ's disciples, and in appearance shewing themselves to profess his religion, yet in very deed do by craft and subtlety their uttermost [endeavour] clearly to overthrow it. So do they salute Christ as their master, that call him master and regard not his commandments. So do those priests likewise kiss him, which consecrate the holy body of Christ, and afterward by false doctrine and evil example of living, kill Christ's members, that is to wit, the souls of Christian men....
>
> Verily all these, whom I have here rehearsed you, do, in their salutation and false traitorous kiss, plainly play us the traitor Judas's part.[74]

In the same work, he offered a striking rebuke of all those "modern men" who had originated and assisted the spread of heresy in those days — not just the Luthers and Tyndales but also now the Henrys.

But, befitting the humility and charity of a saint, he also expressed a fervent hope for their repentance and salvation:

> And yet for all this do there in every corner nowadays still start up amongst us, as it were swarms of wasps or hornets which of a certain pride call themselves, as St. Jerome termeth them, *autodidactons*, that is to wit, of themselves learned without any man's teaching, and boast likewise that without the commentaries of the old doctors they have found all those points open, plain, and easy, which all the ancient fathers, men of as excellent wit and no less learning than they, and over that all given to continual study, and touching the spirit of God (whereof they as much babble as they little have) as far beyond them as they passed them in godly living, confessed to be right hard and cumbrous.
>
> But now these newfound divines, that are thus suddenly sprung up of nought, which would so fain seem to know all things, besides that they vary from all those good godly men in the understanding of scripture, agree not within themselves, neither in the principal points of Christ's religion, and nevertheless every one of them bold bearing folk in hand that they have spied out the truth, as they put other of like sort to rebuke and shame, so by other do they take shame themselves.
>
> And as they altogether labour to destroy and overthrow the whole Catholic faith, so are they all the whole rabble of them brought to confusion themselves, whose wretched and foolish enterprises, God that dwelleth in heaven loud laugheth to scorn, whom I most humbly beseech, that he so laugh them not to scorn as he laugh at their eternal damnation, but inspire into their hearts his wholesome grace of repentance, whereby though they, like unthrifty prodigal children, have strayed too long, alas, abroad, they may yet at length return from whence they came unto their mother the Church afresh, to the intent we and they together agreeing in one true faith of Christ, and knit in mutual love and charity,

may as his true members attain unto the glory of our captain and head, which whosoever hopeth to have out of this body, the Church, and without the right faith, doth with a vain hope lewdly deceive himself.[75]

While in the Tower, Fisher likewise engaged in a great deal of contemplation. He wrote two works, *A Spiritual Consolation* and *The Ways to Perfect Religion*, which were addressed to his sister, Elizabeth.

In his *Consolation*, Fisher encouraged daily meditation upon death and the future judgment, insisting on a life of penance for one's sins and growth in virtue:

> Be you your own friend; do you these suffrages for your own soul, whether they be prayers or almsdeeds or any other penitential painfulness. If you will not effectually and heartily do these things for your own soul, look you never that others will do them for you, and in doing them in your own persons, they shall be more available to you a thousandfold than if they were done by any other.[76]

Likewise, in *The Ways to Perfect Religion*, Fisher offered ten considerations for growing in holiness in the Christian life, all of which were aptly summarized by a concluding prayer:

> O blessed Jesu, make me to love Thee entirely.
>
> O blessed Jesu, I would fain,
> but without Thy help I cannot.
>
> O blessed Jesu, let me deeply consider
> the greatness of Thy love towards me.
>
> O blessed Jesu, give unto me grace heartily
> to thank Thee for Thy benefits.
>
> O blessed Jesu, give me good will
> to serve Thee, and to suffer.

O sweet Jesu, give me a natural
    remembrance of Thy passion.

O sweet Jesu, possess my heart,
    hold and keep it only to Thee.

These short prayers if you will often say, and with all the
power of your soul and heart, they shall marvelously kin-
dle in you this love, so that it shall be always fervent and
quick, the which is my especial desire to know in you.
For nothing may be to my comfort more than to hear of
your furtherance and profiting in God and in good religion, the which our blessed Lord grant you for His great
mercy. Amen.[77]

In February 1535, the Act of Succession was amended to make even
thoughts treasonable — such as considering the king a heretic, a schismatic, a tyrant, or an infidel. This change would, it turned out, have
dire consequences for both More and Fisher, who could no longer
rest under the shadow of any laws that would protect them. All that
remained was the blazing heat of Henrician wrath.

On May 7, 1535, a most ignominious event took place that
would later serve as the basis for Fisher's condemnation at the hands
of the same man — Richard Rich — whose testimony would likewise seal the fate of More. Rich, the solicitor general of England, met
Fisher in the Tower, and assured him that the king would grant his
conscience immunity if only he would fully speak his mind on all the
issues at stake. Fisher, perhaps naively but with a purity befitting his
innocence, believed him. "The bishop," wrote an early biographer,
"thinking assuredly that no manner of hurt nor harm should come
unto him by sending his opinion in this matter by this messenger to
the king was willing thereunto as well for that he was glad to show
himself willing to do to the king his sovereign lord all such pleasure
and service as he possibly could, saving his life and conscience." With

such assurances directly from the king himself, relayed by one of his chief officials, Fisher discharged his mind with love for his king:

> The bishop, I say, for these causes plainly and frankly in few words willing this messenger [Richard Rich] to certify the king from him that he believed directly in his conscience and knew by his learning precisely that it was very plain by the holy scripture, the laws of the church, the general council, and the whole faith and general practice of Christ's Catholic Church from Christ's ascension hitherto, that the king was not, nor could be, by the law of God, supreme head of the church of England.

By the end of that month, news reached England that the new pope, Paul III, had made Fisher a cardinal of the Roman Church. While perhaps intended to help Fisher avoid martyrdom, in fact it sealed his fate as the first and only cardinal martyr. Henry was enraged and sent members of his royal council to the Tower to give both More and Fisher one final opportunity to swear to the king's supremacy over the English Church. Both refused.

A Double Martyrdom

The wrathful Henry sent royal commissioners to confiscate Fisher's estate prior to the beginning of his trial. As they scoured through his belongings, where they expected to find gold, they instead found a hair shirt and penitential whips.

Fisher's trial began on June 17, 1535. The charge was treason for denying that the king was the head of the Church in England. The decisive moment at his trial came with the testimony of Richard Rich:

> Then came forth witness against him only he that had been ... the messenger from the king to this bishop in the Tower [likely Richard Rich], who there openly before the judges and the jury and the whole presence, where were a

great number of people gathered to see this woeful trag-
edy, deposed upon a book that the bishop had by plain
and express words declared unto him in the Tower that he
knew by his learning and believed in his conscience that
the king was not, nor could be, supreme head in earth of
the church of England.

And when this bishop heard this mischievous man
depose this, he said unto him, "Sir, I will not deny that I so
said to you, but for all my so saying I committed no treason.
For upon what occasion I so said, and for what cause, you
yourself know right well." And thereupon the bishop declared openly, not only the message that this man came
with him in the Tower from the king, but also all their communication and talk, and further the earnest and assured
promise that this messenger made unto him on the king's
behalf with also his own solemn oath that he would utter
the answer to none but to the king.... "Now, my lords,"
quoth the bishop, "what a monstrous matter is this, to lay
now to my charge as treason the thing which I spake not
until then; besides this man's oath. I had as full and as sure
a promise from the king by this his trust and sure messenger as the king could make me by word of mouth, that I
should never be impeached nor hurt by mine answer that I
should send unto him by this his messenger, which I would
never have spoken had it not been in trust of my prince's
promise and of my true and loving heart towards him, my
natural liege lord, in satisfying him with declaration of mine
opinion and conscience in this matter, as he earnestly required me by this messenger to dignify plainly unto him."

Whereunto this shameless beast, this mischievous
messenger, said that true it was that he declared unto him
that message from the king and by the king's commandment made him that assured and faithful promise from
the king, and swear unto him also as he had said. "But all
this," quoth this wicked witness, "do not discharge you
any wit."

Here Fisher made a final attempt to appeal to the statute's use of the word "maliciously," declaring that "as touching this his claim of supremacy in the church of England, in such sort as I did, as ye have heard, there was no manner of malice in me at all, and so I committed no treason." His judges were not impressed, declaring:

> The word maliciously in the statute was of none effect, for that none could speak against the king's supremacy by any manner of means but that the speaking against it was treason; and also that message or promise to him from the king himself neither could, nor did, by rigor of our law in any wise discharge him, but that in so declaring his mind and conscience against the king's supremacy, though it were even at the king's own commandment and request, he by the statute committed treason, and nothing might discharge him now of the cruel penalty of death appointed by the statute for speaking against the king's supremacy, howsoever the words were spoken, but only the king's pardon, if it would please his grace, to grant it him.

Prior to the jury rendering its surely predetermined verdict, the judges had harsh words for Fisher, who, they declared, had been utterly presumptuous in contradicting the stance of the majority of his clerical order and the rest of the kingdom (no doubt ignoring the fact that many of the clergy had acted under duress). His humble response contrasts starkly with their temerity:

> But before the inquest of twelve men went from the bar to agree upon their verdict, there was laid to the bishop's charge by some of his judges, high pride and great presumption, that he and a few other did dissent and vary in this matter of the king's supremacy from the whole number of the bishops, lords, learned men and commons, gathered together in the Parliament with diverse other things, unto all which he answered in effect as the

holy fathers Carthusians and Doctor Reynolds had done, wherein he showed himself excellently and profoundly learned, of great constancy and of a marvelous godly courage, and declared the whole matter so learnedly and therewith so godly, that it made many of them there present, and some of their judges also, so inwardly to lament, that their eyes burst out with tears to see such a great famous clerk and virtuous bishop to be condemned to so cruel a death by such impious laws and by such an unlawful and detestable witness, contrary to all human honesty and fidelity and the word and promise of the king himself.

St. Thomas More's Trial and Condemnation

More's trial began just after Fisher's execution, and likewise turned on the treachery of Richard Rich.

Rich claimed under oath that More had denied the supremacy of the king over the Church in England. In fact, More had denied that Parliament could declare *him*, Richard Rich, to be the pope, or head of the Church. More, under oath, responded:

> If I were a man, my lords, that did not regard an oath, I needed not, as it is well known, in this place, at this time, nor in this case, to stand here as an accused person. And if this oath of yours, Master Rich, be true, then pray I that I never see God in the face; which I would not say, were it otherwise, to win the whole world.[78]

Then, speaking directly to Rich, he said, "In good faith, Master Rich, I am sorrier for your perjury than for my own peril. And you shall understand that neither I nor no man else to my knowledge ever took you to be a man of such credit as in any matter of importance, aye, or any other, would at any time vouchsafe to communicate with you."

Once it became clear to More that he would be condemned, his long and studied silence came to an end, and the saint fully spoke his mind on the king's statutes, never once expressing malice toward the king himself but only the presumption exhibited in his ill-made laws:

> More: "Forasmuch as, my lord ... this indictment is grounded upon an act of Parliament directly repugnant to the laws of God, and his holy Church, the supreme government of which, or of any part whereof, may no temporal prince presume by any law to take upon him, as rightfully belonging to the see of Rome, a spiritual preeminence by the mouth of our Savior himself, personally present upon the earth, only to Saint Peter and his successors, bishops of the same see, by special prerogative granted; it is therefore in law amongst Christian men insufficient to change any Christian man....
>
> This realm, being but one member and small part of the Church, may not make a particular law disagreeable with the general law of Christ's universal Catholic Church, no more than the city of London, being but one poor member in respect of the whole realm, may make a law against an act of Parliament to bind the whole realm.... It [is] contrary both to the laws and statutes of our own land yet unrepealed, as [you] might evidently perceive in Magna Carta: *Quod Ecclesia Anglicana libera sit et habeat iura sua integra et libertates suas illaesas* ["That the English Church be free and have all of its rights whole and its liberties uninjured"]; and also contrary to that sacred oath which the King's Highness himself and every other Christian prince always with great solemnity receive at their coronations.... No more might this realm of England refuse obedience to the see of Rome than might the child refuse obedience to his own natural father....
>
> Audley [Lord Chancellor]: But seeing that "all the bishops, universities, and best learned of this realm have to this act agreed," I must marvel that you "alone against

them all do so stiffly stick thereat, and so vehemently argue thereagainst."

More: "If the number of bishops and universities be so material as your lordship seemeth to take it, then see I little cause, my lord, why that thing in my conscience should make any change. For I nothing doubt but that, though not in this realm, yet in Christendom about, of these well-learned bishops and virtuous men that are yet alive, they be not the fewer part that be of my mind therein. But if I should speak of those which already be dead, of whom many be now holy saints in heaven, I am very sure it is the far greater part of them that, all the while they lived, thought in this case that way that I think now. And therefore [I am not] bound, my lord, to conform my conscience to the counsel of one realm against the general counsel of Christendom."

Like Fisher, More was accused of pride in following his own judgment, though it was contrary to that of virtually the entire kingdom. In response, More appealed to the millennium-long witness of the Catholic Faith and Christendom:

More: My lords, "since I have been adjudged to death, whether rightly or wrongly, God knows, for the exonerating of my conscience I would willingly say some words to you concerning your statute. I affirm that I have spent all my study during the whole of the last seven years, and I have never found an approved doctor of the Church to hold that any layman is the head of an ecclesiastical order." ...

Audley (*interrupting More's statement*): "Do you wish to be more prudent and religious than all the bishops, the whole nobility, and all of the people who are subjects of the King and his kingdom?"

More: "For one bishop who agrees with you, I have easily a hundred, including some who are among the saints. And for your one council, Parliament, and your statute — what it is worth the great good God knows — on my side are all the general councils celebrated during the last thousand years. And for one kingdom, the kingdom of France and all other kingdoms of the Christian world agree with me."

Norfolk: "More, now you are plainly revealing your mind's stubborn malice."

More: "What I say, I say because necessity compels me, for I wish to exonerate my conscience and not weigh down my soul. I call on God, the searcher of hearts, as witness.

"I add this besides, that your statute was wrongly made, because you deliberately swore your oaths against the Church, which alone is whole and undivided through the whole Christian world. And you alone have no power to enact anything, without the consent of all other Christians, which is contrary to the unity and concord of the Christian religion."

I am now for the first time revealing my opinion concerning this law by which the king has been appointed Head of the Church in England. I have not done so before this, to avoid giving my enemies further opportunities of lashing out against me, and it would have hindered my defense here today. But I speak out now, "being mindful of my care for England, lest any person therein should imprudently and ignorantly favor this pestiferous law. This law is in contradiction to all human and divine laws. It will be more pernicious to anyone who assents to it than it has been to me, who stand condemned to capital punishment for having dissented from it."

One final word, my lords: "I am not unaware of the reason for which you have adjudged me to death. The one single cause is that I have been unwilling over the past years to consent to the second marriage of the King."

After additional interrogation, More then declared his joy at the prospect of departing "[this] place of discord, dissension, and tumult" to a place "where the root of all strife and dissension is removed, where love, peace, concord, and tranquility will live in all."

He expressed his highest hopes that he and his executors would one day be united in Heaven by appealing to the example of St. Paul and St. Stephen, for Paul, when Saul, had been St. Stephen's executioner, though later the very same man became an apostle and one of the greatest saints. "They are now together in heaven," More reminded the court, and offered his prayer that "all of us, though we disagree in this life, will nevertheless agree in another life with perfect charity." He offered once more a prayer for the king, asking "the great good God to guard the King, conserve him, and make him safe, and send him salutary counsel."

Turning finally to his judges, he magnanimously declared, "More have I not to say, my lords, but that ... I verily trust, and shall therefore right heartily pray, that though your lordships have now here in earth been judges to my condemnation, we may hereafter in heaven merrily all meet together, to our everlasting salvation."

St. John Fisher's Final Words and Execution

Fisher was found guilty and sentenced to being hanged, drawn, and quartered, though the king commuted this to beheading. His serenity as he went from Westminster back to the Tower was noticed by all:

> "I thank you, masters all, for the pains ye have taken this day in going and coming from hence to Westminster and hither again." And this spake he with so lusty a courage and so amiable a countenance and his color so well come to him as though he had come from a great and honorable feast. And his gesture and his behavior showed such a certain inward gladness in his heart that any man might easily see that he joyously longed and looked for the bliss and joys of heaven, and that he inwardly rejoiced that he was so near unto his death for Christ's cause.

When the sheriffs arrived at the Tower to take Fisher to his execution, the aged bishop opened his New Testament, raised his eyes toward Heaven, and said, "O Lord, this is the last time that ever I shall open this book. Let some comfortable place now chance me whereby I, thy poor servant, may glorify thee in this my last hour." He then glanced down at the pages, and the first verses his eye saw were from the Gospel of John: "And this is eternal life, that they know thee the only true God, and Jesus Christ whom thou hast sent. I glorified thee on earth, having accomplished the work which thou gavest me to do; and now, Father, glorify thou me in thy own presence with the glory which I had with thee before the world was made" (17:3–5).

"Here," Fisher said, "is even learning enough for me to my life's end."

Fisher arrived at the scaffold around eleven in the morning, his slender, emaciated body a testament to his life of penance and self-denial. He forgave his executioner, and then uttered his final words:

> Christian people, I am come hither to die for the faith of Christ's Catholic Church. And I thank God, hitherto my stomach hath served me well thereto, so that yet hitherto I have not feared death. Wherefore I desire you help me, and assist me with your prayers, that at the very point and instant of my death's stroke, and in the very moment of my death, I then faint not in any point of the Catholic faith for any fear. And I pray God save the king and the realm, and hold his holy hand over it, and send the king a good counsel.

Then he knelt down, was blindfolded, and praying most devoutly, lifted his hands toward heaven as the ax severed his head from his body.

The dead bishop's body was left in the open for nearly a day. He was unceremoniously buried naked, with no funeral rites of any kind. His head was on display on London Bridge, and later thrown into the Thames.

Fisher died alone, publicly disgraced, and naked in an unmarked grave, abandoned by his episcopal brothers, the only bishop in the entire realm with the courage to stand up for the truth. But as they retained their earthly palaces, he ascended into his heavenly one.

On June 25, 1535, a circular issued in the name of the king commanded clergy to preach in support of the king's supremacy and to remove the pope's name from all service books, as well as "set forth the treasons of the late Bishop of Rochester and Sir Thomas More." This was still a week before More's trial. Even while this layman lay rotting in the Tower of London for the Catholic Faith, letters survive that show bishops remained more than ready to comply with the royal will.

St. Thomas More's Final Words and Execution

After receiving his own guilty verdict and on his way back to the Tower of London, More embraced his beloved daughter Margaret once last time. He was, according to the narration of his execution, "shedding no tears, and showing no distress of countenance or mind." One thing he said to his beloved daughter: "Farewell, and pray to God for the salvation of my soul."

After speaking his mind to his judges, More, like Fisher, was perfectly serene, absorbed with the reality of Heaven. In his final letter to Margaret, on July 5, 1535, he wrote, "Farewell, my dear child, and pray for me and I shall for you and all your friends, that we may merrily meet in heaven."

He carried himself with this same serenity to the chopping block. Like Fisher, More's execution was commuted to beheading. Before the severing of his head, More's last words were reported as follows: "Finally he strongly exhorted them and urged them to pray to God for the King, that he would grant him right counsel and good mind; openly protesting and declaring that he died a faithful minister to him, yet first of all to God Almighty."

Final Reflections

There was great consternation throughout Christendom at the execution of both More and Fisher. The famed humanist scholar, Erasmus, said of them, "They were the wisest and most saintly men that England had." This sentiment was shared by scholars across Europe.

With More, perhaps the greatest irony is that the man who earlier in his life had believed the papacy was likely a human institution and helped a king defend its divine establishment ended up dying for the conviction that the papacy was of divine institution at the hands of the same king who no longer believed so.

In like manner, Fisher was consulted on "the king's great matter" for his holiness of life. But it was his steadfastness in such holiness that caused the same king to make a martyr of him.

All on the anvil of the sanctity of marriage.

Both men died completely abandoned by nearly everyone of their order, either temporal or spiritual. These traitors — baptized Catholics all — had bended to keep from being broken on earth. But More and Fisher preferred breaking on earth for the sake of standing upright in Heaven.

For the truth of the Catholic Faith; for the sanctity of marriage, as much as against the evil of divorce; and finally for the authority of the pope and the liberty of the Church against all temporal powers, these two Englishmen, representing the best of temporal and spiritual, shed their blood.

"What other have you, or have you had for centuries, to compare with Rochester in holiness, in learning, in prudence, and in episcopal zeal?" asked Reginald Pole, an Englishman made cardinal shortly after Fisher's death and who would later serve as the final Catholic archbishop of Canterbury during the reign of the Catholic Queen Mary, Henry's daughter. He continued:

> You may be, indeed, proud of him, for, were you to search through all the nations of Christendom in our days, you would not easily find one who was such a model of episcopal virtues. If you doubt this, consult your merchants

who have travelled in many lands; consult your ambassadors; and let them tell you whether they have anywhere
heard of any bishop who has such a love of his flock as
never to leave the care of it, ever feeding it by word and
example; against whose life not even a rash word could be
spoken; one who was conspicuous not only for holiness
and learning, but for love of country?

Of More, Pope Pius XI spoke as follows at his and Fisher's canonization on May 19, 1935:

Endowed with the keenest of minds and supreme versatil-
ity in every kind of knowledge, he enjoyed such esteem
and favor among his fellow-citizens that he was soon able
to reach the highest grades of public office. But he was no
less distinguished for his desire of Christian perfection
and his zeal for the salvation of souls. Of this we have
testimony in the ardor of his prayer, in the fervor with
which he recited, whenever he could, even the Canonical
Hours, in the practice of those penances by which he kept
his body in subjection, and finally in the numerous and
renowned accomplishments of both the spoken and the
written word which he achieved for the defense of the
Catholic faith and for the safeguarding of Christian morality.... When he saw that the doctrines of the Church
were gravely endangered, he knew how to despise reso-
lutely the flattery of human respect, how to resist, in accordance with his duty, the supreme head of the State
when there was question of things commanded by God
and the Church, and how to renounce with dignity the
high office with which he was invested.[79]

At the conclusion of his sermon, invoking the memory of both saints,
Pius XI issued a rousing call for the separated brethren of England to
return to Mother Church:

Let those who are still separated from Us consider atten-
tively the ancient glories of their Church which were at once
a reflection and an increment of the glories of the Church of
Rome. Let them consider, moreover, and remember that
this Apostolic See has been waiting for them so long and so
anxiously, not as coming to a strange dwelling place, but as
finally returning to their paternal home. In conclusion, let us
repeat the divine prayer of Our Lord Jesus Christ: "Holy
Father, keep them in Thy name whom Thou hast given me,
that they may be one as we also are." Amen.[80]

St. Thomas More, in *The Sadness of Christ*, written while imprisoned
in the Tower, wrote that "good men should be ashamed to be more
timid in good deeds than wicked men are in wicked deeds."

In willingly enduring the suffering of imprisonment and execution, both St. Thomas More and St. John Fisher proved themselves
to be men and saints of the highest holiness, unashamed to outdo the
wicked in their goodness, even to the point of death. They indeed
proved that when the time comes, "The righteous are bold as a lion"
(Prov. 28:1).

CHAPTER 7

The Persecution of St. John of the Cross and St. Teresa of Avila

St. Teresa of Avila and St. John of the Cross were two of the greatest mystics since biblical times. But in addition to achieving the highest heights of prayer, they also were administrators and practical people who spearheaded the refounding of the Carmelite Order, an international religious institution that has endured for more than four hundred years. Despite these remarkable achievements and their heroic virtues, both saints spent much of their lives persecuted by Catholic clergy.

Their Lives and Times

The Carmelite Order began in the Holy Land. The tradition of the order (which has been cited with approval by seven popes[81]) says that it was founded by the Prophet Elijah, who slew the prophets of Baal on Mount Carmel (1 Kings 18). God was found "not in the wind," but in the silence, and thereafter many Jews came to seek God in a life of silence upon Mount Carmel, in a prototype of the Egyptian Desert Fathers centuries later.

Before settling in Samaria, St. Elisha stopped on Mount Carmel (2 Kings 2:25). Informal communities of monks and hermits are recorded to have lived on Mount Carmel continuously since the time of King David. These include Jews, pagans, and later, Christians, such as St. Dionysios, St. Serapion, St. Cyril of Alexandria, and St. Cyril of Jerusalem.[82] According to tradition, the Virgin Mary later instructed that a church be built there in her honor.

The formal beginning of the Carmelite Order as a Roman Catholic institution, however, dates to the age of the Crusades, when Christianity returned to the Holy Land after the Muslim conquests of the seventh century.

St. Albert and the Founding of the Carmelite Order

St. Albert was one of the most talented bishops and administrators in the Church during the Middle Ages. In 1205, Pope Innocent III offered St. Albert the Latin Patriarchate of Jerusalem, one of the most prestigious positions in the entire Church. St. Albert had no ambition, and no desire to leave his native Italy, but he accepted the Patriarchate in the Holy Land in the hope of dying as a martyr at the hands of the Muslims. He is the only bishop of the Holy Land in the Middle Ages to be canonized or beatified.[83]

In 1209, the hermits of Carmel asked St. Albert to write a rule for them to live as a religious community. He did so, basing it on the Rule of St. Augustine and how the hermits were already living. The rule was rigorous, requiring the monks and nuns of the order to have no personal property, to live almost entirely in silence, to eat their meals alone in their cells, to fast from September to Easter, and to eat meat only when absolutely necessary for health reasons, among other things[84] — though it is the shortest rule of any religious order, just sixteen paragraphs long.[i] Pope Honorius III approved the rule in 1226.

---

[i]   Despite being the shortest rule of all the religious orders it has nevertheless been a bedrock for Carmelite life in all its facets for over eight hundred years.

Though St. Albert himself was a member of the order of Canons Regular of the Holy Cross and not a Carmelite, the Carmelites have always venerated him as one of their own. In fact, his statue in St. Peter's Square depicts him dressed as a Carmelite.[85]

The Gradual Relaxation of the Rule

Throughout the thirteenth century, the crusaders continued to make modest gains. But increasing numbers of Carmelites also began to return to Europe with crusaders who had been their patrons. In 1238, the first Carmelite houses in Europe were founded in Sicily, France, and England.[86] St. Louis IX of France visited Mount Carmel in 1254 and brought back six French hermits with him to Paris. In 1263, the hermits built a new monastery and a church on Carmel — but the last crusader kingdom fell to Muslims just twenty-eight years later, and the remaining brothers died as martyrs.

In 1246, just a generation after the order's papal approval, Pope Innocent IV relaxed the Rule of St. Albert,[87] effectively changing it from an Eastern order of hermits to a Western order of mendicants, like the Franciscans or the Dominicans, which had been founded in 1209 and 1216, respectively. Instead of remaining in a cell, friars and sisters were expected to go out into the world as itinerant preachers, and to survive by begging. This was a completely different vocation, and it prompted a crisis of identity for the order.

Many Carmelites, including several priors general of the thirteenth century, such as Nicholas Francois and his successor Raoul, openly vented their frustration with this change, as they desired to isolate themselves from the world in order to dedicate themselves entirely to prayer.[88]

Additional pressures on all religious orders came with the Great Famine of 1315 and the Black Death of the 1340s, the worst pandemic in history, which killed nearly half the population of Europe in a decade. The clergy (especially good clergy) were more likely to fall ill than others because of their responsibilities to those in dire need.

Both the quantity and quality of priests declined, and this likely contributed to the ecclesiastical culture of abuses decried 150 years later by the Augustinian priest Fr. Martin Luther.

No religious order was spared from the effects of the pandemic, and those which did survive saw the number of vocations plummet and the rectitude of their communities suffer. By 1442, there was already a movement within the order to return to the previous rule in a Carmelite house in Mantua, as a way of restoring its integrity. In 1451, Prior General Bl. John Soreth instituted reforms intended to address some of the problems in Germany and the Low Countries. But his reform efforts did not extend to Spain.[89] However, Bl. John also opened the order to women in 1452, just sixty-three years before St. Teresa was born.[90]

By the time of St. Teresa, the Carmelites were one of only three religious orders in Spain that had not undergone a reform in the previous century. An early sixteenth-century report on the Carmelite houses in Toledo and Avila found scandal and deplorable conditions.[91] Every other order in Spain had returned to earlier rules, with an emphasis on asceticism, personal spirituality, and the interior life.

The prior general, Fr. Nicola Audet, supported reforming the order and had already issued his own articles of reform, *Caput Unicum,* at a general chapter in 1524. But after the Audet reforms were put in place in Castile, half of the Carmelites in the province left the order.[92] The unfinished work of reform would fall to a middle-aged nun in Castile, Teresa de Ahumada.

St. Teresa

The role of reformer — or, in a sense, of re-foundress — would have seemed an unlikely one for Teresa of Avila to play, at least when she was young. She writes in her *Vida* that her early desire to become a nun was soon forgotten under the influence of the world. During her teenage years, she became preoccupied with her attractive appearance and with being popular. At one point she even considered giving up religious life and marrying one of her cousins. When she lodged at a house of the Augustinian order as a young woman, she decided not to join it because it was too strict.[93]

Teresa entered the *Encarnacion* Carmelite convent in her hometown of Avila at the age of twenty in 1535, in large part because a friend of hers had already entered the same convent. At the time there were forty nuns in *Encarnacion*. Ten years later, there were 165.[94] While this might appear to be a miraculous boom in vocations, the reality is that during this time many Spanish women entered convents for worldly reasons, such as a desire to avoid marriage or a lack of marriage prospects. (St. Teresa herself repeatedly told her nuns to be grateful that they were nuns and not married.) At this time, many Spanish men, including St. Teresa's brothers, had gone to seek a better life in the New World or to fight in Spain's many wars. As a result, there were large numbers of *abandonadas*, women who had chosen to live a common life with other women. The "abandoned" were not necessarily bad, or insincere, nuns. But their enthusiasm for following the order's rule or living out its asceticism was sometimes muted. (St. Teresa would later forbid convents to have more than thirteen women, since smaller communities were easier to hold accountable.)[95]

Sixteenth-century Spain was an honor society and extremely class-conscious. It sounds surprising to us today, but rooms at *Encarnacion* convent were given to the nuns largely in accord with their social status, and they could also be bought and sold. Teresa's cell had two levels and was large enough to host her sister Juana for several years. Indeed, as Teresa was the daughter of an *hidalgo* (minor nobility), she was also referred to as Doña Teresa, or Lady Teresa, rather than Sr. Teresa.[96]

The wealthier sisters wore finer clothing than the poorer ones, and the wealthiest families could give their daughters as much money as they wanted. The result was extreme inequality and class-consciousness, even in a house of religion. Despite her own social position, this infuriated Teresa more than anything else she saw in the convent, and she stood against the spirit of her age and her own country by seeking to end it.

Another regular trouble was *Encarnacion*'s finances. Some sisters even had to get side jobs sewing or tutoring.[97] The sisters had to raise money to keep the house open, and there were visitors of both sexes chatting in the parlors practically all day long. St. Teresa writes that in this environment she grew lax and backslid into her previous struggles with vanity and the desire to be popular.

> I myself was vain and liked to be well thought of in the things esteemed by the world.... It was a very bad thing for me not to be in a convent that was enclosed. The freedom ... would certainly have led me, who am wicked, down to hell, had not the Lord, through very special favors ... delivered me from this peril. It seems to me, then, that it is a very great danger for women in a convent to have such freedom: for those who want to be wicked it is not so much a remedy for their weaknesses as a step on the way to hell.... Let [parents] be prepared to allow [their daughters] to marry far beneath their stations rather than put them into convents of this kind.... It is better to keep them at home; for there, if they want to be wicked, they cannot long hide their wickedness, whereas in convents it can be hidden for a very long time.

The saint records that eventually an older nun warned her about her familiarity with the outside world on several occasions, but she did not listen. St. Teresa became so preoccupied with receiving visitors and leaving the house that she — history's greatest advocate of mental prayer — left off the practice of mental prayer for a full year.

When the saint began to spend time with one worldly woman in particular, Our Lord appeared to her in a vision as a stern and angry judge. She broke off the friendship, and the terrifying vision haunted her for the rest of her life.

Worldliness and corruption were problems not only in the convent but throughout the Church in Spain at the time. Although it is tempting to imagine a past when all the world was devout, in reality many entered religious life for worldly reasons, and many priests in Spain openly had girlfriends and concubines. The Spanish Inquisition prosecuted eight priests for seducing women through "spiritual counsel," and a local synod reiterated the condemnation of fornication by priests.[98] St. Teresa records her shock upon discovering that her own confessor was entangled with a local woman, and she records her successful prayers for his conversion and repentance.

Her "Second Conversion"

In 1554, at the age of thirty-nine and after nearly two decades as a nun, the saint experienced her "second conversion" after she was given a copy of St. Augustine's *Confessions*, which had only been translated into Castilian earlier that year. "When I read the *Confessions*," she later wrote, "I seemed to see myself in them.... When I got as far as his conversion and read how he heard that voice in the garden, it seemed exactly as if the Lord were speaking in that way to me.... I remained for a long time dissolved in tears."

This moment proved to be the beginning of the reforms of the Carmelite Order. "I began to long to spend more time with God, and to drive away occasions of sin."

Soon after this, in 1556, St. Teresa began to receive visions and locutions from Our Lord, Our Lady, and the saints.

Deceived by the Devil?

St. Teresa's confessors and superiors were rightly skeptical of her extraordinary experiences, and some even thought that she was possessed by the devil. This was an occasion for suffering that she had to endure in obedience.

> Many are the affronts and trials that I have suffered through telling this and many are the fears and persecutions that it has brought me. So sure were those whom I told of it that I had a devil that some of them wanted to exorcize me. This troubled me very little, but I was sorry when I found that my confessors were afraid to hear my confessions or when I heard that people were saying things to them against me.

St. Teresa also records great embarrassment after levitating in front of the other nuns. "I have lain on the ground and the sisters have come and held me down, but none the less the rapture has been observed. I besought the Lord earnestly not to grant me any more favours which had visible and exterior signs."

When St. Teresa's first visions became known by others, and word began to spread, people warned her that she could get summoned by the Inquisition. But she was not concerned.

> They only amused me and made me laugh, because I never had any fear about this. I knew quite well that in matters of faith no one would ever find me transgressing even the smallest ceremony of the Church, and that for the Church or for any truth of Holy Scripture I would undertake to die a thousand deaths. So I told them not to be afraid, for my soul would be in a very bad way if there were anything about it which could make me fear the Inquisition. If ever I thought there might be, I would go and pay it a visit of my own accord.

It was not until 1557, when two canonized saints visited Avila — St. Pedro of Alcantara and St. Francis Borgia — that her visions began to be endorsed as coming from God. Ultimately, her confessor, Fr. Domingo Bañez, O.P., told her that she should venerate an "image" of Our Lord, even if it is painted by a bad man — and even if it is painted by the devil.[99] The saint's canonization documents quote her as saying that she might be deceived by visions, but that she would never be deceived by obedience.[100]

The Teresian Reforms

In the saint's most famous vision, St. Teresa was shown the place reserved for her by the devils in Hell. It terrified her, but she considered it "one of the most signal favors which the Lord has bestowed upon me." It was arguably this vision that prompted the entire Teresian reform. "After I had seen this vision, and other great things and secrets," she wrote, "I desired to flee from others ... by withdrawing myself completely from the world.... I would wonder what I could do for God, and it occurred to me that the first thing was ... by keeping my Rule with the greatest possible perfection."

St. Teresa was not alone in wanting to return to the order's roots. One day, in one of her many parlor conversations, the saint spoke to her cousin, Maria de Ocampo, who suggested the idea of establishing a separate convent under the rule of 1246. The wealthy noblewoman and close friend of the saint, Doña Guiomar de Ulloa, walked in on the conversation at that very moment, and she immediately endorsed the idea, even offering to help fund it.

Soon after that conversation, the saint writes,

> The Lord gave me the most explicit commands to work for this aim with all my might.... [He said] it should be called San Jose ... [and] the convent would be a star giving out the most brilliant light.... This caused me the deepest distress, because I had a fairly good idea of the serious disturbances and trials which the work would cost me.... The Lord appeared and spoke to me about it again and again, and so numerous were the motives and arguments which He put before me, in such a way that I saw

that they were valid and that the project was His will, that
I dared not do otherwise."

St. Teresa wrote to St. Pedro of Alcantara, who by then was her spiritual advisor. (St. Teresa had the rare privilege of having three canonized saints as her confessors.) St. Pedro had undertaken a similar reform of his own Franciscan order, and he strongly urged her to proceed.

Opposition from Within

The Council of Trent, which closed just a year after the founding of San Jose, decreed enclosure for religious and required hermits to enter religious orders.[101] The council also stipulated that reforms should be done by the superiors of orders and that opening religious houses required a license from the local bishop.[102] These two requirements would cause many difficulties for the reform. St. Teresa quickly found herself contending with superiors, fellow nuns, and bishops.

> Hardly had news of the project begun to be known here than there descended upon us a persecution so severe that it is impossible in a few words to describe it: people talked about us, laughed at us and declared that the idea was ridiculous.... I could now see what those saints who had founded religious Orders had suffered: they had had to endure much more persecution than any I could imagine.... Both among people of prayer and in the whole place, there was hardly anyone who was not against us and did not consider our project absolutely ridiculous.
>
> The Provincial thought it would be hard for him to set himself against everybody; so he changed his mind and refused to sanction the plan. He said that the revenue was not assured, that in any case there would be too little of it, and that the plan was meeting with considerable opposition. In all this he appeared to be right.

Priests in Avila were so indignant about St. Teresa's plans that Doña Guiomar was denied absolution unless she would repent of her association with her.[103] Carmelite priests even publicly preached against St. Teresa from pulpits in Avila. The saint's cousin, Teresita, records attending Mass at St. Thomas Church in Avila, where a friar preached against "nuns who left their convents to go found new orders." Teresita was offended, but when she turned to St. Teresa, she saw her "laughing with great peace."

Nevertheless, St. Teresa obeyed her superior and stopped working on founding her convent for about six months, despite the fact that she believed that she had received a direct order from God. After six months, Our Lord told her that her trials were about to end, which she took to mean that she would die. Instead her confessor left, and her new confessor gave her permission to start up the work again.

While remaining obedient, Teresa actively hid her work from her superiors. St. Teresa had her sister buy the tiny house for the convent (so tiny that St. Pedro of Alcantara compared it to the stable at Bethlehem), which created the impression that it was for her own use and not for a convent. "I thought it of great importance to do nothing against obedience, but I knew that, if I told my superiors about it, everything would be ruined, just as it was on the last occasion, and this time things might be even worse." Our Lord told her instead to write to Rome for approval, so she did.

It was at this time that St. Teresa was sent from her convent to Toledo to comfort the widow Doña Luisa de la Cerda, who greatly revered the saint and requested to see her. St. Teresa was founding a new convent in order to stop exactly this sort of practice, but she interrupted her project and obeyed her provincial's order. She realized that her time away from the convent might be part of God's Providence. This understanding was confirmed when, on the very night she returned to Avila, Doña Guiomar received a letter from Rome giving approval for the Convent of San Jose. St. Pedro persuaded

Bishop Mendoza to give his approval as well, and less than two months later Teresa's first Discalced convent had opened.

Like Bishop Mendoza, the people of Avila were dubious that their poor little town could afford to support another house of nuns. Would this new house siphon away funds from the others? The parents of the *abandonadas* had to wonder. The civil authorities, the *corregidor* (imperial officials), and the town council, were enraged at having to shoulder another financial burden. There were already six convents in the small town of Avila.[104]

Biographer William Walsh relates what happened: Teresa listened with sadness as the *corregidor* denounced her at a public meeting after Sunday Mass. The main point of contention was how to pay for everything; but Teresa insisted on founding the house in poverty, although the pope had allowed for an endowment. Nevertheless, the Avila town council insisted that she have the house endowed: the last thing Avila needed was more beggars. In what was probably his last letter, St. Pedro wrote to Teresa that "the Lord would be much served in that monastery, since the devil had tried so hard to have it destroyed." He also urged her not to budge on a vow of poverty. On January 11, 1563, the city council of Avila voted to destroy the Convent of San Jose, claiming that it was blocking a public fountain. St. Teresa wasn't deterred. She built another right next to it.[105]

In addition to battling with the political authorities, St. Teresa had to manage the nuns at *Encarnacion,* who were deeply offended by her. Who did Teresa think she was? After twenty years of living at *Encarnacion,* was she suddenly too good for them? The prioress demanded an explanation, and St. Teresa showed her the approval from Rome. She even had the provincial, Fray Salazar, confirm in person that she had his permission, though he ordered her to stay at *Encarnacion* for a fortnight until the passions of the nuns and the townspeople of Avila had calmed.[106]

From March of 1563 to 1567, Teresa resided at San Jose. She had finally attained the kind of austerity and isolation for which she had longed. The Discalced lived in poverty, wore coarse habits, and wore no shoes (hence "discalced"). She later wrote that they were the most peaceful years of her life.[107]

In 1562, Fr. Audet died and Fr. Giovanni Battista Rossi (known in Spanish sources as Fr. Rubeo) was elected prior general of the Carmelites. Like Fr. Audet, he supported the idea of reforming the order, but wanted to work gradually and avoid conflict when possible. He also favored reforms that followed the rule of 1432, whereas Teresa insisted on going back to the rigors of 1246.[108]

Fr. Rossi met with Teresa and expressed his support for the Convent of San Jose. But he noted that her papal approval was technically invalid, since he had not given his consent. He also reminded her that she was still under his authority.[109] Nevertheless he gave her permission to found more convents, and later, in a letter from Valencia that same year, he gave her permission to found two monasteries for friars.[110]

One and a Half Friars

Just four months after her meeting with Fr. Rossi, Teresa founded the second Discalced convent at Medina del Campo. She again met opposition: "There was much murmuring. Some said I was crazy."[111]

There she met two young Carmelite friars, Fr. Antonio de Heredia and the newly ordained, twenty-five-year-old Carmelite, Fr. Juan de Matias — a man known to us as St. John of the Cross. (She later joked about St. John's short stature, saying that he and Fr. Heredia together were "one and a half friars.")[112]

St. John confided in her that he was already considering leaving the order. He wanted to live a more rigorous asceticism and enter more seriously into a life of prayer, and so he thought that he ought to become a Carthusian. At length Teresa told him that, in order to do these things, he did not need to leave "Our Lady's order," and told him of her reform and her plans to open houses for friars as well as nuns. He agreed to help, so long as he did not have to wait long.

He did not have to wait long at all. Within six months Teresa had already founded a third convent at Malagon, and in August of 1568, she went with John to Valladolid, where she founded a fourth convent. When John saw firsthand the life of the Discalced Carmelite nuns, he was impressed. In fact, conversations between the two saints ultimately led to the founding of the Discalced friars, and St. John became the first. He received his habit from Teresa herself and removed his shoes.

Unwelcome Return Home

Over the course of 1569 and 1570, St. Teresa founded four more convents and one more monastery.

By 1571, the apostolic visitator, Fr. Pedro Fernandez, O.P., ordered St. Teresa back to *Encarnacion*, this time as prioress. The problems at *Encarnacion* had only got worse since she had left, and the success of San Jose proved that Madre Teresa was an effective manager and administrator. However, according to Doña Maria Pinel, a nun of *Encarnacion*, her appointment was actually intended as a snub of both the *Encarnacion* nuns and the Discalced nuns, since those who wanted St. Teresa's leadership would be deprived of it, and those who detested her would be forced to obey her.[113] St. Teresa herself said that she thought Fr. Fernandez wanted her to stop founding convents.[114] She did not leave for *Encarnacion* for several weeks, and reportedly received a vision from Our Lord scolding her for delaying her departure.[115]

Many of the nuns at *Encarnacion* had denounced Teresa a decade before. Indeed, when they heard the news that they would have to obey her, they shouted down the provincial, and some even fainted. They attempted to physically block St. Teresa from entering the building and shrieked at her as she approached. Teresa remained calm.

The sisters feared that she would impose the rules of the Discalced on them and make them live the austerity and silence that

Teresa had lived for the last five years. This fear was unfounded. Teresa did not impose the rule of the Discalced on the nuns of *Encarnacion*. Instead, she merely ordered all the boarders and visitors out before she arrived.[116]

When it came time for her to take her seat in chapter, St. Teresa put a statue of Our Lady in the prioress's seat and sat at its feet. She then told the nuns that she did not want to be prioress but was only taking office under obedience. Speaking to each individually, she said she agreed that she was unworthy.[117]

In the mystery of Providence, it was during this bitter exile at home that the saint began her correspondence with Philip II, whom she later referred to as "my dear friend the king."[118] It was also during this turbulent time that she received the mystical marriage with Christ, the pinnacle of human prayer.[119]

By Lent of 1572, the saint had put an end to the streams of visitors to the 130 nuns of *Encarnacion*, angering some of the noble families. She soon brought St. John of the Cross to *Encarnacion* to hear confessions. He too was met with suspicion and assumed to be a fanatic, because he had become Discalced. Once, in the confessional, a nun asked him suspiciously if he was calced or discalced; John covered his feet with his habit, technically rendering himself barefoot no more. "Calced," he said. She relaxed and was able to make a good confession.[120]

The nuns soon grew to love St. John. Fr. Fernandez noted a dramatic change in the nuns and said that they were now just as holy as the Discalced. In one of her most impressive achievements of all, St. Teresa gradually won the hearts of dozens of women who had spent years hating her. When her term came to an end in October 1574, many begged her to stay. Dozens of nuns attempted to re-elect St. Teresa, but were blocked by the provincial, Fr. Salazar. St. Teresa continued to receive visions, including of Our Lady and of the previously mentioned St. Albert, who told her that ultimately the Calced and the Discalced would have to be separated into two different orders. When her term

as prioress at *Encarnacion* expired, St. Teresa finally was allowed to return to San Jose, where she was elected prioress.[121]

More Foundation Stones, More Stumbling Blocks

St. Teresa continued to found more convents, with miraculous success — and in the face of continued opposition from laity and secular
authorities.

Early in 1574, Our Lord ordered St. Teresa to found a convent in
Segovia. St. Teresa was still at *Encarnacion* under orders from Fr.
Fernandez, and she "knew that he had no desire that I should found
anymore."[122] Our Lord told her to ask him anyway; to her amaze-
ment, he approved.

She had no money and was sick with a fever, but Our Lord soon
provided her with a generous donor. However, when she attempted to
rent a house, she was sued by the Franciscans and Mercedarians, who
were attempting to rent the same house.[123] To make matters worse, St.
Teresa's license from the bishop had been given verbally only. At the
time St. Teresa was not concerned, since the bishop's support for the
reforms was well-known. But the bishop's vicar general was apparently
less supportive and demanded to see the license. He threatened to
imprison a priest who had said Mass at the convent, and for a time he
forbade the convent to keep the Blessed Sacrament.[124] But in the end,
the bishop's will was done: in March of 1574, the Convent of San Jose
in Segovia became the ninth founded by the reformers.

Also in 1574, the apostolic visitator to Andalusia deputed his authority to Fr. Jerome Gracian, who was then twenty-eight years old and
scarcely professed for six months. Fr. Gracian went to Madrid (which
at that time had only recently become the seat of royal government in
Spain) to meet with Bishop Ormaneto. On his way there, he met St.
Teresa for the first time, and she vowed obedience to him. St. Teresa
wrote in a letter that "these days ... are some of the best of my life,
without exaggeration.... Ask His Majesty to give [Fr. Gracian] to us as

prelate.... Such perfection and gentleness I have never seen." She later had a vision of Our Lord in which Christ told her to take Gracian in His place for the rest of her life. Fr. Gracian records that on many occasions she prayed that God would "move the heart of my Prelate, that he may command me, for I cannot disobey him."[125]

On one occasion, when St. Teresa told Fr. Gracian that Our Lord had commanded her to found a house in Madrid, Fr. Gracian told her to found it in Seville instead. This was beyond the authority given her by Fr. Rossi, the prior general of the Carmelites, since she was not allowed to found houses in Andalusia. Nevertheless, the saint reasoned that Fr. Gracian's authority came from the pope and superseded that of Fr. Rossi. St. Teresa obeyed her vowed superior Fr. Gracian rather than the private revelation she had received from Jesus Christ Himself. But soon Our Lord appeared to her and praised her obedience: she had done the right thing.[126]

St. Teresa's Autobiography Reviewed by the Inquisition

Convents weren't the only source of Teresa's troubles. In 1575, a princess denounced Teresa's autobiography to the Spanish Inquisition and it went under official review.[127]

The German Peasants' War of 1524, as well as the defection of millions of Germans from the Catholic Church following the rebellion of Luther, put the Spanish Inquisition on a heightened state of alert.

In 1525, the Spanish Inquisition condemned a list of propositions of the so-called *alumbrados* ("the enlightened"), including the doctrine that union with God erases the distinction between persons (such that one "becomes God") and the idea that someone could, by prayer and meditation, become "beyond sin," or incapable of sin. *Alumbrados* were disproportionately Jewish *Marranos*, who had converted to Catholicism only a generation or two before to avoid Ferdinand and Isabel's 1492 Edict of Alhambra, which required Jews to convert or leave the country.[128]

At a time of mass illiteracy, it was not surprising that many new converts were poorly catechized. But many Jewish converts also became exemplary Catholics: St. John of Avila, St. Teresa, and probably St. John of the Cross were all of Marrano descent.

At the same time, there had been an increasing interest in mysticism and personal prayer among laity and religious alike. This had borne much spiritual fruit (such as publication of *The Imitation of Christ*), but it also created an environment for fraudsters and lunatics. St. John himself served as a consultant to the Inquisition, and he helped uncover the fraudulent "mystic" Maria de Olivares.

In this context, in 1574, a group of *alumbrados* in Extramadura had been found to have copies of the writings of St. Teresa and St. John of the Cross in their possession, as well as writings by Bl. Luis de Granada and St. Ignatius of Loyola.[129] This discovery unsurprisingly brought these writings under suspicion.

By Providence, the review of Teresa's autobiography was assigned to Fr. Bañez, Teresa's lone defender before the *corregidor* in Avila. Her *Vida* was also reviewed by St. John of Avila and, in an official capacity, by the head of the Spanish Inquisition, archbishop of Toledo Gaspar de Quiroga, who immediately became a supporter of St. Teresa and her reforms. When Teresa met then-Cardinal Quiroga in 1580, he assured her of his strong support and asked her to pray for him.[130]

Despite being found free of heresy by the Inquisition, Teresa's *Vida* was held up for publication until six years after her death.[131] An inquisitor named Fr. Alonso de Fuente, O.P., waged a tireless campaign to discredit St. Teresa, even denouncing her to Rome.[132] Fr. Fuente explicitly cited her sex as a reason for his denunciation, arguing that women were not competent in matters of theology because St. Paul says that a woman ought not to teach men (1 Tim. 2:12).

More Stumbling Blocks

In May of 1575, the Carmelite Order held its general chapter meeting at Piacenza. No Discalced were present, and the delegate from Spain did not make it in time. Further, Fr. Rossi's invitations to Teresa to defend herself at the general chapter did not reach her until June 17.[133]

The general chapter therefore moved to restrict what seemed a fanatical Spanish novelty and ordered the closure of all Discalced houses outside of Castile — that is, those founded with Fr. Rossi's permission. All outward expressions of being a reform movement were restricted as well. Even calling oneself "Discalced" was forbidden. In addition, Fr. Rossi ordered St. Teresa back to Castile, to pick a convent and to stay there for good.[134] Provincial Fray Angel de Salazar called St. Teresa "an apostate."

St. Teresa, as with everything else, saw this enormous setback as a blessing of Providence. She embraced this time of forced stillness as an opportunity to rest from her work and to live her vocation, just as she did in the five years before being made prioress of *Encarnacion*.

Despite St. Teresa's and Fr. Gracian's desire to take a conciliatory attitude toward the other Carmelites, Fr. Mariano and other Discalced friars were furious and voted to ignore the orders from the general chapter. They had permission from the pope's representative; they did not need permission from the general chapter.

Fr. Gracian records that the Carmelites of Seville condemned him from the pulpit as a wicked and immoral man, and wild rumors spread of him being killed. Fr. Gracian began to fear poisoning, and so he ate only hard-boiled eggs. The friars accused him of embezzling enormous sums of money and of having an affair with the sixty-year-old St. Teresa. The saint was not offended, except at the way this damaged the reputation of this zealous twenty-eight-year-old priest who looked to her as to a mother — and who was so determined to be pure that he even tried to avoid hearing women's confessions.

By July of 1575, St. Teresa realized that she was putting new wine into old wineskins. The Discalced had to separate from the Calced somehow — perhaps as part of a different province with a different provincial. Otherwise the constant fighting would continue and only get worse. St. Teresa wrote to "my good friend" Philip II to ask his help in dividing the order into Calced and Discalced provinces. She hoped that Fr. Gracian would lead the Discalced as provincial. Philip balked: he wanted the Jesuits to oversee reforms of the remaining unreformed orders. And so the crisis dragged on.

The new convent at Seville quickly met with opposition from within and without alike. A clerical error led to a lawsuit and an enormous tax bill. Before the year was out, a failed novice named Maria del Corro denounced the nuns to the Inquisition, accusing them of being *alumbradas*. St. Teresa and Fr. Gracian quickly found themselves under investigation. Fr. Gracian recorded that, although he was worried by the investigation, St. Teresa was *tranquila*, smiling and saying, "Look, Father, they are burning us for Christ. But don't be afraid, for no one who has the faith ever suffers through the Inquisition." It is said that she even joked with the inquisitor. The matter was referred to two Jesuits, one of whom was a friend and confessor to St. Teresa.

St. Teresa's interview with an inquisitor is preserved among her writings as her Fifty-Eighth Spiritual Testimony, in which she gives a defense of her reforms. (Testimony Fifty-Three, also written from Seville around this time, records her being upset about "false testimony" by others.) Of course, the nuns were cleared of the baseless charge of heresy. The real problem, it turned out, was a single nun who was emotionally unstable.

Excommunication and Imprisonment

In 1577, the nuns of *Encarnacion* voted to elect Teresa as prioress. Fr. Tostado, the provincial of the Carmelites in Spain, then threatened to excommunicate all the nuns who voted for her.[135] Fr. Tostado had been sent to implement the decrees of the disputed general chapter at Piacenza, conducted by the Calced to suppress the Discalced. He had already removed St. John of the Cross as confessor at *Encarnacion* in 1576, which St. Teresa wrote caused a "great scandal" in Avila.[136] St. John refused, claiming his appointment by an apostolic visitor superseded the authority of Fr. Tostado. The nuns of *Encarnacion* also rejected Fr. Tostado's authority and voted for Teresa anyway. Fr. Tostado followed through on his threat and excommunicated fifty-five nuns. The remaining forty-four voted for a new prioress, whom the fifty-five refused to obey. St. John of the Cross defended the rights of the fifty-five nuns, whose excommunication was not only invalid but in violation of the Council of Trent, which had so recently issued its decrees. Philip II also intervened, and Fr. Tostado relented.[137]

Meanwhile St. Teresa continued at her work seemingly unperturbed. By the feast of St. Andrew, she had finished writing another one of her spiritual masterpieces, *Interior Castle*.

Yet, soon after the excommunication controversy, on the night of December 2, 1577, a group of Calced Carmelite priests, soldiers, and lay Carmelites seized St. John and took him to Toledo. Bishop Ormaneto, an ally of the Discalced, was dead and could not protect him; Bishop Sega was alive, but would not protect him. Fr. Maldonado, the Calced Prior in Toledo, had warned John to repent just three days before, even offering him the position of prior if he would return to the Calced.[138] But John had refused. He made no resistance to his captors.[139]

In Toledo the Calced demanded St. John renounce the Teresian Reform. John refused, having taken Discalced vows, and arguing that he was not bound by the decisions at Piacenza that were superseded by the orders of Fr. Fernandez. True obedience meant obeying the higher authority.

The friars declared him a rebel, whipped him, and threw him in prison. While traveling to Toledo in disguise, one of the laymen remarked at how horribly the friars were treating John, to which the saint replied that it was not half as bad as he deserved. When the same layman offered to help him escape that night, John said that he had no desire to escape.

St. Teresa heard the news the next day and immediately wrote an appeal to Philip, saying, "I would rather he were in the hands of the Moors, for they perhaps would be more merciful." Philip summoned her for a meeting at the Escorial Palace. Neither she nor the political authorities knew where John was.

The friars stripped St. John of his hood and scapular and locked him in what had once been a closet, six feet wide and ten feet long, with no windows. He had to wear the habit of the Calced friars and was not permitted to change clothes, no matter how filthy they became. His only food was bread, water, and occasionally sardines.

The only light came from a three-inch loophole, by which John continued to pray the Office. It agonized him that he could not say Mass, and when he requested to say Mass on the feast of the Assumption, Fr. Maldonado refused.

Three nights a week the friars took him into the refectory to eat while kneeling on the floor. After supper, the friars whipped him as they recited the *Miserere*. When later the friars reduced this practice to only Fridays, St. John asked them to do it more often. He had regularly whipped himself — as, with great devotion, did St. Teresa — so why not be whipped by someone else? The Carmelites also had the custom of making accusations to each other — including false accusations — in order to humble them. Why not bear false accusations from these fellow Carmelites?

For months, St. John of the Cross was nowhere to be found. St. Teresa's appeals to Fr. Gracian, to Philip II, and to other notables in Madrid discovered nothing. A rumor even went around that John had been sent to Rome, which it appears St. Teresa found credible.

After six months of this imprisonment and torture, John was assigned a new guard, Fr. John de Santa Maria, one who took some small measure of pity on him: he gave him a change of clothes, and pen and paper.

Over a series of months, St. John wrote a series of poems that are still considered, even by secular scholars, to be among the greatest literary works in the Spanish language.[140]

On the feast of the Assumption, it is said that Our Lady appeared to John and instructed him how to escape. She promised him that he would be able to say Mass again. The next night, August 16, 1578, John escaped from prison at two o'clock in the morning and slept under the porch of a nearby house. When daylight came, he made his way to the convent in Toledo, looking like a madman rather than a friar and scarcely able to walk. In those first few hours, Calced friars came to the door of that most obvious hiding place, but the nuns hid him in an infirmary, which by Providence the Calced friars left as the only room unchecked. The sisters made him a new Discalced habit before sending him to Almodovar del Campo.

There is not one recorded instance of St. John speaking ill of his captors or complaining of his captivity. To him it had been a passive mortification inflicted by God Himself. Such a man was St. John that once, at *Encarnacion*, upon hearing the word "suffering" he went into a rapture for more than an hour.

Weeks after his escape, St. John was in Almodovar with Fr. Gracian for another general chapter, where, over the objections of John of the Cross and Teresa, the Discalced elected Fr. Heredia as provincial of a separate, Discalced province. Bishop Sega nullified this supposed election, summoned Gracian and Heredia for a rebuke, and excommunicated anyone who had participated in this legally dubious general chapter.[141]

Fr. Rossi had died in October, but Fr. Gracian sent two friars to plead their cause in Rome anyway. Bishop Sega had Gracian imprisoned at Alcala, and rumors spread that Gracian would give up the reform and return to the Calced. St. Teresa wrote to him in the sternest terms not to back down, and his own mother — a Polish noblewoman who had borne twenty children — threatened to disown him if he did. Rumors spread that St. Teresa would be imprisoned next.[142] The Discalced reforms seemed on the verge of collapse.

"All This Trouble Came from God"

And then, as if by a miracle, everything changed.

By 1579, St. Teresa had won over the Royal Council to the reform, and one of its members, the Count of Tendilla, scolded Bishop Sega for the outrageous treatment that she and the Discalced were suffering. When Bishop Sega demanded an apology from Philip II, he received a rebuke from the king.[143]

In time, the count apologized, and Bishop Sega's heart softened toward the Discalced. He agreed to Philip's request to appoint an independent commission to investigate the Carmelite controversy. The commissioners were selected by Philip, who had backed St. Teresa from the beginning. By July they had persuaded Bishop Sega to support making the Discalced into a separate province. A year later, Pope Gregory XIII made it official, and in February of 1581, Fr. Gracian was elected the first provincial of the Discalced Carmelites.[144]

Despite the pope's approval of the Discalced province, Spain's bishops and civil authorities remained concerned that Spain was too poor to support even more houses of religion. When St. John went with Ven. Ana de Jesus in January of 1582 to found a convent in Granada, the archbishop refused.[145] A few days later, the archbishop's residence was struck by lightning near the room where he was sleeping. The archbishop took it to be a sign from God and gave them his permission.

St. Teresa's final days were spent in Burgos, contending with an archbishop who thought that there were already more convents than the people could afford. The archbishop even forbade Fr. Gracian to say Mass in Burgos. But ultimately St. Teresa prevailed and founded her last convent — her seventeenth — on April 18, 1582.

On October 3, the saint asked for Viaticum. While waiting for the priest, she adjured her daughters to keep the rule with all rigor. Some of her final words in the presence of Viaticum were an affirmation of obedience: "I am a daughter of the Church. I am a daughter of the Church."[146] She died, to all appearances, in a state of rapture. Afterward it was recalled that she had prophesied years before that she would die of love.[147]

Grant Me to Die Unknown

By 1585, there was already something of a coup d'etat in the young Discalced Province. Fray Nicholas Doria, the head of a faction called the *zelanti* (the zealous) was elected the new provincial at a general chapter in Lisbon.[148] The *zelanti* considered St. John of the Cross and Fr. Gracian to be moderates — not strict enough and engaged in too much outside activity.

Fr. Doria was deeply critical of his predecessor, Fr. Gracian, and accused the man who had been St. Teresa's spiritual director of introducing novelties and watering down her message. The Discalced had started as a movement to return to original rigor; now its own leaders were considered not rigorous enough.

When Fr. Doria was elected provincial, he "reformed" the province by setting up a committee of seven friars to handle all questions and complaints within the province.[149] In effect, there were seven provincials, and Fr. Doria tasked them with investigating the convents and friaries with the utmost scrutiny. This was a great scandal to the nuns in particular, including to Ven. Ana de Jesus, who consulted with St. Teresa's former confessor Fr. Bañez on this question.

By June 1591, St. John was known to be sympathetic to the nuns and therefore considered a rebel against Fr. Doria. The first Discalced friar in history thus received not a single vote for provincial, and found himself out of an office for the first time in his religious life. It was a defeat, but to the eyes of faith it was a victory. John praised God. At a general chapter, St. John pointed out that the new rules contradicted many existing rules, and he defended the nuns and Fr. Gracian.

St. John went to Peñuela, one of the poorest and most austere houses in the order at that time, where he was always found in prayer and practiced extreme mortifications that weakened his health.

Soon he was ordered to the Indies, which the other friars found absurd for someone of his ill health, but which rejoiced him as an opportunity to die.

But it was not to be. When his health deteriorated even further, his provincial begged him to recover his health in Spain at either Baeza or Ubeda. Suffering from a fever and inflammation of one of his legs, he went to Ubeda — even though he could have better medical care in other places — "for in Ubeda, nobody knows me."[150] The prior at Ubeda, Fray Francisco Crisostomo, openly complained about John being a burden and gave him the worst cell in the monastery. (Some sources suggest that Fray Crisotomo already hated St. John before he came to Ubeda, and that St. John chose to go to Ubeda because of this.)

Some pious women in Ubeda sought to assist the saint and wash the linens that were used to dress his wounds, but Fray Crisostomo forbade them. This scandalized the friars, and when Fray Crisostomo finally ordered the infirmarian to stop treating him at all, the friars were so outraged that the scandal broke out into the open. All the while St. John did not complain, and even told one of his surgeons — who despaired of saving his life — that he was ready to suffer more.

The provincial, Fray Heredia, rushed to Ubeda and ordered that the doors of the infirmary be opened to all of the friars and even to the general public, that all might see this *alter Christus* who was suffering with "the peace that surpasses understanding."

"My sufferings are nothing," said St. John. "The Lord has laid His Hand lightly on me."[151]

Like St. Simon Cyrene, Fray Crisostomo underwent a dramatic conversion of heart as he witnessed this joyful pain. At last he came to John and begged for forgiveness. Just hours later, on December 14, 1591, St. John of the Cross died, praying, "in manus tuas, Domine, commendo spiritum meum."

In his last hours, Fr. Heredia asked for a blessing, but St. John refused, since Heredia was his superior. Finally Fr. Heredia ordered him, as his superior, to bless them all, and he obeyed.

He had prayed to die not as a superior, somewhere he was unknown, and after suffering much. These prayers were answered.

Their Glorification and Legacy

In 1593, Clement VIII finally made the Discalced Carmelites a separate order with a separate prior general.[152] Then, in 1622, just forty years after her death, St. Teresa was canonized by Pope Gregory XV alongside St. Philip Neri and two other Spanish saints, St. Isidore the Farmer and St. Francis Xavier.[153]

In 1970, Pope Paul VI honored St. Teresa as the first female Doctor of the Church.[154] It is recorded that Pius XI would have made her a Doctor of the Church in 1925, at the same time as St. John of the Cross, but refrained because of her sex.[155]

St. John's own beatification process was delayed because of accusations of being an *alumbrado*. With time this accusation was seen to be patently false. St. John was beatified in 1675, canonized in 1726, and recognized as a Doctor of the Church in 1926. He is known as the Mystical Doctor.[156]

The legacy of the Discalced saints continues to grow. St. Thérèse of Lisieux, whom St. Pius X called "the greatest saint of modern times," was a Discalced Carmelite. In 1997, Pope John Paul II declared her a Doctor of the Church, the second woman so designated. St. Teresa Benedicta of the Cross, born Edith Stein, was also a Discalced Carmelite. In a curious and possibly mystical connection,

St. Teresa Benedicta was born and raised Jewish, became an atheist as a teenager, then converted to Catholicism upon reading the work of St. Teresa. She became a Carmelite in 1934. She was murdered at Auschwitz in 1942.

Today, more than four hundred years after St. Teresa's canonization, more than two thousand Carmelites live and pray on all of the inhabited continents of the world.[157]

CHAPTER 8

The Persecution of St. Alphonsus Liguori

EVEN AMONG THE SAINTS, the bishop and Doctor of the Church St. Alphonsus Liguori "shine[s] like the brightness of the firmament ... like the stars for ever and ever" (Dan. 12:3). He is best remembered today for his voluminous writings, more than a hundred books, and especially for his moral theology, which became the standard for confessors around the world within decades of its publication.

St. Alphonsus is a Doctor of the Church twice over: he has been declared the Church's Doctor of Moral Theology and the Doctor of Prayer, subjects which hold preeminence in the Church's mission of saving souls. This honor is exceeded perhaps only by those given to St. Thomas Aquinas and St. Augustine of Hippo.

Although today St. Alphonsus is synonymous with orthodoxy, while he lived and wrote and preached, he was a controversial figure. He suffered at the hands of governments and of his own family, while enduring chronic illness — and some of his greatest suffering was at the hands of the Catholic hierarchy.

St. Alphonsus spent decades fulminating against rampant heresy and immorality among Catholics, and castigating corrupt or complacent clergy (lay theologians were practically unheard of at this time, as they were throughout the Church's history before Vatican II). At the end of his life, the saint was denounced by fellow priests, which ultimately resulted in his being punished by the pope. The saint wrote to the Roman Curia, "I wish before I die to obtain the forgiveness of the Holy Father ... so that I die in peace."[158]

This wish was not granted.

An Aside on St. Francis Jerome

In 1696, the Liguori family was visited by a Neapolitan missionary, Padre Francesco de Geronimo, S.J. During the visit, the Jesuit prophesied to Donna Anna Caterina, the pious new mother, that her firstborn son would live to be ninety years old and that he would spend his long life "doing great things for Jesus Christ."[159]

We now know Padre de Geronimo as St. Francis Jerome, a saint who was in several ways a precursor to St. Alphonsus. Both men wanted to become overseas missionaries yet instead became missionaries in their own land of Naples. Both men preached in a simple style: St. Alphonsus said he aimed to preach so as to be understood even by "the poorest old woman in the congregation."[160] In 1839, both Neapolitan saints were canonized together at St. Peter's Basilica in Rome.

Indeed, both men suffered at the hands of Catholic priests and bishops. St. Francis's ministry to slaves, servants, and people of the streets led many to murmur against him, as the Pharisees had murmured about Jesus eating "with tax collectors and sinners" (Matt. 9:11). Fellow priests even conspired against him, as they later did against St. Alphonsus, convincing the local archbishop to put a stop to the saint's street preaching.[161] The archbishop soon discovered that the accusations against Francis were baseless and removed the restrictions in 1694, not long before the saint came to stay with the

Liguoris — a parallel we will soon see in St. Alphonsus's final and most humiliating trial.

The Centuries-Long War against Jansenism

St. Alphonsus was born in an age of religious controversy. An unprecedented tide of Christian blood had finally begun to ebb after more than a century of war. Luther's so-called Reformation had divided the body of Christ after a millennium of established Catholicism in Western Europe. The result was millions of dead Christians, thousands of new denominations, and a myriad of novel religious doctrines.

Less than a generation after Luther, a young lawyer named John Calvin extended several of Luther's doctrines (such as the validity of individual interpretation and the denial of free will) to their logical conclusions. Luther himself had essentially denied the freedom of the will, writing that "the human will is placed between [God and Satan] like a beast of burden. If God rides it, it wills and goes where God wills.... If Satan rides it, it wills and goes where Satan wills; nor can it choose to run to either of the two riders or to seek him out, but the riders themselves contend for the possession and control of it."[162]

To Luther and Calvin, man was a helpless puppet on a string, perhaps redeemed, perhaps unredeemable, but in any case not free — which leads, logically, to one conclusion: as St. Vincent de Paul would later write, Calvin "makes God the author of sin."[163]

"Having the form of godliness but denying the power thereof," Calvinism spread like a pestilence across Western Europe, more widely even than had Lutheranism, advanced rapidly in France and Switzerland, then to Germany, the Netherlands, and Scotland, and finally to the New World.

Calvin's influence was so widespread that it even infected many Catholics who remained within the Church, preeminently the bishop of Ypres, Cornelius Jansen, whose eponymous doctrines were echoes of Calvinism.

Calvinist ideas defended by the Jansenists include *limited atonement* (the idea that Christ died only for those who will ultimately reach Heaven, not for all), the previously mentioned *denial of free will*, and *irresistible grace* (the idea that God saves all whom He desires to save).

Jansenists held a Calvinistic view of human depravity. They became so afraid of causing sacrilege to the Eucharist that they restricted reception only to those "in whom there is the purest love of God, unmixed with any lesser affection."[164] The result, as St. Vincent de Paul decried, was that in Paris "no longer do we see persons frequenting the sacraments, not even at Easter."[165]

According to Fr. John Hardon, S.J., Jansenist priests feared eucharistic sacrilege so much that some stopped saying Mass altogether, the age of First Communion was sometimes delayed well into adulthood, and some Jansenists even refused to give or receive Viaticum.[166]

It is a matter of spiritual arithmetic that as Communion is reduced, popular morals decline. As the *Catechism of the Catholic Church* teaches, "The Eucharist ... preserv[es] us from future sins" (no. 1393). Jansenist doctrine convinced Catholics to abstain from Communion and to delay Confession, reducing the grace in their souls, which only convinced them to stay away from the sacraments even more. Thus began a vicious cycle of irreligion and immorality.

In practice, Jansenists also downplayed devotion to the Blessed Virgin Mary, teaching that "praise to Mary is vain."[167] Her immaculate life, completely free of sin, was incompatible with their Calvinistic theology of total depravity, so that some Jansenists even denied the doctrine of Mary's sinlessness, which has been the constant teaching of the Church from the time of the apostles.[168]

Entire libraries have been written on the Jansenist controversy, but it will suffice for these pages to say merely that the influence of this movement was enormous and lasted for centuries, well into the times of St. Alphonsus Liguori. The last nail in the Jansenist coffin did not come until Pius X's 1910 decree *Quam Singulari*, which allowed children as young as seven to receive Holy Communion, fully 272 years after the death of Bishop Jansen. (It is recorded that St. Pius even gave Communion to a four-year old who knew sufficient doctrine.)[169]

As has been persuasively argued by others, Jansenist ideas remain widespread even today, not only in the New Calvinism of American Evangelicalism, but even within the Catholic Church.[170] Pope Francis's 2016 exhortation *Amoris Laetitia* appeared to some readers to teach the Jansenist proposition that certain requirements of the moral law are impossible, at least for some people.[171] If this doctrine were true, then sin would be morally justified, which is logically impossible.

Even if the Holy Father's letter was misinterpreted, Jansenist ideas are still unquestionably alive and in circulation, which makes St. Alphonsus very much a saint for our time. He spent decades battling Jansenism with his pen and pulpit, as both priest and bishop. In dozens of books, he showed persuasively that God wills all to be saved, that He gives everyone the grace necessary to be saved, and that, if any of God's commandments seems impossible, we need only ask for God's help, and it will become possible.

From 1749 to his consecration as bishop in 1762, St. Alphonsus published forty-four works of theology and devotional literature, an astonishing output, notwithstanding the number of priests who assisted him — and in fact, the editors of the critical edition of his works say that an additional ten books were lost in transit to publishers.[172] In addition to spending hours in prayer, preaching, and in the confessional, he spent up to nine hours a day writing.

Just as he was twice a Doctor, St. Alphonsus had two ministries. His days were spent preaching the most basic gospel message to illiterate farmers, and his nights were spent in correspondence and debate with some of the foremost intellectuals in Europe. In the confessional, he spoke gently in a country dialect; in his writings, he spoke a blunt but heavily allusive Latin.

These two ministries were quite complementary. The saint's concern was above all for the salvation of souls, which he saw endangered by the false gospels of Calvin and Jansen. His hours in the confessional showed him how Jansenist ideas were leading ordinary laypeople into anxiety and despair — with some even giving up on religion altogether — since they doubted whether they were predestined to be among the tiny number of God's elect and had no way to affect their fate in any case.

In his writings for the common people he zealously promoted devotion to the Virgin Mary, despite the mockery of Jansenists. In his more abstract works of theology, he went to battle against now-forgotten men who comprised the theological establishment of their day. St. Alphonsus even battled in the press against Don Ludovico Muratori, one of the greatest scholars who ever lived.

St. Alphonsus knew that he would face opposition from powerful enemies, many more prominent and powerful than himself. His writings were widely attacked and condemned by Jansenist censors across Europe — and even torched in a book burning by Jansenists in Lisbon.

False Brethren, False Shepherds

Yet the saint's clerical enemies were not only scattered through the far reaches of Europe. Those who caused him the most suffering were in his own order — sometimes even in his own family.

In May 1730, on orders of his superior, the saint went on retreat with some fellow priests. They went to Santa Maria dei Monti, a monastery that overlooks the Amalfi Coast. While he was there, he ministered to the local farmers, shepherds, and goatherds.

This was a transformational experience for St. Alphonsus, who was descended from nobility on both sides of his family. The saint had grown up with servants, including one whom the young saint inspired to convert to Catholicism from Islam, a decision as fraught with danger then as it is today.

And while Alphonsus's native Naples at the time was said to have three pastimes — blasphemy, prostitution, and usury — in comparison with the poor and forgotten people of the countryside, it was a paradise on earth. What shocked the young priest most was the people's utter ignorance of Catholic doctrine and the prevalence of superstitions, some of which dated back to pagan times. They had not had a chaplain in years.

By God's providence, it was around this same time that the saint preached a mission to a convent of nuns nearby in Scala. He met each of the nuns and questioned them about doctrine and morality. One of the nuns, Sr. Maria Celeste Crostarosa, claimed to be a visionary.

At first the saint was skeptical, as was her confessor, Bishop Tomasso Falcoia. Yet over the course of months and years, both men came to believe in her visions. The bishop even oversaw the founding of a new order of nuns, which Christ had allegedly commanded Sr. Maria Celeste to found in private revelation.

Then, in 1731, Sr. Maria Celeste told the bishop that Our Lord now wanted him to found a men's order, an order of missionary priests. She told him Our Lord wanted it to be led by Alphonsus, the thirty-six-year-old priest who had preached at the convent. The bishop summoned Alphonsus, and the saint spoke with Sr. Maria Celeste in the chapel. When he heard her proposal, the saint was appalled, and the conversation quickly devolved into argument and shouting.

St. Alphonsus knew that he would, once again, be a fool for Christ. His friends and family had tried to stop him from becoming a priest in the first place. (His father had pressured him to marry into the upper nobility, and St. Alphonsus had even been briefly engaged.) The Church had plenty of religious orders. Now he was taking orders from God through the alleged visions of a young nun, whom many thought was mentally unbalanced. Alphonsus spent five months thinking and praying about what to do.

Though Alphonsus feared he might look ridiculous, after extensive correspondence with Sr. Maria Celeste, he came to believe that she was telling the truth, and that the new order was the will of God. He remembered the great empathy he felt for the ignorant country people he had met on his retreat, and he came to believe that Christ was sending him to spend his life with them.

As expected, even some of the devout laughed at the idea that the Church needed another missionary society. The young priest was already doing missionary work through the local archdiocese. Wasn't that good enough? It seemed ridiculous that yet another nun was hearing messages from God. The saint was derided by the Neapolitan clergy as *uscito de mente* (out of his mind) and as a *pazzo* (fool), which also happened also to be one of the saint's preferred nicknames for God, *Il Pazzo d'Amore*.

Fellow priests, including his own uncle, tried to stop him. Yet with Bishop Falcoia's support, St. Alphonsus founded in 1732 the Congregation of the Most Holy Redeemer, known in English today as the Redemptorists.

The order had an inauspicious beginning. Within a year, eight of the ten original brothers had left because they didn't want to take a vow of poverty. The saint found himself all but abandoned and humiliated, and it looked as if the new order might be stillborn.

When vocations began to recover, the saint faced a new problem: success. Because the order's missions and preaching in the countryside were popular with the country people, rival clergy became jealous. Priests in Naples, both secular and religious, complained to the bishop about this upstart order; they heckled and harassed members of the congregation on their missions, singing profane songs outside their window. One lay brother was even punched in the face while working in the garden. Having failed to persuade the bishop to restrict their missionary work, the resentful priests appealed to the civil government, though to no avail.

Despite the opposition, the order bore much fruit in southern Italy. Over the next forty years, the Redemptorists gradually expanded in the Papal States, and to four houses in the Kingdom of Naples.

The Suppression of the Jesuits

Throughout his battles with the Jansenists, St. Alphonsus had no greater brothers in arms than the Jesuits. One of the slurs against the saint was that his *Moral Theology* was simply plagiarized from the Jesuits, whose defense of casuistry — or drawing out theoretical rules from a particular case to apply to other cases — had earned them a reputation for legalism and hairsplitting that remains to this day.

In the sixteenth and seventeenth centuries, the Jesuits became a *bete noir* of Protestants because of their effectiveness in reconverting Protestants back to Catholicism. (For example, it is widely believed that the nation of Poland is Catholic today because of the work of the Jesuits.) By the eighteenth century, Jesuits had also run afoul of Catholic monarchs because of the rise of royal absolutism, which they rightly condemned from the pulpit as heresy. A Jesuit's fourth vow is loyalty to the pope, and no one at the time more fervently preached the supremacy of pope over all governments than the Jesuits did. Jesuits also angered European governments because they were some of the fiercest opponents of slavery and the mistreatment of Native Americans.

In 1759, the Jesuits were banned from the Kingdom of Portugal; in 1764, the Kingdom of France; and in 1767, the Kingdom of Spain. Finally, in 1773, Pope Clement XIV announced the complete suppression of the Jesuits worldwide. In one of Providence's many ironies, the Jesuits continued their work only in non-Catholic countries such as Prussia and Russia, where the papal brief was rejected by the Enlightenment figures of Frederick the Great and Catherine the Great.

To say that the saint disagreed with the pope's decision would be an extreme understatement. It was a great shock to St. Alphonsus, who feared that the same treatment was in store for the Redemptorists. According to Fr. Alessandro Tannoia, C.S.S.R., a contemporary of St. Alphonsus:

> When he received the brief of the Pope, [St. Alphonsus] adored the judgment of God in silence for some time, then said: "the will of the Pope is the will of God"; and did not utter another word....
>
> One day, the Grand-Vicar and other persons of distinction wished to cast blame on the dispositions of the Sovereign Pontiff. "Poor Pope," exclaimed the saintly bishop, "what could he do in the difficult circumstances in which he was placed, when so many crowned heads united in demanding their suppression? As for us, we have only to adore the secret judgment of God, and be at peace."

The saint was deeply disturbed, but he accepted the pope's decision as something that must be endured. The saint sensed that his own order would be next, and he began to prophesy that he would no longer be superior at his death.

The Regalomento *Disaster*

In February 1777, an official at the court of King Charles III, Duke of Parma, issued a provisional report calling for the suppression of the Redemptorists in Naples. The report argued the Redemptorist rule was practically a copy of the Jesuit rule — which was illegal under Neapolitan law — and that now-Bishop Liguori's theology and preaching were also characteristic of the Jesuits, the notorious enemies of royal power.

The saintly bishop drew upon his training as a lawyer and arranged to have the report referred to a more favorable court. He worked long hours planning his reply, so hard that he feared he would have a stroke. The saint's delegate in Naples, Fr. Angelo Maione, urged the saint to come to Naples in person to defend his case, but the saint wrote back that he was too ill. Despite his absence, the court proved favorable and the case went nowhere.

In 1778, the political situation of the order took an unexpected turn. King Ferdinand obtained a papal bull of crusade against the Barbary pirates, a band of brigands that had terrorized Christian Europe for decades, enslaved more than one million Europeans, and against whom the United States would soon go to war under President Thomas Jefferson.[173] To raise money for the crusade, the king asked the most effective preachers in his kingdom — the Redemptorists — to take to the pulpits.

Bishop Liguori replied that, if the king wanted their help, he must remove the threat of suppression in the kingdom and give them a permanent legal status. The bishop anticipated that some small changes to the Redemptorist rule might be necessary to comply with Neapolitan law — such as substituting an oath in place of a vow — and began negotiations with the royal court.

Trouble ensued. The saint had opened negotiations on these matters without informing the Curia in Rome. To Rome, it appeared that the saint was trying to change a papally approved rule without consent of the pope. Furthermore, he had agreed to the suggestion of Fr. Maione (a priest of his own order) to take an oath of secrecy about the negotiations, despite having been warned about the treachery of Fr. Maione by multiple priests. As a result, not only had Bishop Liguori not informed the pope of the negotiations, he had taken a vow that kept him from fixing that mistake — and the saint took vows extremely seriously.

The saint also gave Fr. Maione blank sheets of paper with his signature at the bottom. He was in fact old and infirm, but as Fr. Maione negotiated on the saint's behalf in Naples, he claimed that the saint was *scimunito* — senile — then he used the blank sheets of paper and agreed to major changes to the rule, such as eliminating the vow of poverty and common life, changes that even he admitted "would ... destroy the Congregation."

The official royal approval came in February of 1780, and Fr. Tannoia describes how it was received:

> The holy old man was stupified [*sic*] with amazement. He looked at the new rules: "It is not so!" he exclaimed, "it cannot be!" Then turning to Father [Andrea] Villani [an ally of Fr. Maione], he said reproachfully: "Don Andrea, I did not expect such deception from you." Afterwards addressing the community, he said: "I deserve to be dragged at a horse's tail, for I ought to have read everything myself, as I am superior." Then looking at the crucifix, he exclaimed: "My Jesus pardon me! I trusted to my confessor. In whom could I have more safely confided?"
>
> "You know," he said to the assembled brethren, "how much it costs me to write even a line." Sobs and tears almost choked his utterance. "I have been deceived," said he, sadly. He passed the whole morning in a state of absolute dejection.

He had signed not a new rule but a death warrant for the religious order to which he had dedicated his adult life. Men who had followed after him found that the order they had joined had ceased to exist. Within months, half of the priests in Naples and all of the seminarians in Naples left the order in disgust.

The priests and brothers were outraged at the changes and that they had been secret. Fr. Tannoia tells us many of them turned on the bishop, regarding him as senile.

Where a lesser man might have been tempted to lash out, St. Alphonsus dealt mercifully with Fr. Maione, and after recalling him from Naples did not even remove him from his role as his advisor.

The saint defended him publicly and wrote to him, "Let us forget the past and pass over what has been done."

The saint wrote to former friends, including bishops and superiors of other orders, asking them to intercede for him with the royal court. Cleric after cleric turned him down.

St. Alphonsus called a general assembly of the order. Before the gathering began, Fr. Francesco De Paola denounced St. Alphonsus and called for the order to be split in two. The houses in the papal territories called their own council, deposed Alphonsus as superior, and entreated the pope to divide the order in two. The priests of the order assumed that the purpose of the gathering was to enforce the new regulations. This was the exact opposite of what the saint intended.

When the general assembly actually began, debate became heated between the two factions, who agreed only on one thing: bitter indignation with the founder. Even those of goodwill were furious at the saint for trusting in Fr. Maione and for being so lenient with him. Ultimately the assembly reached contradictory resolutions — some in keeping with the new rule and some opposing — and the saint regretted calling the meeting at all.

Yet the betrayal in Naples was not nearly as bad as the betrayal in Rome. The saint had sent Fr. Francesco De Paola and Fr. Isidoro Leggio to Rome to plead their cause. Fr. De Paola, seeking a promotion for himself, betrayed Alphonsus, denouncing the founder for everything from the *regalomento* controversy to his claim to having been elected as rector major for life (which was illegal). Fr. Leggio resorted to outright calumnies against the founder, blatantly mischaracterizing letters he had received from him about his role in the *regalomento* controversy.

The pope promptly ordered that the papal-approved rule should be followed without alteration. Yet the two Redemptorists continued to defame the founder. To make matters worse, Fr. Tannoia sent a scathing letter to the Congregation for Bishops defending St. Alphonsus, but the letter unintentionally confirmed the facts about the rule change and the existence of complete chaos in the order.

Fr. Tannoia's fiery defense of the founder backfired, and in September, Pope Pius VI cut off the Redemptorist houses in Naples. They were no longer part of the order, and St. Alphonsus was removed as rector general. In effect, the order was suppressed in the Kingdom of Naples, the homeland of St. Alphonsus and the place that inspired the order in the very beginning.

Fr. De Paola got his promotion: the pope appointed him rector general of what remained of the congregation in the Papal States. Fr. Tannoia arrived in Rome to defend the founder, but it was too late. The secretary of the Congregation for Bishops informed him that Alphonsus was "cut off from the Congregation." According to Fr. Tannoia, Fr. Leggio snickered that now the Church would never canonize Alphonsus Liguori.[174]

The pope ruled that no further petitions on the matter would be considered.[175] The case was closed.

Once again, the priests had to break difficult news to the saint; Fr. Villani delivered it while Alponsus was preparing to hear Mass. The saint was startled, but quickly gathered himself. He stated that he accepted the decision — "Good is good enough for me" — and went back to preparing for Mass.[176] He remained at peace, but on the way back from Mass he broke into tears and began shouting that he was on the verge of despair, for he had destroyed a work of God and would surely be punished in Hell.

His Death

There began a dark night of the soul that would last for the rest of his life.

The saint lived for nearly six more years. He was already nearly deaf, nearly blind, and in constant agony from rheumatoid arthritis, which cocked his head down and at an angle, a posture which is memorialized in many icons and statues of the saint. In his final years he was known around the house at Pagani as *il cadavere parlante*, the talking corpse.

As death approached, it was accompanied by temptations and spiritual afflictions. He began to worry about his own salvation more than he had in decades, telling one priest, "I am enduring the pains of hell."[177] He frequently woke Fr. Villani in the middle of the night to request the Sacrament of Confession. Eventually, the priest simply stopped answering the door past a certain hour, though the saint had told him, "At every word I say, God seems to reject me."

He suffered from hallucinations. One day he became convinced that his writings had spread error and heresy, and he became extremely anxious. Once, after he prayed "Jesus, I love Thee," he heard a voice that said, "That is not true." At other times, he saw a man who told him that he would be damned. On another occasion the devil walked into his room in the form of a young temptress. At these disturbing visions, the saint was often heard sobbing or shouting for help, both day and night. He was openly treated as a burden by the other priests, including Fr. Villani, who said, "If is his temptations and scruples were a heavy cross for him, they were equally so for us." The brothers assigned to assist him were called "martyrs of patience."

By then the saint needed to be carried everywhere or pushed in a wheelchair, and yet he could (and did) preach in the pulpit for hours at a time. Fr. Tannoia records that one of his final sermons touched on the subject of obedience:

> I recommend two things to you, obedience and poverty:
> obedience, were it even to the cook; obedience is that
> which preserves us; he who lacks obedience is wanting as
> regards his duty to God, and God will drive him out of the
> Congregation; I also recommend poverty to you, for it is

that which unites us to God. I regard faults against obedience and poverty as capital offences.

Whenever his caretakers wanted him to do something, they needed
only to invoke the words "obedience" and "the will of God," and the
strong-willed saint would comply.

During this same dark night of the soul, Alphonsus was at times
rewarded with ecstasies and consolations. Multiple priests of the
house at Nocera claimed to have seen his face light up during prayer
like that of Moses on Sinai. He was also recorded to work miracles,
healing an eight-year-old girl of a serious illness and curing a young
boy of deafness.[178] One resident of the house, Br. Anthony, claimed
the saint healed thousands of local children of illnesses, although Fr.
Tannoia records the bishop joking humbly, "If I were a saint, and if I
knew how to work miracles, I should cure myself, who am so crip-
pled and worthless."

By 1784, the saint's confessor ordered him to stop saying Mass,
since it had become physically impossible. This was a devastating
blow and made him even more eager to die. He often sat before a
crucifix and prayed, "*Gesu Mio,* it seems like a thousand years before
I die and come to be with You in paradise." Nevertheless he continued to attend daily Mass and spend hours each day in prayer. He
made the Stations of the Cross daily until he was eighty-eight.

One of his caretakers, Brother Raffaele, often heard him talking
in sleep, as if he were back in the confessional. He was heard saying
that, as long as the penitent had confessed all his sins with confidence in God's mercy, then he should be confident in God's forgiveness. He was also heard reciting acts of contrition and charity for the
penitent to repeat after him. One night the imaginary penitent was
not sorry for his sins, and the saint was heard saying, "Do you want
to go to eternal damnation — you and your confessor?" He told him
to pray to the Virgin Mary, who was his last hope.

He spent his last years reading over and over the life of St. Joseph Calasanz, who had also been deposed from his own order in his old age, as well as the life of St. Teresa of Avila, who also suffered at the hands of her own order.

During this final period, the saint frequently said, as he had when the Jesuits were suppressed, that "the will of the pope is the will of God." The saint obeyed not only the pope but also his new superior, his betrayer, Fr. De Paola. Once, when a priest seemed to look at him with pity, Alphonsus said, "You must accept everything because it is the pope's will."

Alphonsus's affection for and submission to the pope, despite his disgrace at the pope's hands, were emphatic. In his final years he is recorded as saying, "After God is the pope. Without him, in what confusion should we not be! It is the pope who makes known to us the will of God, and puts our consciences in peace." The saint's letters from these final years are filled with entreaties for his priests to "pray for the pope." Those who came to the saint for his advice about the *regalomento* were told simply, "Obey the pope."

He told his priests, "We cannot judge the pope in our own cause; let us humbly bow our heads in submission. If the pope has cast us down by one decree, he can raise us up by another; we must obey, and not put interpretations of our own on what he does."

Finally, on July 31, 1787, the saint entered into his last agony. His room was swarmed with priests, lay brothers, and eventually local laypeople looking for relics. In the morning, he died quietly, peacefully, with hardly anyone even noticing. He was ninety years old.

His Glorification

The Redemptorist order was suppressed in Naples, yet it grew in the Papal States. Pius VI opened three more Redemptorist houses, including one near Santa Maria Maggiore in Rome. Even though St. Alphonsus had long opposed opening a house in Rome, before he died he had been happy that the pope's will was now known and would be carried out.

Bishops in the Kingdom of Naples had mourned the loss of the missionaries, and they eventually defended Alphonsus to the pope and the cardinals directly. They told him of the loss to their dioceses of not having the missionaries anymore, and Pius VI restored the rights and privileges of the missionaries in the Kingdom of Naples in 1783. Nevertheless, the order was conflicted over who should lead it, with at least three candidates in contention.

The saint predicted reunification would happen sooner or later, and three years after his death, in 1790, the pope and the king reached an agreement that reunited the order under the rule approved by Benedict XIV, the exact same rule followed by St. Alphonsus for decades.

As is often the case with history's greatest men and women, St. Alphonsus suffered enmity in life only to be loved after death. Within months of his death, Fr. Villani and Fr. De Paola — men who had caused him so much difficulty and who did not get along with each other — themselves began the process that would lead to his canonization.

During the canonization process, some of the cardinals raised the question of the *regalomento* controversy. Fr. Leggio in particular remained critical of the saint for his mishandling of the situation. Just when it looked as though this argument would carry the day, in April 1796, Pius VI declared that the saint was not to be blamed for his handling of the controversy and it was not to be considered as a factor in the decision for canonization. The same pope who had removed him as rector then declared that he had lived a life of heroic virtue and made him Venerable.[179]

Months later, Napoleon invaded Italy, and Europe was engulfed in fifteen years of bloodshed. Napoleon kidnapped and imprisoned both Pius VI and later Pope Pius VII. The Congregation of Rites, which handled the process of canonization of saints, essentially shut down for several years, which undoubtedly delayed St. Alphonsus's canonization.

When the wars had finally come to an end, Pius VII beatified Alphonsus in late 1816. In 1830, Rome cleared him for canonization, and the pope named him "Prince of Moral Theologians." Nevertheless, the Redemptorist order could not afford a canonization ceremony, and it delayed the process nine years in order to share the expenses with the Jesuits. Finally, St. Alphonsus was raised to the altars.

In 1870, Pius IX named him a Doctor of the Church. In 1901, Pope Leo XIII declared Sr. Maria Celeste — the visionary who called on Alphonsus to found the Redemptorists — Venerable. In 1950, Pius XII made St. Alphonsus the patron saint of confessors.

Today, seventeen Redemptorists have been canonized or beatified, including St. John Neumann, and St. Gerard Majella, one of the most popular and beloved saints in the Church.

Despite suffering greatly, the order that was once Alphonsus and two lay brothers flourishes, now including 5,500 priests and brothers worldwide.[180]

CHAPTER 9

The Persecution and Excommunication of St. Mary MacKillop

ST. MARY MACKILLOP — a lover of children and education — was revered by Catholic laity and non-Catholics alike in her time. Yet for most of her life she struggled under the predations of bishops who wanted the order she founded firmly under their control. Ironically, the humble woman whom Australia's bishops so often saw as a thorn in their sides would eventually be recognized as Australia's first saint.[181]

Her Times and Formation

St. Mary MacKillop was born in 1842 to poor Scots immigrants to British Australia. St. Mary's parents were native Gaelic speakers, descendants of Jacobite Catholics who had risen up against King George I just a century before the saint was born. Her father, Alexander, was a Roman seminary dropout who assisted in May 1839 at the first Catholic Mass in the history of Australia. St. Mary's upbringing was very devout: she received First Communion at just eight years old, which was rare before the twentieth century.[i]

According to Mary's diary, it was after her First Communion that the Virgin Mary told her that she would enter religious life.[ii] Her father's seminary training had enabled him to give Mary an excellent education in the Faith. The idea that he had nearly become a priest haunted St. Mary, who had an inner conviction that she was called to take his place in consecrated life.

Alexander MacKillop had quit the Pontifical Scots College in Rome because of a perceived slight to his honor. It was an impulsive decision that ended nearly a decade of training. This same impulsiveness later gave Mary a taste for poverty when it precipitated disastrous financial decisions. Just months after Mary was born, Alexander was forced to sell the family home for half of what he had paid for it. He later made a series of unsuccessful land deals, an unsuccessful attempt to join Australia's and New Zealand's gold rushes, and several unsuccessful runs for public office. He wound up in bankruptcy court. The family was forced to move to Richmond, Sydney, and Melbourne, and were repeatedly forced to stay with relatives. In Collingwood, Flora MacKillop — Mary's mother — opened a boarding house, which quickly went out of business. In 1849, Alexander impulsively returned to Scotland for more than a year without telling his wife.

Poverty in South Australia was even worse than poverty in Scotland. The British Empire had only begun to settle Australia some fifty years before Mary was born, and there was little there that could be called civilization.

Tensions ran high between English, Scots, and Irish immigrants, and these tensions only grew during the saint's youth. Only 10 percent

---

[i] August 15, 1850, at St. Francis Church.

[ii] "You told me I was to be a consecrated spouse of your Son, you told me I had great work to do, you said you marked me as your child since my birth."

of South Australians were Catholic at the time. Mary's brief time in school was cut short when she stood up to a Protestant teacher who spoke ill of Mary Queen of Scots.

The MacKillop family's misery instilled in Mary a love of poverty and simplicity. It also brought her into contact with South Australia's education system, which became a matter of great controversy for Australian Catholics at the time.

In 1851, the colony of South Australia ended funding for religious schools; public money could only be used for licensed nondenominational schools. (This anticipated the later movement in the United States for the Blaine Amendments, which blocked taxpayer funding of religious schools — overwhelmingly, Catholic schools — in almost every state.) By 1900, all six of the Australian colonies had similar laws on the books. However, fees were still charged, even for secular public schools, which meant that the poorest of the poor didn't go to school at all and remained trapped in a cycle of poverty.

At just fourteen years old, Mary was forced to become the breadwinner of the family due to her father's financial ineptitude. She became a governess to a family in Sydney and then at nineteen she became governess to her Aunt Margaret's daughters in Penola. It was there that she met Fr. Julian Woods, the local parish priest. Fr. Woods was an immigrant from England, a tall, charming man, and a widely published scholar.

The two bonded almost immediately over a shared concern about the lack of education in South Australia, and especially the lack of Catholic education. As the saint would later write to Bishop Laurence Sheil of Adelaide, "Circumstances as well as choice having for many years compelled me to live as a teacher, I saw so much of the evils attending a merely secular course of education."

Mary's collaboration with Fr. Woods would have to wait for a few years, as one group of her cousins reached the age of maturity and another needed her help in Portland. Mary soon found a teaching job at the local Catholic school. According to Fr. Woods's niece Mechtilde, who later became a confidant of St. Mary, it was during her time in Portland that Mary "suffered through the attention paid to her by a gentleman of wealth and position" who desired to marry her. We know little about this incident, but we do know that Mary had already sensed a vocation to religious life before this time and wouldn't be swayed from her conviction.

In January 1864, St. Mary opened a Catholic girls' school, the Bay View House Seminary for Young Ladies, employing her sister Maggie as a teacher and her mother as a housekeeper.

She also obtained for her sister Annie a job teaching at another local Catholic school. Soon Divine Providence used Alexander MacKillop's hot temper to its own purposes once again. After hearing that one of the teachers in the school had falsely presented the school's worst students to the school inspector as Annie's students, Alexander MacKillop stormed down to the school committee and told them that Annie was quitting. This loss in income came at a time when Alexander had already spent the family into debt.

The family's time of stability — and indeed, their ability to live under the same roof — came quickly to an end, forcing Mary to take much more responsibility within her family than most of her peers.

Fortunately, Fr. Woods was able to get Annie another teaching job in Penola. In 1866, Mary moved to Penola with Annie and Lexie. Mary rented a cottage and a stable from a Scots Presbyterian and had it renovated by her brother John. Thus began the first St. Joseph's School.

To the astonishment of the locals, the girls offered to teach even the children whose parents could not afford to pay. Working together, the siblings taught more than fifty local children.

Mary did not just want a career as a teacher; she wanted to live as a religious sister. In the late 1850s, she considered joining the Sisters of Mercy, but she decided against it in large part because the sisters made no vow of poverty. Her confessor told her that to join the kind of order she wished, she would probably have to move to France.

Three months after founding St. Joseph's, on the feast of St. Joseph, Mary got rid of all her fashionable clothing and began to wear all black, which caused a minor scandal in the little village. In November, on the feast of the Presentation of Mary, a local girl named Blanche Amsinck, who became Mary's first follower, did the same.

After Christmas, Fr. Woods left Penola to serve as secretary to Bishop Sheil. In April, the bishop put Fr. Woods in charge of the diocesan schools and announced that Catholics in the diocese were not to participate in the secular government schools.

Fr. Woods saw that this would improve the prospects for Mary's project of founding Catholic schools. However, with everything going their way, he predicted "the crosses must be to come after." St. Mary agreed and even began to pray for crosses. Her prayers were soon answered.

After Fr. Woods left, Annie wrote to him that Mary had a vision of Bishop Sheil as a shepherd and herself as his sheep. "The Bishop went to pull her up with his crook ... and then he altered his mind and the crook looked like one of those things they use to dip sheep with when they are washing them, and Mary was a sheep getting dipped in the same way.... Can you make anything of her vision? It is time to put a stop to such nonsensical fancies." But the vision would make sense soon enough.

Fr. Woods sent for Mary to begin opening schools in Adelaide, and in the summer of 1867, Mary moved to a house on Grote Street. Even Mary was shocked at the poverty in the city, where there were no jobs and every day new poor immigrants arrived from Britain and Ireland.

Fr. Woods drew up a rule for an order of religious sisters inspired by the rule of the Sisters of Auvergne, whom he had met in France. On Mary's favorite feast day, the feast of the Assumption, she made the public vows of obedience, chastity, and poverty. She was twenty-six years old and the cofounder and first of the Sisters of St. Joseph. For her fourth vow, Sr. Mary vowed to promote to the utmost of her abilities the love of Christ in the hearts of little children.

Mary quickly won over the affection of the people of Adelaide, of whom only about 9 percent were Catholic. Sr. Mary gave them a free education and rarely used corporal punishment, which was unusual for the time. By the end of the year, there were seven postulants in the order. Bishop Sheil approved the rule on December 17, 1868. Within two years, seventy Sisters of St. Joseph were teaching children at twenty-one schools in South Australia.

The sisters slept on straw mattresses, rising at five in the morning for an hour of meditation before reciting the Office. They spent their days teaching dozens of children. They ate little, wore cheap alpaca habits, and were forbidden even to have carpets on the floor. Their rule did not permit any property. The sisters also cared for unwed mothers, former prostitutes, neglected children, and the elderly, ministering to Catholics and non-Catholics alike. The order spread quickly. Within four years, 130 sisters were working in more than forty institutions across South Australia and Queensland.

But as is so often the case, the sisters seemed to meet with more opposition from fellow Catholics than from non-Catholics. Fr. Woods, as head of education for the diocese and as de facto superior of the order, began closing Catholic schools that were not run by the sisters. This outraged the other priests of the diocese. Most of the priests hoped to split the schools into two tracks, with one track for the poor, which they hoped and expected would be subsidized. But the sisters refused to accept such subsidies, and Mary emphatically opposed all distinctions of class within the order and in her schools.

Father Keating

Fr. Patrick Keating was one of the many Irish priests who had been sent to South Australia in the mid-nineteenth century. While he was serving in Kapunda, Fr. Keating was accused of committing sexual offenses in the confessional, offenses which only a bishop can absolve.[182] The Sisters of St. Joseph reported these accusations to Fr. Woods, who then reported it to the vicar general, Fr. John Smyth.

The sisters succeeded in getting Fr. Keating expelled from the diocese. He was removed and sent back to Ireland, officially for alcoholism rather than his crimes against the sixth commandment. Indeed, Fr. Keating continued to work as a priest for the rest of his life.

Contrary to widespread belief, it was not St. Mary herself who reported the abuse, but other sisters of the order. St. Mary was in Queensland at the time and so could not have had firsthand knowledge of the situation. Nevertheless, according to Fr. Joseph Tappeiner, S.J., who replaced Fr. Woods as superior of the order in 1872, it was the Keating affair that poisoned relationships with a powerful group of Irish priests sent to Australia, including a Fr. Charles Horan. This was "the beginning of the hatred of Fr. Horan for Fr. Woods and the Sisters," Fr. Tappeiner said.[183]

According to the postulator of St. Mary's cause, there is evidence the Fr. Horan "swore vengeance" on Fr. Woods and on the Josephites.[184] Even though St. Mary was not the accuser of Fr. Keating, the other sisters' accusations, coupled with the long simmering climate of tension between Irish, Scots, and English immigrants, together help explain the extreme hostility that St. Mary would experience from the Irish clergy through most of her life.

The "Mystics"

An additional cause of friction between the order and the diocesan priests came in 1868, when two women, Sr. Ignatius and Sr. Angela, joined as postulants. Soon both of them began reporting "supernatural" phenomena: visions, locutions, and other extraordinary claims.

Fr. Woods believed them wholeheartedly and considered them saints. He even hinted that Sr. Ignatius would one day take over as superior of the order from Sr. Mary.

Fr. Woods was a respected scholar, but was not astute in spiritual matters. He once admitted to St. Mary, "I never read spiritual books now, especially those which treat of supernatural things. I don't know anything about the theory and I dread trying to learn." Fr. Woods was ill-equipped to deal with the "mystics," and the other priests of the diocese were infuriated by his credulity.

Tensions with the "mystics" came to a head when Fr. Horan accused Sr. Angela of desecrating the Blessed Sacrament. On April 11, 1870, the Blessed Sacrament went missing from the tabernacle in St. Joseph's Convent in Kensington. At the same time, there appeared blood stains on the altar cloth, as well as unexplained fires in the convent.

Fr. Woods was convinced that these events were all of preternatural origin. Archdeacon Patrick Russell, who at that time was running the diocese while the bishop was in Rome attending the First Vatican Council, set up a commission of nine priests to investigate. The commission quickly pointed the finger not at a preternatural cause but at the "mystic" Sr. Angela, who wrote to Mary accusing Fr. Horan of making sexual advances to her.

Archdeacon Russell filed a report to Rome about the alleged desecration of the Blessed Sacrament, without telling Bishop Sheil first.

The bishop was livid. To save face he assured Rome that the report was merely a petty character assassination, and he fired Archdeacon Russell as administrator. Rome apparently disagreed with the bishop and reprimanded him for removing the archdeacon — another humiliation that infuriated the bishop.

As for the "mystics," Sr. Angela later admitted to being a fraud. Sr. Ignatius left religious life altogether and later founded St. Margaret's Maternity Hospital in Sydney, which she bequeathed to the sisters and served women of all beliefs for more than a century.

The Saint's Excommunication

The day after Bishop Sheil returned from Europe in April 1871, he was presented with a document signed by Fr. Horan and by ten other priests denouncing the Josephite Sisters and Fr. Woods.[185] The document said the order included "ignorant girls" and that most of the sisters were "utterly useless for educational purposes." The letter went on to say that "a host of uneducated and ignorant Sisters would be an unbearable onus" on priests and laity alike. The priests further claimed the sisters took advice from no one but Fr. Woods, the man incompetent enough to have been duped by the purported mystics.

As with most calumnies, there was some truth in each of the allegations. Three of the sisters could not read and two could not write. On the other hand, thirty-six of them had been schoolteachers before they joined the order. The fact of the matter was that many of the girls came from poor backgrounds, and some of the wealthier Catholics resented having their children taught by girls from the lower classes.

Bishop Sheil called a meeting with Fr. Woods, who revealed that the order was buried in £4,000 of debt (more than $600,000 in today's currency). Even worse, the order could not even afford to keep up with the minimum interest payments.

The bishop listened calmly but informed Fr. Woods that he would give them no assistance with the debt. The bishop then appointed a commission to examine the order, a commission made up of three priests who were already some of its fiercest opponents. Bishop Sheil's inner circle of fellow Irish priests then convinced him to send Fr. Woods to Sydney for a mandatory vacation.

Bishop Sheil had always thought well of the sisters. He had boasted of them during his time in Europe. But in his first four years in office, the bishop had only been present in Adelaide for eleven months, and so he relied on his clergy for his information — and many of them were sworn opponents of the sisters and especially Fr. Woods.

Based on what he knew, the bishop visited the motherhouse in Adelaide on September 1, 1871, and informed the sisters that he was going to make significant changes to their constitution. Mary's vision was beginning to come to fruition.

St. Mary was in Kadina at the time (about seventy miles away; a long journey in those days) and the sisters sent word for her to return immediately. A week later, St. Mary met with the bishop, who essentially repeated what he had been told in the letter from the priests. He said the sisters at the motherhouse were "lazy" and those teaching in the schools were "ignorant."

He told her that he wanted to make the order more like those in Europe, with a clear differentiation between lay sisters and consecrated sisters. Each convent would be completely independent of the others and would be put under the authority of the local parish priest. There would be no shuffling of sisters between convents.

The bishop then delivered this sentence of judgment: the teaching sisters would be examined in order to weed out the ignorant, and their schools would no longer accept those who couldn't pay. The motherhouse would be turned over to the Dominicans. Any sister who couldn't accept the new rules should leave.

St. Mary was devastated. She consulted with a number of priests, each of whom concluded that there was nothing she could do. The bishop gave, and the bishop could take away. What made the situation even more complicated was that the sisters had taken a specific set of vows, including poverty, that they could no longer fulfill under the new rules.

St. Mary wrote a long letter to the bishop on September 10 that is as innocent and blunt as that of a child. She told the bishop,

> I longed for a religious life, one in which I could serve God and His poor neglected little ones in poverty and disregard of the world and its fleeting opinions.... When

an opportunity of entering another religious community was offered to me ... in that order I could not find what my heart craved. I looked for a poverty more like unto that practiced in the early religious orders of the Church ... [and] all my desires seemed to center in a wish to devote myself to poor children ... in some very poor Order."

I know that you can withdraw your approbation from [the Constitution] and if our good God wills it I am resigned. But pardon me my Lord if I say that I cannot in conscience see it altered and remain as a Sister. I am your child, my Lord, your humble helpless child. I want to please you, but above all to please God and do His holy will. If then, in any way, it may please God that you should alter the Rule, then, my Lord, I feel I must take the alternative you offered and leave.... Your obedient child in JMJ, Mary of the Cross.

Perhaps seeking reassurance, Mary showed the letter to several priests, who were all encouraging. A Fr. Kennedy told her, "There was not one word in the letter to cause the least offence."

But Fr. Kennedy was wrong. The bishop was deeply offended at the letter and summoned Mary in person for a rebuke, telling her he never expected something like that from her. The bishop's staff and advisors continually blocked the rather stunned St. Mary from meeting with him afterward.

Mary told the other sisters that they had to follow their conscience about whether to stay in the order. Likewise, Mary decided to follow hers and fulfilled the resolution she expressed in her letter to the bishop.

On September 21, the bishop went to the convent looking for St. Mary, but she was not there. He mentioned that he wanted her to go to the convent at Bagot's Gap, about fifty miles away. Later in the day, Fr. Horan and another Irish priest visited the Adelaide convent and told the sisters that there would be an important announcement the next day. Fr. Horan instructed Sr. Teresa to tell St. Mary that the bishop had changed his mind and that she was to go to St. John's, about forty miles away (which conveniently would make her absent for the big announcement). Fr. Horan said there would be some minor changes to the rule but that they were nothing to worry about. St. Mary returned and had a somewhat ambiguous conversation with Fr. Horan about going to St. John's and about changes to the rule. St. Mary very carefully said, "I do not know if I can." Undoubtedly, everyone was in a state of confusion about what exactly was going on.

Fr. Horan left and returned after ten o'clock; the doors were bolted and all but two of the sisters were in bed. He said that he had a message from the bishop and told Sr. Teresa to tell St. Mary that she would be excommunicated if she did not obey the bishop's new constitution. Perhaps because she had just been woken up, Sr. Teresa thought he said that St. Mary was *already* excommunicated, and she rather boldly told Fr. Horan that none of the sisters would obey the new constitution. Fr. Horan left, and the sisters spent a sleepless night trying to figure out what had just happened and what they ought to do.

None of them attended morning Mass. Was only Mary excommunicated or were they all excommunicated? None of them knew. At eight o'clock, the bishop and four priests arrived, demanding to know why they had not attended Mass. The sisters said that they thought they were excommunicated.

St. Mary was sick in bed with a migraine headache and possibly the extreme menstrual pain she suffered every month. The bishop summoned her to the chapel. She arrived, looking pale, and asked for the bishop's blessing. He refused. He told her she was "disobedient, rebellious" — and therefore excommunicated. He ordered her to kneel before him. He scolded her for her "pride" and read the order of excommunication. The bishop then threatened to do the same to any of the sisters who continued to have dealings with her.

As St. Mary obeyed the bishop and walked out of the church, all the sisters followed her, some of them weeping. The bishop then called them back, and they each asked to be dispensed from their vows.

St. Mary moved in with the family of Fr. Woods's brother James, who was a journalist. James was outraged and desired to publicize the entire episode and put the bishop to shame, but St. Mary made him promise "not to write one single word against the bishop and priests." She gave the other sisters the same order to say nothing against the clergy, but rather, as the Suffering Servant, to open not their mouths.

Soon she moved in with a Protestant friend. She began to move about frequently, living with friends and supporters. She changed her manner of dress so dramatically that few recognized her and there quickly arose a rumor that she was dead.

St. Mary had thought that the reason for her excommunication was her letter. But a few days later she found out it was actually precipitated by an even flimsier pretext: an alleged refusal to go to St. John's, a refusal that had never happened.

The convent at Adelaide quickly emptied as sisters were either dispensed or expelled. Dominican sisters took it over on November 21. Bishop Sheil refused to renew the lease. In the exodus from the order, all but eighteen Josephite schools closed. Priests often refused to give the sisters Communion.

Many of the sisters took jobs in the city, working as servants, manual laborers, or governesses. In an act of charity that the sisters were hard-pressed to find among their fellow Catholics, a Jewish member of Parliament, Emmanuel Solomon, donated a small house where they could live rent free.

Priests with whom the saint corresponded assured her that the excommunication could not be procedurally valid. Neither the saint nor any of the sisters knew much canon law and could not assess this possibility. Nevertheless, St. Mary made no effort to clear her name and considered this trial an opportunity to offer suffering to God. She also expected that this trial would not last and that the order would ultimately be vindicated, grow, and perform its much-needed service to the poor of South Australia.

When the saint did speak of the bishop, it was never with bitterness, and certainly not with resentment. Instead, she spoke with pity. "The poor bishop ... there are some about him whom God permits to be bitterly opposed to Fr. Woods and in a manner to myself ... our poor, dear old bishop."

The saint's supporters were not always so forgiving. Her mother, for example, wrote a scathing letter to His Excellency. "The great sin of her life, in my opinion," she said, "has been leaving me and putting herself under your Lordship's protection." St. Mary was horrified, writing to her mother, "That letter vindicates me, but oh at a terrible cost."

After one article defending her was published, St. Mary said, "I would have suffered anything rather than that it should have been published.... Oh Sister, do not say a word against [the bishop] but pray that he may have light. As of the others who are against us, let us not judge them. If we cannot speak well of their acts, let us be silent."

Reconciliation and Further Troubles

Bishop Sheil's health continued to decline, and the effect on his cognitive abilities became more obvious. He became confused increasingly often and regularly contradicted himself. This mental decline further empowered the circle of priests around him, particularly Fr. Horan, his fellow Irish Franciscan. The bishop ran the diocese, but the Irish priests ran the bishop.

By February 1872, the bishop's health was failing and it was clear to all that he would soon die. In an uncanny and perhaps miraculous way, his mind suddenly became clear again, and he realized the duplicity of his advisors. He wrote to a friend, "I am dying with a broken heart.... Those whom I trusted contracted bad habits. At times I acted at their suggestions — I'm sorry. That is why I am so unhappy."

That month, the bishop attempted to rectify his regrets. On February 23, at Willunga, the bishop lifted the sentence on St. Mary, who by Providence happened to be in Willunga at the same time. A Fr. Hughes met her on the road that day and told her the news.

The bishop then moved to ensure that Fr. Horan would not be administrator of the diocese after his death. Instead the bishop wanted as his successor the Irishman Fr. Christopher Augustine Reynolds. When the bishop died on March 1, Fr. Reynolds immediately accepted back all of the sisters who had been expelled or dispensed over the previous six months. Sisters of St. Joseph prayed around Bishop Sheil's casket all night.

The sisters were prepared to forgive and forget, but Fr. Horan was not. He continued to attack the sisters, including from the pulpit. On March 24, he preached against their "ignorance and fanaticism" at two Masses and published his homily in the newspapers. Fr. Reynolds decided that enough was enough, and in his position as acting administrator of the dioceses suspended Fr. Horan.

St. Mary continued to think well of Bishop Sheil, referring to him as "our late and much loved bishop." She not only forgave the priests; she went out of her way to excuse what they had done, presenting it as just a big misunderstanding. "They were young and inexperienced in the ways of Australia, and one unreflecting word led to another."

As Mary proved ready to move on, word of the excommunication episode made it to Rome. In May 1872, Bishop Daniel Murphy of Hobart and Bishop Matthew Quinn of Bathurst were sent to Adelaide to investigate, and Bishop Quinn later praised Mary as "a very holy person." In June, the bishops sent Fr. Horan and two others back to Ireland and replaced Fr. Woods, who had demonstrated administrative ineptitude, with Fr. Joseph Tappeiner. Yet Mary was unassuming in her new prosperity. She wrote, prophetically, "It would not surprise me should God in His strangely mysterious ways permit

[Bishop Quinn] yet to be a cross to me like all those who have ever helped or assisted me in times before."

Fr. Woods wrote to Mary to suggest that she get papal approval of the order and its rule before there could be another repeat of the Bishop Sheil affair. Fr. Reynolds and Fr. Tappeiner agreed, with Fr. Tappeiner insisting that Fr. Woods not be the one to represent the order in Rome. The two priests instead sought to have Fr. Woods visit Adelaide to consult with Mary, but Fr. Woods revealed that the investigatory commission had forbidden him to return to Adelaide. Thus Mary set off for Rome all by herself, an exceedingly rare journey for a woman to embark on alone at that time.

Mary spent two and a half months at sea, falling desperately seasick onboard. She had no money, no plan for lodging in Rome, and no return ticket to get home to Australia.

In May of 1873, while Mary was in Rome, the Italian Parliament had taken over Catholic schools, hospitals, and churches. To avoid legal troubles with the Italian government, Mary traveled incognito under the name of Mrs. MacDonald. In her modest black garb, some mistook the thirty-one-year-old sister for a teenager and some for an elderly woman, which the saint found highly amusing. The ship's purser asked her how many children she had, and she gave the unforgettably strange but enthusiastic answer, "I have a great many."

After landing at Brindisi, she was not allowed through customs because she had no passport. A Protestant friend named Mr. Smythe, whom she had met on the ship, pulled a few strings at the American consulate, got her through, and bought her a ticket to Rome.

In Rome she stayed in a cheap hotel across from the Scots College where her father had once studied for the priesthood. She soon met Msgr. Tobias Kirby, the rector of the Irish College, who was in direct contact with Pope Pius IX. On June 1, 1873, just two weeks after she arrived in Rome, Msgr. Kirby introduced St. Mary to Pope Pius IX. When the monsignor told the pope of the excommunication, the pope put his hand on her head and gave her his blessing. St. Mary wrote to her mother, "What he said and how he said it when he knew I was the excommunicated one are things too sacred to be spoken of, but he let me see that the pope has a father's heart, and when he laid his hand upon my head, I felt more than I will attempt to say." She recorded in her diary, "A day never to be forgotten, a day worth years of suffering."

Mary fell seriously ill almost immediately after, and the Italian summer heat proved too much for her. On July 24, she met with the pope a second time, this time in a smaller group. Conversation was limited this time, however, because Msgr. Kirby was not there to translate.

She met with Fr. Bianchi, the procurator general of the Dominicans, who was assigned her case by the Congregation of Rites. Fr. Bianchi told her he had written a new rule from scratch, and that the new rule wasn't necessarily approved yet; but the sisters were to try it for a few years and then resubmit it for approval. Until then, it could not be amended, even by a bishop.

Surprisingly, Fr. Bianchi's rule allowed the order to remain self-governing, which was a relief to St. Mary. His most significant change to the rule was eliminating the vow of poverty, a vow which was so dear to St. Mary and her followers. Because of the political crises in Italy and throughout Europe at that time, the Vatican wanted orders to be self-funding, in order to prevent governments from confiscating Church property, as had just happened in Rome months before. A vow of poverty put religious orders too much at the mercy of secular governments offering — and then removing — financial support.

On July 27, Msgr. Kirby broke the news that the new bishop in Adelaide would be Fr. Reynolds, who had been so favorable to Mary as acting administrator of the diocese. It was a relief. Msgr. Kirby shared a letter from Cardinal Barnabo saying that there was no need for her to stay in Rome while the decision was pending.

On August 1, St. Mary set out alone again through Loreto, Belgium, and Germany, en route to London. Fr. Reynolds had wanted her to visit

European schools, and she found with pleasure that German schools had much in common with her own. But the trip had its difficulties. She had almost no money and was sick much of the time. After a fruitless attempt to fundraise and recruit in London, she joined a friend for a trip to her ancestral homeland of Scotland. She was the first religious sister to set foot in the West Highlands in three hundred years. There she met distant relatives and priests who had gone to seminary with her father. Her visit to Scotland was the most moving and consoling of her life. Yet, as a fundraising and recruiting trip it was an utter failure. St. Mary struggled to raise the funds to get back to Rome, never mind Australia, and debated asking her non-Catholic friends in London for help.

The Bishops Quinn

While in Scotland she received a letter from Bishop Matthew Quinn of Bathurst expressing his desire to make changes to the rule for sisters in his diocese. In particular, he wanted to ensure that the order would be subject to the local bishop — namely, himself. He made it clear that he would write to Rome to make his case. "I feel it my duty ... to carry out these views. I have very strong convictions on this matter, and most of the bishops to whom I have spoken are of this opinion."

Mary received word from Rome to remain in Europe until the order received official approval; and so, with no money, she moved around London as she'd moved around Adelaide, staying with friends, both Catholic and non-Catholic alike.

In December, Msgr. Kirby wrote to tell her that the constitution had been amended by the Vatican again without her knowledge. In March 1874, she returned to Rome, and on April 20, she was granted another audience with the pope. Cardinal Alessandro Franchi, prefect of the Propaganda, gave her the order's new rule, in Italian. She carried it with her, but she did not know how to read it.

Once someone finally translated it, Mary learned that the institute was still technically not approved but would resubmit its application after a few years' trial period. But in a significant victory — and a significant relief — central government was maintained, against the wishes of Bishop Quinn.

With the new constitution in hand, St. Mary left Rome, first for an unsuccessful fundraising trip to Lyons, then to Ireland, where she spent three months and recruited fifteen girls to join the order as well as two priests to come to Australia. While in Dublin, she met with Bishop Quinn of Bathurst, who informed her of his plan to remove the sisters from his diocese and start a separate order under his own control. Mary shrewdly agreed to remove the sisters from the diocese after one year to give him time to replace them, expecting that this order would ultimately never be carried out.

After she returned to Australia on Christmas Day 1874, St. Mary called a general chapter of the order, which by then comprised 196 sisters. In her letter to the sisters, she alluded to the troubles facing the order because of the local bishops and the lack of final approval, saying,

> The trial is deeply painful to all, but coming from Rome it comes from God. Let us humbly wait and pray; it will not always last, and when it has passed away we will find ... that it has been the means of drawing our hearts more completely to God.... Our Heavenly Spouse ... sends such trials to prove our love ... let us humbly thank Him alike for the trial and for the blessing, for the bitter and for the sweet.

Bishop James Quinn of Brisbane (brother of Bishop Matthew Quinn of Bathurst) sent a sister of St. Joseph to attend the general chapter, and reportedly scoffed at the idea of a woman running an order of some two hundred sisters and writing a rule. "The formation of such a [constitution] is hardly woman's work," he told St. Mary. Clearly, despite her trip to Rome, Mary still faced significant headwinds.

The sisters met on March 19, 1875, to iron out the details of the new rule. They voted against any compromise on the rule and almost unanimously elected Mary: hers was the lone vote in opposition.

Bishop James Quinn was furious at the rejection of his desire to put the sisters under the bishop's authority. He renounced all ties to the sisters in their headquarters of Adelaide (within the diocese of Bishop Reynolds), called Mary "a sentimental young lady," and took over the Josephite house in his diocese. Against his wishes, St. Mary sailed to Brisbane in April 1875, and had what she called "a painful interview" with the bishop. He threatened to have her arrested if she tried to enter the local Josephite house.

Mary later said, "Of course I did not mind his threats." Instead, she obeyed the bishop, and said she would withdraw the sisters from Brisbane. Just as with his brother Matthew Quinn, St. Mary gave James Quinn one year to prepare for their absence.

Bishop James Quinn was worried about how the news would be portrayed in the press. He asked Mary to write to the newspapers to make clear that this was her own decision and not his. She refused, saying that this was simply not true.

The bishop's instinct for self-preservation proved correct, however. Closing the Josephite schools triggered an outcry from the public, Catholic and non-Catholic alike. More than a thousand people signed a petition to the bishop to keep the sisters in the diocese, while he publicly blamed Mary.

In their place, Bishop James Quinn started the Black Josephites, his own version of the order. They wore black habits, in contrast to the Brown Josephites (affectionately known as "Brown Joeys" in Australia). Bishop James Quinn got Fr. Woods to write the rule for his new order, which included the requirement of poverty. A number of the sisters considered this a manipulative act, since the bishop knew of the sisters' loyalty to their cofounder and former father superior, who at the time was preaching missions in the Diocese of Brisbane.

The bishop called Mary "obstinate and ambitious" and said he would do everything in his power to ensure that she was removed as head of the order. Bishop James Quinn complained to Rome of "fanaticism and insubordination" in the order and said Mary's only goal was "to subvert the whole system here."

Yet Mary's strategy worked. Within two months, the bishop backed down and agreed to a compromise. The motherhouse in Adelaide, not the bishop, would appoint the head sister in Brisbane. He would let the sisters live under their rule until a final decision came from Rome.

St. Mary sent a Sr. Josephine to lead the house in Brisbane, and gave her a word of advice based on her experience: "Be guarded with the priests but make friends with them.... Do not yield anything even in opinion to [the bishop] concerning the things in dispute. But don't argue with him, coax him rather by telling him how much the sisters really do love him and now more than ever since he is going to work with [me] and not against [me]."

When the provincial in the Bathurst diocese died, Bishop Matthew Quinn refused to accept another. He also accused St. Mary of breaking her agreement with him in Dublin for visiting his diocese while he was absent. On Christmas Eve, the bishop disbanded the convent in Perthville, scattering the sisters among various smaller convents. When Mary arrived in Bathurst, he told her that he had already informed Rome of his decision and that it would not be revoked. With the unanimous support of her four main advisors in Adelaide, Mary decided to withdraw the sisters from the Bathurst diocese altogether.

Even as the assaults upon the Josephites by the Bishops Quinn continued, one sister said, "I have never heard her say an unkind word about the bishops." This wasn't just a sentiment. To Mary, it was central to the order. "If a Sister spoke unkindly of a priest," Mother Mary said on one occasion, "I would not consider her to have the true spirit of a Sister of St. Joseph."

The saint prophetically predicted, "I often think that rest will come to my dear Sisters when I am gone. Many prejudices are directed against myself, for bishops and priests think me some extraordinary and bold woman. Sometimes it wearies me that they think thus."

The disbanded sisters from Bathurst fled to Sydney, where the English Archbishop Roger Vaughn was a strong supporter. Yet even there, Mary met with difficulties from priests. The new bishop of Armidale, the Capuchin Elzear Torregiani, eagerly sought for more sisters to teach in his diocese, which inevitably required pulling sisters from South Australia. This of course caused offense in South Australia, and Mary had to endure a new round of criticism from her opponents. Further, this decision by Mary was taken as a perfect example of why the order should not be allowed to govern itself, since pulling sisters from South Australia upon the request of another bishop left the former jurisdiction short staffed. In one of the only bitter phrases to drop from her pen, St. Mary wrote, "I can scarcely keep my patience with some of them. They are so selfish."

Debt and Drink

In July 1883, Bishop Reynolds conducted another visitation of all the convents in the Adelaide diocese, with Archdeacon Russell as the top member of his commission.

Despite Bishop Reynolds's more positive relation with the sisters, the investigation seemed rigged from the start. Over five months, the commission consulted with only about half of the sisters, and they were overwhelmingly the younger and less experienced ones. Each sister was required to take an oath of secrecy, so Mary was kept completely in the dark about what was being said. The commission also spoke with a disgruntled former sister named Clare.

As the apostolic visitation began continued, questioning focused on two topics: debt and drink.

The order's finances were so poor that Mary was suspected of fraud. At one point, Archdeacon Russell tried to put her in a debtor's prison over an unpaid fifty-pound account with an Adelaide bootmaker.

The apostolic visitation also asked whether Mary drank in excess. In 1873, a Protestant named James McLaughlin — who was successfully sued for libel by the sisters on an unrelated matter — wrote to Rome accusing Mary of being a drunk. This letter — by a known liar — was admittedly based on hearsay. McLaughlin cited the high authority of his mother-in-law: "Mrs. O'Sullivan most solemnly assured me that she helped to carry in Sister Mary to her [convent] when she fell off a vehicle hopelessly drunk. She is ready to appear before God on the truthfulness of this statement that she had gone into the [convent] twice and Sister Mary and others of the sisterhood were so drunk that they neither knew what they did or said."

A Mrs. MacDonald told the commission that once she had seen Mary slip on the stairs. This was taken to be proof of drunkenness, but a Sr. Annette, who had been with St. Mary at the time, said that she hadn't had anything to drink when she slipped. Another three or four sisters are said to have told the commission that they had seen Mary drinking often and had seen her vomiting.

As previously mentioned, St. Mary was frequently ill and suffered from migraines as well as extreme menstrual pain. To treat the pain, her doctor prescribed her two spoonfuls of brandy. The saint had another sister administer the brandy to her and keep it behind a lock and key. It is no surprise that sisters saw her taking brandy and no surprise that they saw her vomiting.

On September 13, the bishop told Mary that the result of the apostolic visitation had been favorable and that everything was well in the convents. However, two months later, on November 14, Mary found out that just the opposite was the case. She received a letter from the bishop informing her that she was not just removed from the diocese but banished from it. The bishop falsely claimed that this was an order from Rome.

He scolded her bitterly. "Hoodwink the bishop — that is our motto. I am but too well aware of how you have violated religious poverty, how you have squandered (I will refrain from a stronger term) the means of the diocese.... I therefore notify your maternity to prepare at once to leave for Sydney as you no longer have the confidence of the sisterhood."

A friend in Rome pointed out to Mary that the bishop had no legal right to do such a thing. Mary therefore had to choose whether to press her case and fight or to suffer. She chose to accept the bishop's orders and suffer.

With Mary exiled, Bishop Reynolds soon asked each sister at a convent in Kensington to join a new order under his control. They all refused.

In Easter week, 1885, Bishop Reynolds visited the convents and insisted that he was "absolute superior" over the order. He told the sisters that they had one day to decide: either stay there under his control or leave. When the sisters said they would go to Sydney, Bishop Reynolds falsely claimed that Archbishop Moran wouldn't take them, despite Moran having told him precisely the opposite. Bishop Reynolds again falsely claimed to have Roman support for an illegal action. When a Sr. Mary de Sales asked to see documentation from Rome, the bishop refused: "My word is sufficient and they will get nothing else."

The constant attacks from bishops took a toll on St. Mary. She confided her anguish to another sister, writing, "I am so sorry for [Bishop Reynolds], but night or day I cannot forget his cruel writings to me.... Last night is the first time that I did not wake up dreaming of something or other that he wrote."

With a bishop claiming orders from Rome, it was inevitable that Rome would have to intervene. In October 1884, Pope Leo XIII dispensed the vow of silence on the sisters and Rome ordered Archbishop Moran (who would soon become Australia's first cardinal) to open his own investigation. Archbishop Moran's investigation quickly cleared Mary of any wrongdoing. But Bishop Reynolds was never punished. Instead, he later became an archbishop when his diocese became an archdiocese.

In October 1885, now-Cardinal Moran brought word from Rome that Mary was to be removed but not because of Bishop Reynolds: Mary had exceeded her term limit as superior (something she had raised to the other sisters as an objection to her re-election in 1881). With authorization from Rome, Cardinal Moran replaced the term-limited St. Mary as mother general with Sr. Bernard Walsh.

Mary had been vindicated, and her only loss was the position of superior, which she willingly accepted since she had concerns about violating the term limits. Yet the good news was tempered. Bishop Reynolds may not have been able to illicitly gain control over the Josephites, but an Australasian plenary council called by Cardinal Moran nonetheless voted 14 to 3 to oppose central government of the Josephites, leaving the order yet again in a governmental limbo, neither under the bishops nor ruling themselves. It was a tension that was soon to be resolved by the pope himself.

Papal Approval and Re-election

The bishops were quickly overruled. In July 1888, Cardinal Moran brought news from Rome that Pope Leo XIII had fully approved the rule of the order, including a central government. After fourteen years of struggle, the order finally had papal approval and could be troubled by meddling bishops no more.

Yet even then there was a disappointment for Mary. Rome ruled that Mother Bernard would remain in charge for ten more years. Rome would issue the same ruling in 1897. Mary knew that Sr. Bernard was well-liked by the bishops, and that she wasn't. She was disappointed, not because she wanted power, but because she was genuinely concerned about the dissatisfaction of the sisters with Sr. Bernard as their superior., since she was not elected by the sisters but imposed by Rome.

One sister even remarked to Archbishop Carr of Melbourne, "Mother Mary is our real Mother even though Mother Bernard may be our nominal one." The archbishop then wrote to Mary that this kind of factionalism could destroy the order if she didn't put a stop to it. In response, Mary always went out of her way to show her obedience and veneration of Mother Bernard.

Finally, in January 1899, after the death of Mother Bernard, Mary was unanimously re-elected mother general. In 1905, even while paralyzed on her right side from a stroke, Mary was re-elected again. She served until her death in 1909.

Just as Mary showed charity toward Mother Bernard, she continued to show charity toward the bishops who had opposed her. In 1892, after Mary had recovered from a long bout with bronchitis, she heard that Archbishop Reynolds, her old enemy, was dying. Her response was to have Masses said for him, pray for him, and offer Communion for him. Still, she tactfully kept her distance, even though she wanted reconciliation. "Sometimes I have thought of writing to him, but fear I might do more harm than good," she explained.

Cardinal Moran was present at Mary's deathbed, and eyewitnesses say he referred to her in that hour as a saint. He called her a saint again in his homily at her funeral. In her last hours, the saint was miraculously strengthened enough to receive Viaticum, which would have been impossible given her health just a day before. And in a particularly beautiful image conferred by Providence, a sister bringing flowers to her unknowingly spilled a trail of petals from the chapel to her deathbed.

These weren't the only signs of Mary's sanctity. When Mary died, an associate of hers named Fr. Lee was saying Mass. Those in attendance noticed that he paused for a long time at the consecration. According to a Sr. Annette, Fr. Lee said that this was because he saw Mary to the side of the altar, smiling. After Mass, in the sacristy, he announced that Mary was dead.

Her Glorification and Canonization

Mary's cause for canonization was opened sixteen years later, in 1925, but it would take another seventy years to come to fruition. In 1931, the cause was put on hold because Cardinal Moran's document on the drinking question had gone missing — a document that was only found in 1951.

It took until January 19, 1995, for Pope John Paul II to beatify Mary MacKillop. Fourteen years later, in 2009, Bishop Sheil's successor as archbishop of Adelaide, Archbishop Philip Wilson, publicly apologized to the Sisters of St. Joseph for St. Mary's wrongful and invalid excommunication.[186] One year after that, Pope Benedict XVI canonized her — the first Australian to be so honored.[187]

Mary was correct in her prediction: in her death, the persecution stopped. Today the Josephites are present in Australia, New Zealand, Ireland, Peru, East Timor, Scotland, and Brazil.[188] They continue to embrace poverty. They continue to self-govern. And they continue to promote the love of Christ in the hearts of little children.

CHAPTER 10

The Persecution of St. Padre Pio

DURING HIS EIGHTY-ONE YEARS as a pilgrim on earth, Padre Pio embraced a life of spiritual warfare. He spent the vast majority of his days in San Giovanni Rotondo, a small town nestled in the Foggian hills of southern Italy. Yet this humble priest, Capuchin friar, and stigmatic would one day become perhaps the most famous and beloved saint of the twentieth century. He did so without giving speeches, writing books, or owning anything of material value. Rather, he daily contended against the forces of darkness, quietly embracing the Christian paradoxes of happy suffering, joyful resignation, and loving pain. But despite serious health challenges such as recurring headaches and bouts of vomiting — as well as assaults by demonic forces — some of Padre Pio's most grievous wounds were inflicted by the very Church which he loved and served with the utmost obedience and affection. While priests, monsignors, bishops, cardinals, and even popes weighed heavily upon the humble Capuchin friar, Padre Pio was a model of the imitation of Christ.

A Victim for Christ

Born Francesco Forgione in the village of Pietrelcina in the province of Benevento, Italy, on May 25, 1887,[189] Padre Pio was raised in a poor and pious family. His parents ensured that all their children went to church frequently and prayed the Rosary together every day as a family[190] — a devotion Padre Pio kept with fervency throughout his whole life.[191]

Little Francesco was set apart from a young age: for as long as he could remember, he saw and communicated with his guardian angel.[192] When he was still a young priest, he was visited by Jesus, Mary, and angelic beings, and he conversed with them all as if they were members of his family sitting in his room. These meetings would strengthen him for his disturbing encounters with fallen angels. Demons would beat Padre Pio, strip him near-naked in the cold, and tempt him against purity. They would confront him in terrifying, fantastical forms, and sometimes take on the appearance of the padre's friends and associates in order to deceive him.[193]

The attacks were continual and brutal, but not necessarily unexpected. The Lord Himself had revealed Padre Pio's mission to him. In 1903, shortly before he donned the Capuchin habit and was ordained, Francesco had a vision. "A man majestic and of rare beauty was seen at his side, resplendent as the sun," Padre Pio wrote of the vision, describing himself in the third person. The man "took him by the hand and he heard him say, 'Come with me, because it is fitting for you to fight a valiant warrior.'" Padre Pio was then brought to a field where two opposing forces stood, one dressed in the purest white and the other hideous and dressed in black.

Padre Pio's luminous guide placed him in the space between the two forces. Then, a horrible dark figure — whose head reached as high as the clouds — appeared. As the figure approached, Padre Pio's guide told him that he would have to fight the tall figure. Padre Pio begged to be spared, but his guide was firm. "All of your resistance is vain. It is fitting for you to fight him. Take heart: Enter the fight with confidence, advance courageously for I will be close to you; I will help you and I will not allow him to knock you down. As a prize for the victory that you will bring back, I will give you a splendid crown to adorn your brow."

Padre Pio fought the creature and, with the help of his beauteous guide, won a victory. But it was not a final victory. His guide presented him a crown of indescribable beauty — then immediately took it back, promising Padre Pio an even more beautiful crown if he would withstand the attacks of this enemy who would continually assault him to try to regain his lost honor. The vision ended with the beautiful man promising Padre Pio that he would always overcome the enemy, and with the forces of darkness fleeing as the great host in white cheered the guide who had helped Padre Pio in the battle.[194]

Spiritual Desolation and Stigmata

Padre Pio was fifteen, still only a boy, when he had his life laid before him in this vision, a life of fierce struggle against darkness but also of certain victory. As prophesied, the years that followed were indeed filled with more direct confrontations with satanic forces. Eventually, the demonic manifestations became less frequent, but then Padre Pio faced other pernicious assaults from the enemy, coupled with a sense of spiritual desolation that left him uncertain if God was accepting his sacrifices.

His own words in his letters to spiritual directors convey the regular agony that Padre Pio endured. "In truth, I am full of sorrow and there is not one part of me that is not deeply distressed," he wrote.

> The sensitive part is in a bitter and terrible aridity; the powers of the soul are all empty of all their apprehensions, and this fills me with the greatest fear. The spirit lies in the black darkness and the body itself is not excluded from all these sufferings.... In certain instants, my Father, it is so

awful that the soul seems to see hell and eternal damnation open up beneath its feet.[195]

Again he wrote:

> I search for God, but where can I find him? Every idea of God as Lord, master, creator, love, and life has faded. He has completely flown, and I, alas! am lost in the thickest of thick darknesses, going over the scattered remembrances of a lost love again and again, and not able to love anymore. O my Good, where are you? I have lost you, I have become lost by looking for you, because you accepted the open offer I made you.[196]

Padre Pio's "open offer" was to become a victim soul for God, offering himself, like Christ, to endure pains, sorrows, and tribulations, not for his own benefit but for the redemption of others.[197] The clearest external sign that God accepted Padre Pio's offer came in the marks that would make Padre Pio famous and draw the critical attention of ecclesial authorities: the stigmata.

Under holy obedience, Padre Pio wrote to his spiritual director, Padre Benedetto, about what happened to him on Friday, September 20, 1918:

> After the celebration of the holy mass, I was overtaken by rest, similar to a sweet sleep. All of my internal and external senses as well as the faculties of my soul were found in an indescribable quiet. In all of this there was total silence around me and inside me; a great peace and abandonment to the complete privation of everything immediately took over ... This all happened in an instant. While all of this was going on I saw before me a mysterious person ... who had his hands and feet and his side dripping with blood. His sight terrifies me; I don't know how to tell you what I felt in that instant. I felt like I was dying, and I

> would have died had not the Lord intervened to sustain
> my heart, which I felt leap from my chest. The sight of the
> person withdrew, and I noticed that my hands, feet, and
> side were pierced and dripping with blood.[198]

The presence of the stigmata, despite being a mark of sanctity, actually added to Padre Pio's spiritual desolations. Not only did the wounds bleed regularly, requiring frequent cleaning and dressing, they also caused abiding pain. When he first received the stigmata, Padre Pio was left nearly immobile. He limbs bled and hurt so much that he could not get up.[199] While the agony was not always as intense as when he was first pierced, the pain still regularly intensified Thursday nights and Fridays.[200] Yet even this torment was preferable to the internal turmoil he felt. "I will loudly raise my voice to [Jesus] and will not stop begging him until, in his mercy, he withdraws from me not the torment or the pain," Padre Pio wrote, "but these external signs that are to me an indescribable and unbearable humiliation."[201]

Critics accused Padre Pio of creating or using the stigmata to gain fame or wealth. Yet from the start, the stigmata brought unwanted attention and a backlash that only compounded the saint's physical pain. First, it was fellow Capuchins who took lingering, curious looks. Then local women who came to Padre Pio for spiritual direction saw that his hands appeared to be burnt. When his superior, Padre Paolino, entered Padre Pio's room as he sat at his desk writing, he could clearly see his pierced hand holding steady the paper.[202]

A Decade of Persecution

As the First World War ended and word of Padre Pio's miraculous wounds spread, larger and larger crowds began to stream into San Giovanni Rotondo — and the news made its way to the Vatican. Letters signed by "a group of faithful at San Giovanni Rotondo" were sent to the Holy Office in Rome (now the Dicastery for the Doctrine of the Faith) claiming that, while Padre Pio was a good man, the crowds around him were erecting "a false and unacceptable cult" and there may exist "full paganism" where "idolatry is professed on a large scale."[203] At the same time, a local archpriest said that he was under great pressure to denounce the padre, pressure that seemed to have its source in Pasquale Gagliardi, the archbishop of Manfredonia (the diocese governing San Giovanni Rotondo).[204] Perhaps because he considered the friar a fraud who peddled fake miracles and false stigmata for fame — or perhaps because Padre Pio's notoriety drew parishioners and donations away from his diocese and toward Padre Pio — the archbishop became a vicious opponent of Padre Pio for years.

The letters and rumors had their intended effect. Pope Benedict XV sent his personal physician to examine the stigmata in March of 1920. Soon after, he sent a small team of additional examiners, and then some Vatican officials. All the reports that came back verified the authenticity of the stigmata, and Pope Benedict XV declared that Padre Pio was "an extraordinary man, the like of whom God sends to earth from time to time for the purpose of converting people."[205]

But not every visitor's reaction was equally laudatory. Padre Agostino Gemelli arrived at San Giovani Rotondo in April of 1920, having heard of Padre Pio's holiness. While some dispute whether Padre Gemelli even examined the stigmata, what is beyond dispute is the caustic report he sent to the Holy Office after he left. While acknowledging Padre Pio had an "elevated religious life," Padre Gemelli said he viewed Pio as a man of "very limited intelligence" who suffered from "a notable degree of mental deficiency" and was led to believe fantastical things about himself because of the malicious influence of his spiritual director, Padre Benedetto. Padre Gemelli's conclusion was stark: "I believe that Padre Pio is a psychopath ... [who should] be studied by a team of experts in medicine, psychology, and theology."[206]

At the same time Padre Gemelli was reporting to Rome, Bishop Salvatore Bella of the adjacent Diocese of Foggia received a sworn declaration from a local pharmacist that Padre Pio had secretly pro-cured carbolic acid—an antiseptic agent that, when used in large enough doses, can burn the skin.[207] Bishop Bella forwarded the re-port to the Holy Office, and the slew of negative information to-gether with the spread of increasingly widespread devotion to Padre Pio—not just in Italy, but around the world—sparked the first of many formal apostolic visitations to San Giovanni Rotondo.[208]

The apostolic visitor, Bishop Rafaello Rossi, arrived at San Giovanni Rotondo for an eight-day investigation in June 1921, and by all accounts his visit was positive.[209] Bishop Rossi described Padre Pio himself as "a serious religious" who was "serene, jovial, and even humorous."[210] After interviewing other friars, the bishop described Padre Pio's commitment to chastity as "angelic" and wrote that he is fully obedient to superiors.[211] Bishop Rossi then did a thorough review of the wounds on Padre Pio's hands, feet, and left side. At the end of his examination, the bishop declined to make a definitive judgment on the stigmata themselves, yet rejected outright the idea that the wounds were self-inflicted or the result of some diabolical intervention.[212]

The inquisitor did note, however, that Padre Pio was frequently surrounded by a sweet smell that some called "the aroma of paradise," that he reportedly faced bouts of extreme fevers reaching up to 118 degrees Fahrenheit, that he ate very little, and that he received reams of mail offering thanksgiving for graces received by virtue of his prayers. One of Bishop Rossi's primary concerns had little to do with Padre Pio, but instead concerned his spiritual director, Padre Benedetto, whom the inquisitor thought was too credulous when it came to anything supernatural that happened surrounding Padre Pio.[213]

Bishop Rossi returned to Rome with his report. But a few months later, Benedict XV died of pneumonia and Pope Pius XI suc-ceeded to the papal throne. With the accession of the new pope,

Archbishop Gagliardi, Padre Pio's recurring opponent, launched new waves of calumny against the friar, calling him "demon-possessed" and a "country Rasputin" who used nitric acid to create the stigmata and bottles of perfume to create a false miracle. In short order, the allegations extended to the whole community of friars at San Giovanni Rotondo, with Archbishop Gagliardi claiming that the Capuchins were "beating each other bloody with white weapons and fire,"[i] a fight he said was precipitated by an argument over the large sums of money donated to Padre Pio.[214]

Though Archbishop Gagliardi's defamation of Padre Pio became more and more outlandish, the continual reports and contradictory opinions compelled the Holy Office to investigate yet again. It conducted a comprehensive review of all the findings, accusations, and materials it had received so far to determine what should be done in light of the growing controversy.[215] Once more, Padre Pio was cleared of any direct wrongdoing, but his innocence did not exempt him from punishment.

The Holy Office remained worried about the often-fanatical crowds surrounding Padre Pio — crowds the Capuchin priest himself found overbearing and frustrating. (For example, some pious local women fought obsessively for front-row seats at his Masses and monitored the flow of people in and out of the confessional, sometimes even marking who had received absolution and who didn't.)[216]

Despite Padre Pio's innocence, the Holy Office held authority over the friar, not the crowds. Accordingly, it was Padre Pio who was made to suffer in an attempt to curb the actions of others. The punishments the Holy Office imposed on Padre Pio in 1922 were grave, categorical, and severely curtailed his public ministry: Padre Pio had to regularly change the time he celebrated Mass and not disclose the

---

[i] "White weapons" are weapons that don't involve fire or explosives, also called "cold weapons."

time to the public; he was barred from answering letters from the devotees who wrote to him; he was forbidden from showing or discussing his stigmata; he was encouraged to request a transfer to another friary; and he was to cut off all communications with his spiritual director and one of his closest friends, Padre Benedetto.[217] And this was only the start of what would become a decade of pain and suffering.

According to Padre Pio's confessor, Padre Agostino, the friar submitted "with holy resignation," even though the severe restrictions on his ministry made him pray for death.[218] As the months of effective confinement wore on, Padre Pio never lost his zeal for obedience. At the mere suggestion that he had disobeyed orders to leave San Giovanni Rotondo (he had not been ordered, merely encouraged), Padre Pio dropped to one knee, vowing, "I have never received such an order. If my superiors ordered me to jump out of the window, I would not argue, I would jump!"[219]

When close associates denounced the churchmen who were the authors of Padre Pio's plight, only then did the padre exhibit holy anger: "We must respect the decrees of the Church. We must be silent and suffer." And to another he said, "All in the church, only in the church, woe to those who put themselves against the Mother.... We must kneel before the Church.... Sweet is the hand of the church, even when it strikes you."[220]

In May of 1923, the Holy Office reiterated that Padre Pio was not allowed to answer letters and only allowed to celebrate Mass in private.[221] A few months later, in August of 1923, the Vatican formally decided to transfer Padre Pio, and a Padre Luigi was sent to convey to Padre Pio that he must "receive his obedience." When Padre Luigi arrived near midnight one evening, he read Padre Pio the order. Padre Pio's response, according to Padre Luigi, was swift: "I am yours to command. Let us depart at once. When I am with my superior, I am with God." Yet Padre Luigi was not there to take Padre Pio away that instant, only to inform him that a decision was reached. Padre Pio's response left Padre Luigi incredulous. He asked Padre Pio where they would go in the middle of the night. "I don't know," Padre Luigi recorded Padre Pio responding, "I go with you when and where you want."[222]

Ultimately, the townspeople got wind of the transfer and threatened violence and chaos if their padre was ordered to leave.[223] The threats and the obvious fanaticism of the townspeople caused the plan to be tabled, only to be picked up again the next year by the Holy Office and the Capuchin minister general. Yet when local authorities refused to offer their support to suppress any violence, the intended transfer was again delayed. Meanwhile, the restrictions on Padre Pio were tightened. Two years after the original order from the Holy Office, another directive was put into effect forbidding Padre Pio from speaking to laypeople after Mass and barring visitors from gathering in areas that Padre Pio would pass through or frequent.[224]

Even these restrictions were insufficient for Padre Pio's opponents. In 1926, Archbishop Gagliardi and others within the diocese began to slander the padre anew, telling the Holy Office and the Capuchin superiors that he was refusing orders to be transferred, was working with locals to spread calumny and insults against them, and was continuing to see women outside of the confessional.[225] When the Capuchin provincial, Padre Bernardo, informed Padre Pio of the accusations, Pio denied them vehemently.[226] Even so, Padre Bernardo imposed even more restrictions, ordering Padre Pio to refrain from showing himself to visitors at all. If he ran into someone, he was simply to nod his head and not say a word. The provincial also threatened that if overzealous women failed to keep their distance while Padre Pio was hearing others' confessions, then the padre could be banned from hearing confessions altogether.[227]

As it turned out, the threat was carried out not by the provincial but by the pope himself. In 1931 — nine years after the initial restrictions were first imposed on Padre Pio — the pope, the Holy Office, Capuchin superiors, and local clergy were still concerned about the large number of souls that remained devoted to Padre Pio. By that time, Archbishop Gagliardi had been deposed for "mismanagement" of the diocese. (The pope had received a petition from local clergy decrying "disorder, immorality, and clerical degeneracy" in the archdiocese, and after more abuses were publicized, an apostolic visitation took place revealing "outrages against morality.") Yet Gagliardi's removal did not improve Padre Pio's situation, as the next archbishop, Alessandro Macchi, also believed the padre to be either deluded or a fraud.[228]

With Padre Pio's enemies unable to remove him from San Giovanni Rotondo, Pope Pius XI imposed still more sanctions on the troubled friar. Padre Pio was banned completely from hearing confessions and stripped of all the privileges of a priest, except the ability to say Mass, which he was restricted to doing only in private in the inner chapel of the friary.[229] With his public priestly ministry halted, Padre Pio was subjected to two years of what he called his "imprisonment." Yet, just as when the first sanctions were imposed, he endured with a sense of holy resignation. "God's will be done," was all he said when he was informed of the restrictions.[230]

Immediately, Padre Pio's supporters decried the decision and attempted to get it reversed. Petitions were sent to the pope.[231] Padre Pio's spiritual children prayed fervently. And one of his friends even attempted to fight fire with fire: Emmanuele Brunatto, a longtime associate of Padre Pio, proposed publishing a book detailing financial and homosexual scandals in the highest ranks of the Church as a way to blackmail the hierarchy into removing the restrictions on Padre Pio. The saint rejected the plan swiftly and categorically. "I absolutely cannot allow you to defend me or try to free me by throwing mud, and such mud in the face of people that I, you, and everyone have a sacred duty to respect," he wrote on March 15, 1933. Again a few weeks later he added, "I forbid you in any way to involve my name in any publication of that kind, which should make you blush for shame and tremble with fear."[232]

Whether caused by Brunatto's threat, Padre Pio's long-suffering obedience, Pope Pius XI experiencing a change of heart (or being informed of the truth), or the appointment of a new archbishop, Andrea Cesarano, to the Archdiocese of Manfredonia, the Vatican eventually reversed course. Only July 12, 1933, the Holy Office once again allowed Padre Pio to celebrate public Mass and to hear the confession of clergy. Eight months later, Padre Pio was granted permission to hear the confessions of men, and in another two months, women.[233] Over a decade of trial had finally ended.

But Padre Pio's long *Via Crucis* was not quite over. Thirty years later, in the 1960s, another wave of persecution fell upon the then-aging priest.

Treated Like a Prisoner

After decades of ministry and countless hours in the confessional sanctifying the lives of his spiritual children, Padre Pio endured yet another abusive attack at the hands of Holy Mother Church during the final years of his life. As before, this new round of trouble was sparked by the alleged bad behavior of the pious followers of the friar.

It began in the spring of 1960, when a priest at San Giovanni Rotondo, Padre Giustino Gaballo, began secretly recording Padre Pio's conversations, particularly those with women. Padre Giustino feared that Padre Pio was covertly fornicating, and even believed that he had caught Padre Pio on tape receiving a kiss from one of the women. Padre Giustino was so convinced of Padre Pio's sin that he and another friar are reported to have attempted to perform an exorcism on Padre Pio in his room while he slept.[234]

Though the recordings of Padre Pio were said to be unintelligible, they were nonetheless taken to Rome, and more recording devices were placed in Padre Pio's cell and in a guest room where he spent time with others. By the summer of 1960, Pope John XXIII was informed of the allegations against Padre Pio and the recordings, and he wrote in his journal that "the discovery by means of tapes, if what they imply is true, of his intimate and improper relations with the women who make up the impenetrable praetorian guard around his person, point to a terrible calamity of souls, a calamity diabolically capable of discrediting the Holy Church in the world, and here in Italy especially."[235]

Padre Pio never blamed John XXIII for the persecution that followed, saying that "he judges on the basis of what they tell him."[236] But whatever the pope believed personally, the Holy Office took these and other allegations seriously enough to call for another apostolic visit by Msgr. Carlo Maccari. It began in July 1960, and stretched Padre Pio almost beyond what he could bear.[237]

When Msgr. Maccari arrived, he immediately took in the environment at San Giovanni Rotondo, noting the crowds that gathered for Mass, the religious images of Padre Pio being sold, the chaotic scenes of people crowding around the confessional, and the disreputable actions of the pious women to secure their privileged spots near Padre Pio by physically removing those who took "their" spots.[238] Maccari also heard allegations that Padre Pio was regularly having sex with one of the pious women, Cleonice Morcaldi, multiple times a week. However, as Maccari dug deeper, those surrounding Padre Pio vehemently attested to his lifelong chastity.[239]

Maccari then allegedly confronted Padre Pio multiple times, questioning his relationships and communications with the pious women and urging him to confess his errors. After one of these painful confrontations, Padre Pio exclaimed that he was "watched constantly, like somebody who has committed who knows how many crimes." The burden of these accusations weighed upon Padre Pio so heavily that he was reportedly unable to sleep or eat.[240]

When he finished his investigation, Maccari concluded the worst. After Pope John XXIII met with Maccari upon his return to Rome, Maccari's lurid allegations led the pope to conclude that "Padre Pio is revealed as an idol of straw. Spare us, Lord. Spare your people." The Maccari report also sparked yet another Holy Office investigation, this time by Paul-Pierre Philippe in early 1961, who derided Padre Pio as "a wretched priest who profits from his reputation to deceive his victims."[241] Despite the padre's years of fruitful toil in the Lord's vineyard and the legions of faithful who defended his holiness, the Vatican yet again turned against him, imposing renewed restrictions just as punitive as the first.

Padre Pio was once again required to celebrate Mass at varied times and was banned from seeing women outside of the confessional. A railing was built outside his confessional to limit crowds, and priests and bishops were barred from serving at his Masses. Numerous friars who were friends of Padre Pio were removed from the convent and transferred to different locations.[242] Fr. Gabriele Amorth, a friend of Padre Pio, expressed the outrage common among the faithful at the time, writing that the restrictions "could not have been more odious and inappropriate."

"Just think of the iron railing, which is still there today, around Padre Pio's confessional," he wrote. "For some accustomed to those places, it seemed like nothing less than a prison. And then bishops and priests were prohibited from serving at Padre Pio's Mass; I believe never in the history of the Church has there existed such a prohibition." Additionally, the Holy Office went so far as to mandate that Padre Pio limit the length of his Masses — which could sometimes last for up to four hours as the friar became enraptured in prayer — to only thirty or forty minutes.[243]

Just as during Padre Pio's previous trial, Emmanuele Brunatto jumped to the padre's defense: he again threatened to publicize scandalous materials if the Vatican did not relieve its restrictions. But again, Padre Pio urged Brunatto to stay quiet, writing to him, "You can't love the son by mortifying the mother."[244] This time Brunatto was more receptive Padre Pio's wishes and desisted immediately upon his request.[245]

Fr. Amorth likewise wrote that Padre Pio rejected any criticism whatsoever of the Holy See in these matters. "To those who told him they had imprisoned and spied on him, he answered that he felt as free as could be," Amorth wrote. "To those who complained that with these measures they had put him behind iron bars, he answered that everything had been done to protect him. Woe to anyone who in his presence dared to advance criticism against the ecclesiastical authorities and against the provisions of the visitor."[246]

It was not until the election of Pope Paul VI in 1963 that the restrictions were finally lifted and Padre Pio was able to freely interact with the laypeople who came to see him. Paul VI believed the restrictions were unjust and that Padre Pio was being imprisoned "like a criminal."[247] Yet even before the election of Paul VI, the accusations against Padre Pio were crumbling. Near the end of his life, John XXIII admitted his mistake, saying repeatedly, "On Padre Pio, they deceived me!"[248]

But despite these personal admissions, the Vatican apparatus nonetheless sought to save face — after all, it had punished one of the most popular and venerated priests in the world on the basis of false accusations. In order to portray the Maccari investigation as a success, leaders within the Vatican reportedly worked to appoint Msgr. Maccari a bishop.[249]

The Sweetness of the Cross

Chronicling the decades of persecution endured by Padre Pio at the hands of the hierarchy and detailing the saint's many other physical and spiritual sufferings risks portraying him as a man of sorrows. Yet Padre Pio was no sour-faced saint. He embraced the Cross with love, and his life was suffused with consolations, graces, miracles, and the joy of serving God.

Nothing revealed this more than his celebration of the Mass. Padre Pio's Masses would last for hours, and much of the time he struggled to hide his own agony. It seemed, according to those present, that Padre Pio relived Jesus' Passion each time he celebrated the Mass, sometimes jerking as if he were suffering blows to the head, while other times tears would stream down his cheeks. Yet those who attended noticed a remarkable change after he had received Christ's Body and Blood. A fellow friar said that after receiving Communion, Padre Pio's face was "transformed and became truly radiant." Adoring the host and the chalice, his former agony was forgotten, and he would at times slumber "like a baby on his mother's breast," in one onlooker's description. Those in attendance often remarked that Padre Pio's lengthy Masses felt like they lasted only minutes.[250]

Padre Pio was also frequently taken up into ecstasies. The world around him would fade away and he would experience immense peace and even visions of heavenly things.[251] His connection to the divine was often obscured by dark nights of the soul. Yet God repeatedly assured him of His love and comforted him. Indeed, Padre Pio was the conduit of numerous recorded and verified miracles, from bilocations to readings of the heart in the confessional. He had the joy of knowing that his work had snatched souls from the jaws of the devil.

Amidst these extraordinary supernatural phenomena, the waves of restrictions from the upper echelons of the Vatican, and the heavy burden of divinely imposed stigmata, Padre Pio was nonetheless a man who also drew enjoyment from the hours of routine human affairs that occupy the vast majority of mankind's time. A fellow friar remarked in reference to Padre Pio that "as for his life, I do not have anything to remark. I do not see anything extraordinary, no apparent signs of an extraordinary life. It's a simple life, common, ordinary."[252]

In that ordinariness, Padre Pio was often found smiling and even playing practical jokes on his companions. Neither the workings of ecclesial politics nor the machinations of demonic forces could curb Padre Pio's joy of life. But it would be wrong to presume that he was happy because his consolations outweighed his crosses, as if happiness was determined by an abundance of pleasure that eclipses the pain. Through Christ's mysterious work, the Cross itself became a source of life and strength for Padre Pio.

"All have their cross," Padre Pio wrote. "All ask that it be taken away. But if they knew how precious it is, they would be asking that it be given to them."[253] Why precious? First, because through carrying the cross, Padre Pio helped relieve the sufferings of Christ, whom he loved and still loves profoundly. Second, and often forgotten, is that each cross is specifically tailored by God to the particular person chosen to carry it. The yoke of God is not only easy, but it is well-fitting, carved with precision by a great carpenter to the contours of our souls, crafted to humble us where we are proud and strengthen us where we are weak. The cross — especially the unchosen cross — is the regimen that God imposes on our souls to help us get to Heaven.

Like any good Christian, Padre Pio struggled in the conflict between his desire to serve God and the natural aversion to suffering. As he wrote to a spiritual father, "I have a very great desire to suffer for the love of Jesus. How is it, then, that when it comes to the test, against my every wish, I search for some relief. I must use much strength and violence against myself in these trials in order to silence nature which, so to speak, cries loudly to be consoled." Despite this natural, human aversion to pain, Padre Pio nonetheless found joy in it, demonstrating in his life the mystery of the Cross that can never be fully grasped by the intellect alone. As Padre Pio once wrote, "All that happens in you is the result of love, of God's great love for you; it is a most loving trial that God gives to his elect; it is a vocation to co-redeem, and is therefore a source of glory."[254]

Padre Pio bore happily the great weight of physical pain and continual persecution throughout his life, and he felt no bitterness toward the Church. He kissed the hands of his abusive mother and refused ever to condemn his abusive ecclesial fathers, because he saw with spiritual eyes the work of God in the injustice he endured. He did not always understand God's work; he sometimes struggled to accept it. But his trust in God's infinite mercy made the sorrowful burden light, made the suffering sweet, and lifted a poor stigmatic friar to the greatest heights of sanctity.

CHAPTER 11

The Persecution of
Ven. Fulton Sheen

VEN. ARCHBISHOP FULTON SHEEN lived a long life of holiness. But the second to last decade of his life was defined by a great and hidden trial. America's most famous bishop, a beloved preacher, and a gifted fundraiser for the poor had been cast down from the glittering heights of New York City and removed to the provincial diocese of Roches- ter — a place where his talents were so ill-suited that he would resign his position in abject failure in just three years.

The cross that catalyzed this fall was fashioned from a long-running dispute between America's most famous bishop and his su- perior Francis Spellman, America's most powerful cardinal. In Archbishop Sheen's words, it was a dispute between "two men of God, both with a vivid sense of the world's need of the Christian gospel ... [a dispute that was] unworthy of the One Who forgave the crucifiers."[255] In his lifetime, Sheen continually chose to keep silence about his dispute with Cardinal Spellman. Yet in learning his story, we can see that his silence speaks volumes.

The Most Recognizable Man in the American Church

Fulton Sheen was born in 1895 in El Paso, Illinois, the eldest son in a devout Catholic family.[256] Priests visited his home frequently; he was an altar boy at the cathedral; and every evening his family prayed the Rosary together, a habit common to many saints. By all accounts, Sheen had a family life infused with faith, and he admitted that from his earliest memories he wanted to be a priest. In 1919, he was ordained at the age of twenty-four. Soon afterward he embarked on years of study at the most intensive levels, learning philosophy at the Catholic University in Washington, D.C., and earning a doctorate at the University of Louvain in Belgium with the honor of "very highest distinction."

Sheen was young, ambitious, learned, and those around him knew that he had a bright future ahead of him. Yet his first assignment was to be an assistant at a parish in a neighborhood so poor that the streets were unpaved. While some members of the community inveighed in the papers against the bishop that sending a man of such learning to such a parish was a "waste," Sheen acknowledged that "it was my first test, as a young priest, in obedience." He wrote that he was "resigned to being a curate" despite his desire for a more intellectual vocation, because he understood that "the will of God was expressed through the Bishop as a successor of the Apostles."

This first test was brief. His bishop had already planned to send Fr. Sheen to become a faculty member at Catholic University. But Sheen was right: his year at the poor parish in his home diocese was a test in obedience, and his bishop was pleased that Sheen served without complaint.

At Catholic University Fr. Sheen quickly rose in prominence, revealing the prodigious talents that would catapult him to the greatest heights of the episcopacy, namely, his powers of preaching and public persuasion. He was soon receiving numerous requests for speaking engagements and radio appearances. He was asked to deliver sermons in St. Patrick's Cathedral in New York, and by the early 1930s, he was giving a regular radio talk on the program *Catholic Hour*.

Almost immediately, his radio addresses began bearing great fruit. Horace Mann — a campaign manager for Herbert Hoover's largely anti-Catholic presidential campaign in 1928 — was converted to the Church after listening to Fr. Sheen on the radio and talking with him about the authority of the Church. Sheen himself later estimated that his show helped spark the conversions of some fifty souls a week.

However, Sheen never took credit for any conversion attributed to him. In fact, he once told a young priest who spoke glowingly of the seventy-two converts he claimed to have made within six years, "I would advise you to stop counting them, otherwise you might think you made them and not God." Likewise, when Pope Pius XII asked Sheen how many converts he had made in his life, Sheen followed his own advice: "Your Holiness," Sheen answered, "I have never counted them. I am always afraid if I did count them, I might think I made them, instead of the Lord."

Within a few years, the *Catholic Hour* broadcast had expanded to 196 radio stations. Sheen was receiving anywhere from three to six thousand letters a day, he was regularly instructing dozens of converts, and he was traveling around the world to give lectures and sermons. He had been named a monsignor, and many even considered him a fitting successor to lead what was then and perhaps remains America's most important diocese, New York. All the while, Sheen gave away large sums of money from his speaking fees, book royalties, and gifts sent to him from adoring listeners to help fund building projects, like churches and hospitals for the poor.

While the *Catholic Hour* broadcasts ended in 1952, Sheen was already moving on to a growing new medium: television. In early 1952, Sheen filmed the first episode of his soon-to-be famous *Life Is Worth Living* program, a show that would run for the next thirteen years.[257] In each episode, he would appear in full episcopal regalia and speak without notes (although after hours of preparation) to an audience that quickly ballooned to two million a week watching on seventeen stations.

The show was simple: a Catholic bishop speaking in front of a chalkboard. But the American people loved it. The same year *Life is Worth Living* launched, Sheen was featured on the cover of *Time* magazine.[258] He was named the "Man of the Year" on television in a poll by *Radio and Television Daily*. During his first year on the screen, he won an Emmy for "Most Outstanding Television Personality." (True to Sheen's style, the next day a family member noticed that the Emmy had been left haphazardly on a radiator in Sheen's home.)

Sheen purposefully designed his shows to be ecumenical, drawing people from common presumptions about morality into more defined Christian philosophy. Ultimately, he trusted the Holy Spirit to accomplish a conversion. He merely provided an opening. As he wrote of his broadcasts, "Never once was there an attempt at what might be called proselytizing. It was for the audience to decide that I stood for something which they needed as a complement in their lives. The illumination that fell on any soul was more of the Spirit and less of Sheen."

Despite his growing fame, Sheen constantly strove to achieve Christian virtue and closeness to Christ. Over the course of his life, he made dozens of pilgrimages to Lourdes, and every day of his priesthood he kept a continuous holy hour before the Blessed Sacrament. In fact, he frequently prepared his sermons before the Eucharist in the tabernacle and preached a daily holy hour of companionship with the Lord to all who would listen.

Fulfilling his personal holy hour promise often came at a great cost. At times he would have to wake up at exceedingly early hours in the morning before long days of travel and work. He sometimes faced long droughts where prayer seemed, in his words, "unprofitable and lacking in spiritual intimacy." Yet even in those moments he could still find some consolation in being "at least like a dog at the master's door, ready in case he called me."

Gathering the Sheep

Sheen's interior desire for closeness to Jesus manifested itself in many exterior acts, most prominently his lifelong mission to bring others into relationship with Christ, and the countless hours he spent instructing catechumens in the Faith. The list of converts Sheen helped shepherd into the Church included many luminaries — and many surprises.

There was Fritz Kreisler, the world-renowned violinist and composer whom Sheen had met by Providence. Sheen was making a call to a grieving widower, but when he rang the doorbell to the apartment, nobody answered. When he asked the elevator attendant who lived next door and learned it was Fritz Kreisler, he called on the famed musician instead. At their first meeting, Sheen boldly asked if Kreisler and his wife would like to take instruction in the Faith. Not only did the couple do so, they became lifelong friends with Sheen.

Sheen was also instrumental in the conversion of Congresswoman Clare Boothe Luce, a woman known for her high-flown lifestyle and loose sexual morals.[259] After Luce's one and only child, a daughter named Ann, died in a car accident, Sheen called Luce to invite her to dinner. Near the end of the meal, Sheen told her, "Give me five minutes to talk to you about God, and then I will give you an hour to state your own views." Luce agreed. After a few minutes Sheen mentioned God's goodness. "If God is good," Sheen remembers Luce responding with anger, "why did he take my daughter?" Sheen responded: "In order that through that sorrow, you might be here now starting instructions to know Christ and His Church." It was a bold statement, brimming with the real-world certainty that God truly is greater — and that knowing His love is more satisfying — than anything else on earth. Luce received instruction for the next five months, and her conversion shocked the nation.

In another surprising coup for the army of Christ, Sheen also played an essential role in the conversion of a man named Louis Budenz, a prominent and outspoken communist and the editor of the Communist Party's *Daily Worker* in New York City. Budenz initiated contact with Sheen — a stridently outspoken anti-communist — under the direction of the Central Committee on Communism, which hoped to convince Sheen to join the Reds. As their conversation began, Sheen told Budenz he wasn't interested in talking about communism — he was interested in his soul. That statement stuck with Budenz who, six or seven years later, reached out to Msgr. Sheen again in order to receive instructions to enter the Church. The Holy Spirit had clearly been at work. Budenz's instruction happened in such secrecy that when the Associated Press reported the imminent conversion not only of Budenz but of his entire family, Budenz's atheist soon-to-be-former comrades at his communist paper had no idea; he was still listed as the editor of the *Daily Worker*.

But most of Sheen's converts, by far, were ordinary people. He held classes annually in New York City and Washington, D.C., with fifty to a hundred catechumens. Whether for groups or individually, Sheen would typically spend twenty to twenty-five hours on instructions from start to finish. The prominent names of converts made the papers, but Sheen helped a host of unnamed souls who were searching for God, from prostitutes to mothers, from nurses to lepers, from soldiers to bank robbers, from mechanics to musicians.

Sheen was as generous with his money as he was with his time. Historian Thomas Reeves covered the bishop's generous spirit in his detailed (if often critical) biography of Sheen entitled *America's Bishop*. For example, as Reeves relays, after receiving nearly $70,000 in an inheritance from a wealthy benefactor (over $1.4 million in today's dollars), Sheen immediately donated it, mostly to help erect a maternity hospital to serve black women in segregated Alabama. One winter he literally gave the coat off his back to a poor priest on the train. Later in life, as the bishop of Rochester he was touring a downtrodden neighborhood when a woman approached him saying, "You ought to see where I live." Seeing the poverty of this woman and her family, Sheen purchased a house for them using his own funds. On another occasion he was given a clock and urged not to give it away. Years later, when the person who originally gave him the clock admired it — forgetting that she was the one who bought it — Sheen re-gifted it back to her.

Imperfections

Sheen was a generous man and had a zeal for souls, but he was no plaster saint. He had imperfections, many of which he openly admitted. For example, he had a refined taste and an aversion to self-denial, going so far as to bring his personal chef with him from New York to Rochester when he was transferred. While a professor at Catholic University, his sizeable earning from the speaking circuit and his book royalties allowed him to purchase a lot in a wealthy Washington neighborhood and build a home custom-designed by the head of the Catholic University School of Architecture. He acknowledged that "no great mortifications ever stand out in my life" and that while he always kept the standard fasting and abstinences prescribed by the Church, "there was not a taking on of the burdens and sins of the world as a priest is supposed to do as a co-victim with Christ." Unlike saints who endured great deprivations and mortifications, Sheen admitted that "only two or three times in my life, at the most, did I ever take on extra and rather extreme penances in order to save a soul," such as a week of fasting or embracing the trial of a torturous journey as payment to convert an atheist.

This fear of having failed to fully imitate our crucified and humble Christ loomed in Archbishop Sheen's mind at the end of his life. "In my own heart I knew that I received fewer blows than I deserved," he wrote in his autobiography. Even more dangerous were all the ways Sheen acknowledged by which pride had seeped in. "When I was a priest, I thrilled at being called 'Father,'" he wrote,

> I found the title "Monsignor" mellifluous, but was I a victim? I enjoyed the prestige of being a university professor, and of appearing on radio and television not only at home, but abroad; I was popular, I was sought after, I was loudly applauded after lectures and banquet talks, I was friend of both royalty and the masses, my features became so recognizable that I would be identified by a passerby in a revolving door.... But how close was I to the Cross? I was the priest; was I the victim?

Sheen passed judgment on himself, answering "no" — or at least "not fully." He wrote, "I should have resembled more closely Christ, Who had nowhere to lay His head. I should have fled from some applauding mobs as the Lord fled from the enthusiasms at Capharnaum after the multiplication of bread; maybe I was like Peter, who at one point 'followed the Lord far off.'"

Even acknowledging his faults, Sheen was undoubtedly a virtuous and pious man. He may not have lived a life of physical mortification. He may have delighted in little luxuries and the adoring attention of the masses. But men do not give away large sums of what they earn in this life without having hope in the next; and no man spends an hour every single day before the Blessed Sacrament without loving the Word-made-Flesh.

Sheen and Spellman

As Sheen's star rose, he had a powerful patron in the man who would later become his nemesis, Cardinal Francis Spellman of New York. At the height of his radio fame in the early 1950s, then-Msgr. Sheen was both consecrated a bishop and named the national director for the Society for the Propagation of the Faith (SPF), an organization devoted

to the Church's international missionary activities. The former especially was granted to Sheen, as he acknowledged, "through the good
graces of Cardinal Spellman."

Sheen was clearly one of Spellman's personal favorites. In 1948,
they and a number of other priests took a roughly three-month world
tour and praised each other effusively in public. Sheen noted in his
autobiography that tremendous numbers of people on their tour
came out not to see him but Cardinal Spellman, a very charitable
interpretation of events. Meanwhile, to a crowd in Sydney, Cardinal
Spellman described Sheen as someone "who in America is doing
more than any archbishop or any bishop to make the Faith known
and loved.... I brought him on this trip to give him some recognition
and to pay a debt. But I find that I have only increased the debt — if
there be such a thing." Perhaps the cardinal counted the debt increased because everywhere Sheen spoke he brought crowds of tens
of thousands of people.

It didn't seem to bother the cardinal that Sheen was apparently
more sought after than was his superior. Sheen wrote in his diary on
the trip, "There is absolutely no jealousy in that man."

The relationship clearly benefited Sheen as well, who confessed
that from his early priesthood he had prayed to become a
bishop — something Spellman, with his influence in Rome, had the
power to make happen. Yet when it finally came, he admitted he felt a
"sense of false euphoria" at the trappings of the office: the place at table,
the reverence people bestowed on him, the ring and zucchetto he
wore. But the euphoria did not last. "In a very short time," he wrote, "I
discovered that I was no different than before ... that the esteem people paid me was not necessarily the way the Lord looked on me."

Still, Sheen's positions as auxiliary bishop of New York and national director for the SPF gave him significant influence within the
Church and an even higher perch from which to preach the gospel to
the ends of the earth. At the SPF, Sheen represented the United

States in Rome in the congregation that oversaw worldwide evangelization. During those postwar years, the United States supplied approximately two-thirds of the funds for the entire organization, and Sheen himself donated his own earnings (including his $26,000 per show fee for *Life is Worth Living*, an inflation-adjusted sum of nearly $300,000 today) to the SPF. As a result, Sheen was clearly marked as the first among equals of the different national representatives for the Church's worldwide evangelization efforts.

Coupled with his international fame from radio and TV, Sheen had far more power than an ordinary auxiliary bishop. And it showed. He had multiple private audiences with several popes. He was chosen to participate in Vatican II. He was appointed to the Commission on the Missions by Pope John XXIII. He helped distribute the often-vast funds donated to the SPF. He was beloved by the people, held in high esteem within the Church, and preached with a reach that the first apostles could only have dreamed of.

But then, a series of personal disputes with Cardinal Spellman made it all come crashing down.

Milk Money

While Sheen declined to discuss his long-running dispute with Cardinal Spellman in his autobiography, historian Thomas Reeves had no qualms about doing so. By his account, tensions began to rise within a few years after Sheen's elevation to the episcopacy and to his leading role within the SPF.

Their first major quarrel was in 1955. Spellman wanted Sheen to use funds from the SPF for an aid program in Europe (which was still recovering from the Second World War) that distributed surplus food from the federal government through Catholic Relief Services. Sheen refused, and the general council of the SPF supported Sheen's decision, writing that "this refusal is motivated solely by the intention to use the limited financial resources at hand to the greatest possible advantage in the spreading of Christ's kingdom on earth." Spellman was furious, later writing that "the matter of the surplus foods is the first direct act of non-compliance with a suggestion that I have made, and incidentally it's the first act during the 17 years I have been privileged to be the Archbishop. Someday, perhaps I shall congratulate him on this distinction."

Tensions rose to a boiling point two years later in 1957, in a now infamous dispute over powdered milk. For some time the federal government had been donating surplus powdered milk to Cardinal Spellman, who would then donate it to the SPF to distribute to the poor. Despite the fact that the milk was donated free of charge, Spellman demanded that Sheen pay him millions of dollars of society funds for the milk, which Spellman claimed to have purchased. When Sheen again refused his cardinal's request, Spellman exploded with anger, this time appealing to Rome. In the meantime, Spellman reportedly launched an investigation into Sheen in an apparent attempt to find information that could be used as blackmail while simultaneously offering Sheen a position at a wealthy parish if he would resign from the SPF. The investigation came up empty, and Sheen refused the new assignment.

With the conflict between these two bishops still unresolved, the Holy Father felt obligated to get involved. When the two American bishops appeared before the pope, Sheen produced documentation proving that Spellman had never paid for the milk — demonstrating clearly that Spellman had lied to the pontiff. Pius XII sided with Sheen, and Spellman allegedly swore he would exact revenge. "I will get even with you," the cardinal reportedly told his auxiliary bishop. "It may take six months or ten years, but everyone will know what you're like."

Sheen soon began to experience the wrath behind those words. When Sheen announced later that year that he was retiring from his immensely popular TV program, he stated publicly that his decision was "dictated by spiritual considerations."[260] But rumors circulated that he was forced out by Cardinal Spellman, an explanation that Reeves wholeheartedly endorsed.

Meanwhile, brother priests who wanted to stay in Spellman's good graces apparently gave Sheen the cold shoulder. Sheen's hopes of ascending the ladder in the Church were effectively halted as Spellman held the keys to clerical advancement in America. But all the while, Sheen kept silent. The press had no inkling that anything was amiss; the laity had no idea there had been a break between the two men; and Sheen quietly endured what he called "one of his crucifixions."

A Bishop in "Exile"

Cardinal Spellman's *coup de grace* against Sheen took more time to arrange. As promised, nearly ten years after the milk controversy Spellman had maneuvered to remove Sheen from New York, convincing the pope to make the seventy-one-year-old superstar priest the bishop of Rochester. Furthermore, just as he had allegedly compelled Sheen to leave his popular TV show, now Spellman forced him to resign his position as the national director of the SPF, despite the fact that during his sixteen-year tenure he had raised hundreds of millions of dollars for the world's poor and unevangelized.

Sheen put on a perfect face after the decision, praising and embracing Cardinal Spellman during his goodbye Mass at St. Patrick's Cathedral. Perhaps he saw the trial from a heavenly perspective, heeding his own words: "If we are right in a conflict, the Lord bids us absorb any wrongs like a sponge; if we are wrong, we are to see others as the instrument of working His Will." His public statements reveal only pleasure in the appointment. In his autobiography, he wrote that his move to Rochester "brought a new joy, namely, close association with people and with priests in particular." But however genuine that joy was (and it can't be ignored that Sheen must have felt at least some relief at moving three hundred miles away from Cardinal Spell-man), Sheen nonetheless faced a bitter trial during his brief time as the bishop of Rochester, the sort of trial he had been unaccustomed to up to that point.

After all, notwithstanding the long-simmering ire of a cardinal, Sheen had nonetheless lived a comfortable, productive life in New York. Not only was he famous and well-respected, he also had the pleasure of being exceptionally good at what he did. Nobody could deny that as a speaker and a fundraiser Sheen had excelled beyond measure. By contrast, in Rochester Sheen would face what he had never experienced before: failure and popular disdain.

A few stories reveal how far the once-beloved Sheen had fallen. Shortly after his transfer, Sheen rented out the largest auditorium in the city to deliver a series of talks to his flock. But they were sparsely attended. Sheen allegedly commented in private that "the whole world comes to hear Fulton Sheen, except his own diocese."

Sheen would soon experience something far worse than apathy. When he announced the closure of a downtown Catholic school, a large crowd gathered to protest the decision. As their new bishop drove by, people pounded his car, cursing him and shouting. He had apparently not consulted anyone about the decision, and by the next day he announced that the school would stay open.

His most embarrassing defeat came in what he hoped would be a case study for a partnership between the Church and the federal government to help house the poor. The plan was to offer an old par-ish with a dwindling congregation to the Department of Housing and Urban Development as a site for public housing. The parish had been under consideration for closure for years. But once again, Sheen made his decision after minimal discussion with members of the local church or the city government.

The community in Rochester, allegedly blindsided by the move, immediately rallied to save the parish from closure. Sheen said that he was greatly surprised there was opposition to his announcement, call-ing it "artificially stimulated." Artificial or not, the response was zeal-ous. "That evening when I visited a school, I was surrounded by several hundred people who had been organized to protest against 'the de-struction of our parish,'" Sheen wrote. Rocks were thrown at his car. Diocesan priests, who had previously felt snubbed by their bishop for his swift implementation of changes and his perceived refusal to listen to contradictory advice, quickly drafted a letter urging their bishop to change his mind. Soon, more than a hundred priests had added their names to the letter in a diocese that had only about six hundred clergy. Clearly Sheen had not won the loyalty of his priests. The night of the protest, Sheen reversed his decision, rescinded his offer to the federal government, and kept the parish open.

Reportedly, Sheen later told a fellow priest that when he saw the protestors gathered against his decision and the brewing storm around him, "that night, that very night, I resigned as bishop of Rochester. It took Pope Paul VI some time to accept it. But that night, as far as I was concerned, I left Rochester." At that time, Sheen had been bishop of Rochester for just over a year.

A little over a year and a half later, in October 1969, the Vatican announced Sheen's retirement. In his autobiography, Sheen attrib-uted his retirement to more mundane considerations. "As I reached my seventy-fifth year [1970], I knew I should offer to resign, because this was the wish of the Second Vatican Council for bishops who headed diocese," he wrote. "I did not cherish the thought of receiving a letter some day reminding me ... so I prepared for that day by going to Rome for a long audience with the Holy Father, Pope Paul VI, dur-ing which I submitted my resignation."

After his resignation, Sheen returned to New York City to con-tinue working and preaching. But in the years since he had graced America's TV screens, the nation had changed. The last episode of *Life is Worth Living* had aired in 1957.[261] When Sheen reentered the

New York City scene in the 1970s, social norms and cultural tastes had changed dramatically. His attempt to start another TV show, entitled *What Now America?* and hosted on a public broadcasting station in Ohio, lasted only thirteen episodes, quickly scrubbed despite being offered for free to other public broadcasters.

The now eighty-year-old Sheen would continue to preach retreats and deliver speeches, but the TV magic was gone. As Sheen's life drew to a close, he was still publicly recognized and honored at the highest levels, including by receiving a ceremonial archbishopric from Pope Paul VI and appearing at the National Prayer Breakfast with President Jimmy Carter in 1979. Yet he had lived long enough to see some of his personal magic fade away.

A Yoke Well-Fitting

Sheen was committed to the Blessed Sacrament, to the Church, and to the poor. Yet God undoubtedly knew what Sheen recognized in himself: that even in his old age he was far from perfection. He had delighted in fame. He had enjoyed applause. He loved serving God — but he also experienced many benefits of being in God's service, and he loved those benefits too. In Rochester and upon Sheen's return to New York City, God humbled His bishop and deprived him of many of his lesser loves. Like Christ, Sheen had experienced the adulation of crowds and the praise of the masses for preaching the coming of the Kingdom of God. For so much of his life, he felt the thrill of the popular acclaim of Palm Sunday. But just as the high priests and religious leaders subjected Christ to the Cross, Sheen's religious superior urged Sheen up the hill of Golgotha to face the jeers and rejection of the people, and to climb his own unbloody cross.

Yet in failure, there is God's mercy. True, Sheen's crosses in Rochester were often of his own making, or at least the products of his own shortcomings. But they were no less redemptive. The Romans may have cut and fit together the wood on which they hanged

Jesus, but Christ made the tree. So too God uses worldly materials — the work of our own hands as well — to fashion us into the saints He designed us to be.

"That portion of us which is tried and tested, which is subjected to many trials, is not a waste," Sheen wrote in the final months of his life. "The tears, the agonies, the frustrations, the toils are not lost. All of these which seem to militate against life, are worked into new forms. Life may be marred into a broken thing, but God can make it into a thing of beauty."

Did Sheen have any regrets in life? The world says we are to live without regrets, which ultimately means to live without repentance and without reform. Archbishop Sheen expressed only one: "If I were asked if I had my life to live over again, would I live the priesthood as I have, the answer is: 'No, I would try to love Christ more.'"

In a final mystery of grace, Sheen was given the chance to love Christ even more profoundly in the last months of his life through physical suffering that yielded further purification. Open heart surgery led him to experience what he called "a new dimension of pain." Yet in some ways, Sheen believed that this physical pain was much easier to accept than what he had endured before. He called the pain of his heart surgery "pure," as distinct from the "impure sufferings" that come from others. "It is easier to see pure pain as coming from God than it is to see impure pain as the work of His Mind," he wrote. In his suffering after open heart surgery, Sheen came to recognize that there were times he did not acknowledge God's Providence in the impure pains he endured. As he put it, "there were some corners of my soul that were not swept clean of atheism."

It would appear the weight of his trials under Cardinal Spellman still pressed upon him and he struggled to forgive those who had trespassed against him. He wrote of his internal struggle: "The keeping of the scorecard of past wrongs, the chewing of a cud of resentment, licking of the wound, and the memories of how we received them, the playing of the tapes of injustice real or imagined, were so many proofs that I had not thoroughly digested what my Faith taught me and my lips confessed, that all trials come from the Hands of the Loving God."

Armed with his new clarity of vision, Sheen was being prepared for his final trial. A year and a half after his surgery, Sheen died at prayer before the Blessed Sacrament.[262] In recognition of his life of heroic virtue and after an approved miracle whereby a stillborn baby was revived through his intercession after an hour without showing signs of life,[263] Archbishop Sheen was declared "Venerable" by Pope Benedict XVI in 2012, and his cause for canonization continues to this day.[264]

As Fulton Sheen takes his seat among the saints, his life demonstrates how different God's Kingdom is from the edifices of bitterness and pride that we build here on earth. Even now, God willing, both Archbishop Sheen and Cardinal Spellman are together in Heaven. There, they would see each other as friends and brothers, united without reserve or rancor in the Body of Christ. If so, their friendship will be sweetened during the resurrection: then, these once-rival souls will travel together and find their bodies both laid to rest within the same walls of the crypt beneath St. Patrick's Cathedral.

Conclusion: To Follow Bad Shepherds

IN THE FACE OF persecution from within, one virtue abides at the center: obedience. Internal persecution is painful because it comes at the hands of those whom we want to trust, whom we want to love, and whom we want to follow. Yet more important than our desire is our obligation. Persecution comes at the hands of those whom we are so often *required* to follow.

Jesus appoints shepherds over his flocks. That some shepherds of Christ's flock are unworthy or incapable is no surprise, as man is fallen. But that fallen shepherds must still be obeyed — that is much harder to swallow. Our pride rejects rebukes. Our sense of justice disdains wrongs done. Yet the Church, in her wisdom, nevertheless preaches "obedience, obedience, obedience" as the default for a Christian.

Even so, many questions remain. What does it mean to submit our will to the hierarchy, and how must we do so? When, if ever, are we allowed to resist? Are we ever *obliged* to resist?

We can only answer those questions if we understand what obedience really means.

Obedience in the Divine Plan

The Church has preached obedience from her very inception, because obedience is at the center of nature and salvation.

In the beginning, God made the world out of nothing, and at every moment He sustains it in being. Everything owes every moment of its existence to God. God did this not as an end in itself, but for His own glory. We are not our own. "What have you that you did not receive?" (1 Cor. 4:7). Everything belongs to God, and He has rights over all things as His personal property.

Obedience is therefore part of the cardinal virtue of justice, which gives to all what they are owed. This includes those who exercise authority, all of which is derived from the ultimate authority of God. Through obedience to God, we, His creatures, give to Him, our Creator, that which He is owed. Plants and animals — even inanimate objects — obey the will of God without even knowing it by acting in accord with their God-given natures.

Man, alone among physical creatures, was stamped with the image of God. This image imparts to us a certain likeness of God through our rational soul. This rational soul, unlike plants and animals, possesses an intellect and a will. By the intellect we know. By the will we choose. We are therefore accountable for our actions. We must choose in accordance with what we know to be true.

With the Fall of our first parents, however, nature was damaged. Adam and Eve broke man's relationship with God through sin and passed down a broken and disordered nature to all succeeding generations. Therefore, man's obligation to obey God is unique. Unlike both animals and angels, man has a duty to continually struggle against his fallen tendencies.

Yet, in this struggle we can find salvation. Our Lord's redemption of the human race has made it possible for us to participate in the very life of God. He wishes to make each of us an *alter Christus*, another Christ, and to give His Father the greatest glory possible. We become that other Christ through obedience to a will superior to our own.

Through grace, we can have charity in our souls and give God more than a legalistic or external obedience, as was the norm in the Old Testament. Such external obedience can maintain the appearance of love, even if it proceeds from ulterior motives, yet it cannot attain for us eternal life with God. Rather, God desires that we approach Him as children, obedient not just in our external acts but in our will as well. This obedience of a loving child gives God even greater glory than would the obedience of unfallen Adam. St. Thomas Aquinas goes so far as to say that "obedience, whereby we contemn our own will for God's sake, is more praiseworthy than the other moral virtues, which contemn other goods for the sake of God."[265] Even in the Old Testament it was written that "to obey is better than sacrifice, and to hearken than the fat of rams. For rebellion is as the sin of divination, and stubbornness is as iniquity and idolatry" (1 Sam. 15:22–23).

We can see then why obedience has been traditionally known as "the mother of virtues": mortifying our will habituates us to placing God's will above our own. This naturally inculcates greater humility, rendering us more pliable to God's loving will, even when it requires suffering. God has ordered human life and salvation such that it is impossible without obedience. Whether it be obedience to parents, to rulers, or to the Church — all of which stem from and are ultimately ordered to obedience to God — none of us will get to Heaven unless we obey a will that is higher than our own.

Obedience is difficult in practice. It requires a constant struggle against our fallen nature. But as we grow in perfection, our faith enables us to accept it joyfully. After all, God is perfect. God only requires that which is good for us. To obey God is to act in our own best interests. Even if obeying is painful or the good achieved is hard to perceive, we nonetheless have confidence that "in everything God works for good with those who love him" (Rom. 8:28).

True Obedience

But what of obeying our fellow men? The heart that yearns to obey God can still bristle at the idea of obeying a fallen man, even those invested with divine authority. Yet Christ's Church throughout the ages teaches that we must. The author of Hebrews (likely St. Paul) commands the laity to "obey your leaders and submit to them; for they are keeping watch over your souls, as men who will have to give account" (Heb. 13:17). Our Lord Himself enjoined obedience: "The scribes and the Pharisees sit on Moses' seat, so practice and observe whatever they tell you, but not what they do; for they preach, but do not practice" (Matt. 23:2–3). What was true of the Old Covenant priesthood is even truer of the New Covenant one.

But to follow Christ's command in justice, we must distinguish between different types of obedience, as outlined by St. Thomas Aquinas in his *Summa Theologica*: perfect obedience, sufficient obedience, disobedience, and false obedience.

First, there is perfect obedience. St. Thomas frequently makes a distinction between that which is necessary for salvation, and that which demonstrates perfection. That which is necessary allows people to remain in God's grace, keep His commandments, and live virtuously. That which demonstrates perfection, however, goes beyond the minimum that is necessary to maintain a state of grace. For example, it is necessary to go to Mass on Sundays. But the perfection of charity goes beyond this minimum to participate in the fullness of sanctity, such as going to Mass and receiving Communion daily. When it comes to obedience, one who obeys perfectly obeys every lawful command, no matter how displeasing. Obeying a command even when unnecessary mortifies the will, leading to greater holiness by imitating Christ's own perfect obedience. Below this is sufficient obedience, which is when one obeys when one must, not going beyond what is strictly necessary. Then there is disobedience, when one refuses to obey even when obedience is necessary.

But St. Thomas goes a step further and describes an additional type of obedience: false obedience, what he calls "indiscreet obedience," when one obeys even when it is unlawful to do so.[266] False obedience is impossible in our relationship with God, because God never demands that which is unlawful.

However, false obedience is always a risk with respect to commands from men. If those in authority command what is contrary to God's will, it is disobedience to God to obey such a command, as their authority comes from God and can therefore never contradict His. No one can demand, for example, that you steal your neighbor's property, commit murder, worship a false god, or reject the Catholic Faith. To obey those commands would be to sin. To enjoin them in the name of obedience would be to command false obedience.

This follows from a simple principle of hierarchy: one who is inferior cannot demand disobedience to one who is superior. As St. Augustine wrote, "If a commissioner issue an order, are you to comply, if it is contrary to the bidding of the proconsul? Again if the proconsul command one thing, and the emperor another, will you hesitate to disregard the former and serve the latter? Therefore if the emperor commands one thing and God another, you must disregard the former and obey God."[267] God is the ultimate superior; therefore His law is supreme above all others and must be obeyed above all others.

To the rule of hierarchy, St. Thomas adds another qualification to obedience: limits on jurisdiction. For example, a government cannot command citizens of another country to pay taxes, nor can an abbot order a layman to do chores in his abbey. Governments have a right to tax, but only their own citizens. Likewise, abbots have the authority to direct men to do abbey chores, but only if those men are monks under the abbot's jurisdiction.

Limits on jurisdiction apply not only to who can be commanded, but also to what can be commanded. A government can demand a citizen pay taxes, but it cannot rightfully demand that same citizen go to Mass on Saturday instead of Sunday. The state has no authority to make such an order. Likewise, the abbot can order his monk to eat in silence during mealtimes, but he cannot order the monk to change the speed limit signs on the state road leading up to the abbey. Those in power have authority, but only over certain people, and only within certain confines. As St. Thomas put it, "A subject is not bound to obey his superior if the latter command him to do something where he is not subject to him."[268] Note, however, that St. Thomas said the subject is merely "not bound." Depending on the circumstance, the subject can still choose to obey without sinning.

For example, imagine an abbot has the authority to order monks to do chores, but the abbot's own superior mandates that no single monk can be ordered to clean the filthy latrine daily. Such a command is outside the abbot's jurisdiction. However, a monk would not be sinning by taking up a mop and obeying such a command from the abbot. In fact, it could be meritorious to obey and do what is displeasing — even if the abbot acted improperly by demanding obedience when he had no such authority. By cleaning the latrine despite being "not bound" to do so, the monk is acting in perfect obedience. He is going beyond what is strictly necessary for salvation, mortifying his will to achieve an even greater degree of perfection, by which to attain a closer union with God.

As St. Francis de Sales, a Doctor of the Church, wrote:

> Therefore do you obey their [ecclesial, civil, and domestic superiors'] commands as of right, but if you would be perfect, follow their counsels, and even their wishes as far

as charity and prudence will allow: obey as to things acceptable.... Obey in things indifferent.... Obey in things hard, disagreeable, and inconvenient, and herein lies a very perfect obedience. Moreover, obey quietly, without answering again, promptly, without delay, cheerfully, without reluctance; and, above all, render a loving obedience for his sake who became obedience even to the death of the Cross for our sake.[269]

To these two qualifications to obedience — hierarchy and jurisdiction — we can add a third: trust.[i] Trust does not expect that the person in authority will always treat those beneath him with kindness, gratitude, or even respect. Rather, trust means a belief that the person in authority seeks to do the will of God and acts in accord with the common good. In other words, it is the trust that the person in authority will not demand the false obedience of violating God's law.

Extending our example in the abbey, we can see how trust can alter the monk's vow of obedience. Say the abbot orders the monk to bring a member of the boys' choir to a rehearsal room in the abbey where the abbot will teach him music. When the boy gets there, the abbot orders the monk to depart for the rehearsal. Under normal circumstances, the monk would have no reason to disobey. But suppose the abbot has demonstrated a proclivity to sexual sins and shows improper interest in minors. Because the abbot has broken a bond of trust, the monk should not obey this command and leave the boy unattended with the abbot. By refusing to offer false obedience to his abbot, the monk demonstrates higher obedience

---

[i] St. Thomas distinguishes the three categories as such: Superiors have authority — that is, the moral power to command — when they command (1) that which is compatible with God's will (hierarchy), (2) those who are under their obedience (jurisdiction), and (3) that which is within their competency (trust). See *Summa Theologica* II–II, q. 104.

to Jesus' command to never "scandalize one of these little ones that believe in me" (Matt. 18:6, DRA).

The Personal Struggle of Obedience

At first, these distinctions can appear confusing. There are subtleties to determining what is perfect obedience, sufficient obedience, disobedience, and false obedience, as well as what limits on obedience are imposed by hierarchy, jurisdiction, and trust. Yet making these distinctions allows us to understand the saints in this book — and helps us discern our own course of action in these confusing times. Indeed, these distinctions inform our ability to act prudently, which we must do if we are to respond to persecution within the Church while at the same time seeking to please God.

The *Catechism* defines prudence as "the virtue which disposes a person to discern the good and choose the correct means to accomplish it."[270] That is a good definition, but it can quickly become obscure in practice. How does one know when a superior is violating God's law? How does one know when the line has been crossed and an authority's commands are no longer within his jurisdiction? When does a breach of trust cause a command that would otherwise be acceptable to become unlawful? Knowledge of God's law and commandments, study of Sacred Scripture and Tradition, the aid of the sacraments, and an intimate life of prayer are all necessary for prudence. But we can also learn by example, the example of the saints.

In the previous chapters we have considered the examples of Our Lord, eleven saints, and one venerable bishop on the road to canonization. The models include men and women who lived across twenty centuries and spanned the entire globe from Australia to Alexandria. Some were bishops, some religious, and two were laymen. Each had a different relationship to the hierarchy; each encountered different challenges but prudently lived out the same virtue in different ways.

At first glance, that diversity may appear to reveal contradictions between the words and actions of one saint in contrast to another. How can St. Paul publicly rebuke St. Peter while St. Alphonsus Ligouri could say "the will of the pope is the will of God"? How can we commend St. Padre Pio for silently obeying his lowest superiors while honoring St. Bruno, who all but said that Pope Paschal II allowed for heresy? These apparent contradictions are illusory: in the framework of St. Thomas, we can see in every case the sparkling splendor of the gem of obedience.

The Only Exception

When in doubt, saints obey. They know that man is prone to act in pride, equating his own will with God's and putting his own preferences above Divine Providence.

However, when saints take the extraordinary step of contradicting ecclesial authorities, it is because they are convinced that the Faith itself is at stake, and to do otherwise would directly violate the will of God or risk the salvation of souls. Their "disobedience" is thus always animated by a higher obedience.

This is the key to understanding nearly every act of apparent disobedience within this book. Why did St. John Fisher contradict every other bishop in his nation — including his metropolitan archbishops — and deny King Henry VIII's assertion of civil supremacy over the Church? Why did St. Bruno likewise contradict his pope on a similar question of Church liberty? Because they had to. In their cases, they understood that no matter what bishops or cardinals or popes may say, ecclesial authority cannot be subservient to the laity. They cannot transfer their jurisdiction.

Relatedly, what gave St. Athanasius the right to reject the majority of Church leaders who promoted the Arian heresy — even local church councils that condemned him? God gave St. Athanasius the right, and God is hierarchically above everyone in the hierarchy.

Thus, Sts. Athanasius, Bruno, and John Fisher contradicted their human superiors and peers to defend the integrity of Catholic doctrine, which comes from God Himself.

While the examples above are all bishops, St. Thomas Aquinas implies that any subject — not just the successors of the apostles — should rebuke his superiors if there is a danger to the Faith itself. As St. Thomas put it, drawing on similar observations from St. Augustine:

> If the faith were endangered, *a subject ought* [emphasis added] to rebuke his prelate even publicly. Hence Paul, who was Peter's subject, rebuked him in public, on account of the imminent danger of scandal concerning faith, and, as the commentary of Augustine says on Galatians 2:11, "Peter gave an example to superiors, that if at any time they should happen to stray from the straight path, they should not disdain to be reproved by their subjects."[271]

It is not just that we have the right to rebuke our superiors — and even the pope — but rather that, if the Faith is endangered, we have the *obligation.* Indeed, many popes themselves have concurred with this statement. For example, Pope Innocent III observed in a sermon delivered at his consecration as Supreme Pontiff: "So necessary is faith for me as Pope, that, while I have God alone as the judge of my other sins, I can be judged by the church only for any sin committed against the Faith. For 'he who does not believe, is already judged' (John 3:18)."[272]

St. Robert Bellarmine, a Doctor of the Church, concurred, stating that in the case of a pope who may invade a territory "or endeavor to slay souls by his example," "just as it would be lawful to resist a Pontiff invading a body, so it is lawful to resist him invading souls or disturbing a state, and much more if he should endeavor to destroy the Church. I say, it is lawful to resist him, by not doing what he commands, and by blocking him, lest he should carry out his will." But even while a pope can be resisted in such circumstances, Bellarmine still insists, "It is not lawful to judge [juridically] or punish or even depose him, because he is nothing other than a superior."[273]

Likewise, St. Francis de Sales responded to Protestant accusations against the papacy and its authority by brilliantly explaining the balance between obedience and fraternal correction, truth and error, when it comes to how the faithful relate to the pope:

> Under the ancient law the High priest did not wear the Rational [breastplate of judgement] except when he was vested in the pontifical robes and was entering before the Lord. Thus, we do not say that the Pope cannot err in his private opinions, as did John XXII, or be altogether a heretic, as perhaps Honorius was. Now when he is explicitly a heretic, he falls *ipso facto* from his dignity and out of the Church, and the Church must either deprive him, or, as some say, declare him deprived, of his Apostolic See, and must say as S. Peter did, *Let another take his bishopric* (Acts 1:20). When he errs in his private opinion he must be instructed, advised, convinced; as happened with John XXII, who was so far from dying obstinate or from determining anything during his life concerning his opinion, that he died while he was making the examination which is necessary for determining in a matter of faith....
>
> But when [the pope] is clothed with the pontifical garments, I mean when he teaches the whole Church as shepherd, in general matters of faith and morals, then there is nothing but doctrine and truth. And in fact everything a king says is not a law or an edict but that only which a king says as king and as a legislator. So everything the Pope says is not canon law or of legal obligation; he must mean to define and to lay down the law for the sheep, and he must keep the due order and form.
>
> Thus we say that we must appeal to him not as to a learned man, for in this he is ordinarily surpassed by some others, but as to the general head and pastor of the Church. And as such we must honor, follow, and firmly embrace his

doctrine, for then he carries on his breast the *Urim* and *Thummim*, doctrine and truth. And again, we must not think that in everything and everywhere his judgment is infallible, but then only when he gives judgment on a matter of faith in questions necessary to the whole Church, for in particular cases which depend on human fact he can err, there is no doubt, though it is not for us to control him in these cases save with all reverence, submission, and discretion. Theologians have said, in a word, that he can err in questions of fact, not in questions of right, that he can err *extra cathedram*, outside the chair of Peter, that is, as a private individual, by writings and bad example.[274]

However, it must be continually remembered that circumstances in which we are obligated to disobey are rare exceptions, not the rule. The episodes in the lives of the saints within this book focus on moments of conflict and confusion, singular experiences in lives largely led in harmony with the leaders of the Church.

A defining moment of St. Bruno's life may have been his letter condemning Pope Paschal II's submission to the emperor — but that letter was one act amidst decades of faithful service to the pope. St. Teresa of Avila was directed by God to reform the Carmelites — but she refrained for six months from founding a Discalced convent until her confessor gave approval. Obedience to her superiors was a law of St. Teresa's life. Likewise, St. Padre Pio exhibited courageous obedience, living with limited priestly faculties and a severely restricted ministry for a decade. The ecclesial authorities who imposed these restrictions were undoubtedly wrong. Yet their actions were valid and legitimate. They did not demand that Padre Pio sin. Nor was he so proud as to believe that his personal ministry was necessary for the salvation of souls — "God is able from these stones to raise up children to Abraham" (Matt. 3:9), whether Padre Pio helped or not. Ultimately, he saw the difference between hierarchs with bad judgment — perhaps even bad will — and those who violated God's law. As a faithful son of the Church, he was willing to endure terrible shame in this life for the sake of his vow of obedience.

This is the key to understanding Padre Pio's declaration that "when I am with my superior I am with God." At no point did his superiors ever issue a command contrary to God's will. Padre Pio had every reason to trust that, however displeasing their demands, his superiors would never require him to disobey God, whom he owed ultimate obedience. The same can be said of St. Alphonsus Liguori's assertion that "the will of the pope is the will of God." Liguori was not saying the pope determines what God wills. If he believed that, he would be a heretic, not a saint. Rather, implicit within that statement is the understanding that his pope would never demand that his subjects contradict God's explicit commandments.

The saints teach us that obedience to ecclesial authority has its limits, but those limits are not easily reached. Rebuking Peter is a last resort, not a common tactic. The vast majority of the time, we see the saints striving to obey, even when not strictly necessary.

When being examined for days by an overtly hostile bishop, St. Joan of Arc nonetheless answered with clarity and simplicity, only withholding information her heavenly interlocutors told her explicitly to keep secret. She showed respect to a bishop who showed little respect for her.

In one extreme circumstance, the bishop of Adelaide banished St. Mary MacKillop from his diocese, falsely claiming it was an order from Rome. Though the bishop had no legal right to do this — in a word, it was outside his jurisdiction — St. Mary still obeyed. She would not have sinned had she ignored the bishop, but neither would she sin in following his wishes. At great cost, she submitted, demonstrating St. Thomas's perfect obedience — that love that readily complies with the apostolic injunction, "outdo one another in showing honor" (Rom. 12:10).

Likewise, St. Thomas More heroically attempted to remain obedient even to his schismatic king by remaining silent as long as he could. He was willing to affirm that Parliament had the right to declare who would be the legal heirs of the king — even if they were the fruit of his unlawful "second" marriage to Ann Boleyn. But when the time came, and the adulterer king gave him no option but to affirm his second "marriage" and thereby deny the authority of the pope, More refused. Indeed, he only broke his silence and rebuked the king's actions with full rhetorical force after being formally condemned to death.

Except in the most exceptional moments, the saints chose obedience.

Do we live in exceptional times? Each era has its own heresies. Sometimes they concern false claims about God. At other times, heresy centers on the battle between Church and state. In our own age, we contend perhaps most of all with the widespread rejection, even among clergy, of divinely ordered creation in human sexuality, biology, marriage, and family life; anemic belief in the Real Presence and other Catholic dogmas; an "ecumenism" that often blurs the lines between truth and error, communion and schism, and infallible teaching and heresy; and generally a widespread and shockingly defective catechesis among the laity, no doubt aided and abetted by rampant liturgical abuses.

To use St. Thomas's words, we live in times when "the faith [is] endangered." Bishops in Germany approve blessing same-sex couples. Parish priests commonly treat the Most Blessed Sacrament as if it were not Christ Himself but a communal cracker, spilling Hosts and dropping Our Lord on the ground. Protestant clerics have been allowed to celebrate a false "Mass" within the papal cathedral of St. John Lateran in Rome. The Vatican invited an "artist" famous for submerging a crucifix in his own urine to the Sistine Chapel to be honored. The pope opened the door to idolatry, allowing the

Pachamama "goddess" into the Vatican (a grotesque scandal, regardless of his intentions). The litany of abuses and errors shock every well-formed Catholic conscience.

We are living through a crisis of the Church perhaps unprecedented in history where, to paraphrase St. Jerome's words about the Arian crisis, the faithful groan, astonished to find a great multitude of their shepherds are hirelings and wolves. In such times, it is more important than ever to obey as much as we humanly can, mortifying our wills, remembering always how easily our weak human nature can fall into pride and sin. It can help to remember that wicked shepherds are often put over us as a judgment for our sins. During this time of trial in the Church, we must remove the log in our own eyes (Matt. 7:5), confessing that we, through our sins, have contributed to the marred condition of the Church Militant, including the state of the priesthood.

For example, in 1522, as the Protestant revolt was getting underway, Pope Adrian VI instructed his legate to the Imperial Diet of the Holy Roman Empire to not only condemn the errors of Luther, but to frankly admit that the scourge was being permitted by God as a judgment on His people, and especially for the sins of priests:

> You will also say that we frankly confess that God permits this persecution to afflict His Church because of the sins of men, especially of the priests and prelates of the Church. For certainly the hand of the Lord has not been shortened so that He cannot save, but sins separate us from Him and hide His face from us so that He does not hear. Scripture proclaims that the sins of the people are a consequence of the sins of the priests, and therefore (as Chrysostom says) our Savior, about to cure the ailing city of Jerusalem, first entered the Temple to chastise first the sins of the priests, like the good doctor who cures a sickness at its source.[275]

Yet, as we relentlessly strive for perfect obedience, it is also more important than ever to be clear on the limits of that obedience. Obedience to shepherds is always ordered toward obedience to the Good Shepherd. Where the shepherds are vague, ambiguous, contradictory, and doubtful in their doctrine, we may rely on what the Church has authoritatively taught in every age, an authority Christ assured us can never err. Through such teachings, and the constant understanding of the Church, we hear His voice. He knows us, and we follow Him (John 10:27). And where the shepherds are doctrinally wrong, scandalous, abusive, and heretical, we — attuned to the voice of the Good Shepherd through the constant Magisterium of the Church — can discern them as hirelings and wolves. Then, as the faith, doctrine, and morals of Christ's Church require, we must have the wisdom and fortitude to refuse their call. They, like each of us, will answer to Christ directly on the Day of Judgment. In the meantime, their sins do not cancel or overcome Christ's promises to His Church.

Pray for Those Who Persecute You

When we must refuse obedience to, or even rebuke, our leaders, how are we to act? Again, the saints can guide us. First and foremost, the saints preach constantly never to bear ill will against those who persecute us — or even those who lead others astray. Confronting a wrong does not mean condemning the wrongdoer in fiery terms. "The tongue is a fire," St. James warns us (James 3:6). It makes no sense to offer correction to another soul if in the process we throw our own into the fires of Hell by an over-fiery tongue.

As St. Paul taught us, "Let no evil talk come out of your mouths" (Eph. 4:29), and, "You shall not speak evil of a ruler of your people" (Acts 23:5). When Paul rebuked Peter, he did not call down fire from heaven or hurl *ad hominem* attacks at the pope. Rather, he presented the pope with a *dubium*: "If you, though a Jew, live like a Gentile and not like a Jew, how can you compel the Gentiles to live like Jews?"

(Gal. 2:14). St. Paul had no authority to force the pope to change his actions; so he trusted that by confronting Peter clearly with his error, the Holy Spirit would do the rest of the work within Peter's heart.

Likewise, when Pope Paschal II surrendered to Emperor Henry V, allowing a secular authority to appoint bishops, St. Bruno said flatly that lay investiture "is heretical" and "no one can say that this is not heresy." Yet he made a clear distinction: while those who participate in lay investiture are sinners, it is only those who defend the practice who are heretics, because they dissent from irreformable doctrine. By this, St. Bruno was giving his pope the benefit of the doubt, recognizing that he signed the agreement under duress and making clear that he was not his enemy, despite the pope's bad judgment. Bruno wrote to the pope personally, reiterating his loyalty and love for the pontiff.

Even when the saints were attacked personally, they refused to respond in kind. Saints are quick to defend the truth, but slow to defend themselves. When Mary MacKillop was erroneously excommunicated by Bishop Sheil in Australia, her mother wrote a scathing letter condemning His Excellency. St. Mary could not help but acknowledge that "the letter vindicates me," but she lamented that her personal vindication was not worth the cost of attacking her bishop. She warned one of her sisters never to say a word against the bishop or anyone who is against them: "If we cannot speak well of their acts, let us be silent." She said all this despite the fact that her "excommunication" was utterly baseless.

Padre Pio exhibited the same steely determination never to defend himself at the expense of the hierarchy, no matter how wrong the hierarchy might be. When his friend Emmanuele Brunatto threatened to blackmail Rome to get Padre Pio's faculties restored, the friar told Brunatto he should "blush for shame and tremble with fear" for what he planned to do. "I absolutely cannot allow you to defend me or try to free me by throwing mud, and such mud, in the face of people that I, you, and everyone have a sacred duty to respect."[276] The hierarchy was completely within its jurisdiction when it deprived Padre Pio of his faculties. He would not undermine God's appointed ministers to stop them from doing what God's authority permitted them to do.

Archbishop Fulton Sheen similarly gave a lesson in humble submission when he left his award-winning TV show and powerful position at the Society for the Propagation of the Faith with a smile and abundant praise for Cardinal Spellman, the very man who had reportedly forced him out.

St. John of the Cross transcended all worldly wisdom when he not only accepted abuse from his persecutors, but begged for more. While imprisoned by the Calced Carmelites for refusing to renounce his vows, St. John was whipped by the friars on Fridays as they recited the *Miserere*. Yet, he was so convinced that his penances were for his sanctification and the greater glory of God that he asked them to do it more often.

Each of these saints imitated Christ, who stood before His accusers "like a sheep that before its shearers is dumb" (Isa. 53:7). To those who condemned Him, Christ was silent. To those who spit upon Him, Christ spoke with gentleness. To those who crucified Him, Jesus asked pardon. Only to those who disrespected His Father and His Father's ways did He show his zeal for His Father's house (John 2:17). Jesus violently drove out those who turned the house of prayer for all nations into a den of thieves (Mark 11:17). He roundly rebuked those leaders who would put false burdens upon the people that they themselves refused to carry (Matt. 23:4). To those who slandered the power of His Father, attributing Christ's miracles not to the Spirit of God but to the demon Beelzebub, Jesus declared that such obstinate sin "will not be forgiven, either in this age or in the age to come" (Matt. 12:32). The Lamb who was slain is also the Lion of Judah.

Thus St. Padre Pio and St. Mary MacKillop in their silence did not contradict St. Bruno and St. Athanasius in their protests. Rather, each embodied a different aspect of Christ — the former Christ's humble submission in the face of personal attacks, the latter Christ's fearless defense of the Father and fervor for the salvation of souls. They were obedient to authority on earth to the greatest extent possible, and in doing so, were obedient to Our Father in Heaven — including when the limits of that obedience had been reached.

Wise as a Serpent

While the saints embody complete abandonment to the divine will and trust that God can draw good from evil, their faith never negated their obligation to use reason. We cannot imagine God will resolve our problems without our cooperation. Jesus calls us to be "innocent as doves" but also "wise as serpents" (Matt. 10:16). Those who refuse to exercise their God-given reason fall even when attempting to follow God's plans. For example, when St. Alphonsus Liguori, a bishop, gave the nefarious Fr. Maione blank sheets of paper with his signature on the bottom, Fr. Maione overhauled the rules of the order, making changes that he acknowledged would "destroy the Congregation." Liguori had been warned about Fr. Maione's treachery beforehand. His failure in judgment nearly killed the religious order he spent his life building. God later made whole what was broken, but Liguori had good reason for regretting his lack of wisdom.

To the contrary, those saints who acted "wise as serpents" navigated the confusions of their times without sacrificing their missions. When St. Teresa was told by Our Lord to found a house in Madrid, Fr. Gracian told her to found it in Seville instead — a place outside of her authority. Our Lord is higher than Fr. Gracian, yet she had vowed obedience to Fr. Gracian, who himself was operating under the authority of the pope and was the one Our Lord directed Teresa to obey. The great mystic didn't have a vision telling her what was right. Instead, she reasoned that, in light of her vow of obedience, God was speaking through Fr. Gracian. So to Seville she went. Only after making her decision did the Lord appear to St. Teresa to confirm her choice and praise her for her obedience.

In St. Mary MacKillop's case, when Bishop James Quinn of Brisbane took over the Josephite house in his diocese, Mary didn't fight it. Yet by her obedience she heaped hot coals on his head. Predictably, the general public wasn't pleased about being deprived of free education from their beloved Brown Joeys — and they didn't buy the line that Mary acted of her own volition. Catholics and non-Catholics alike protested. Within two months, the bishop backed down, allowing the sisters back.[ii] His perfidy was publicly established, and her meekness was vindicated.

Perhaps most shockingly, St. Athanasius teaches that when confronted by heretical clergy, even laymen should use their wisdom to contradict error. St. Athanasius trusted that laymen had the ability to distinguish between orthodoxy and heresy, based on their being taught what the Church had always taught. Thus, he encouraged laymen to flee from parishes taken over by heretical priests, and even to disobey bishops who broke with the Faith, because manifest and pertinacious heresy, according to countless Fathers, Doctors, saints, theologians, and canonists, necessarily entails a loss of office within the Church.

A Narrow — and Lonely — Road

As the saints mirrored Christ's words and actions in His life, their persecutions were likewise an imitation of Christ in His Passion and death. Just as Jesus was abandoned, crucified with only His Mother, the Beloved Disciple, and a few faithful women nearby, so too the saints often suffered alone. St. Athanasius was, at various times, all but one man against the world, experiencing multiple exiles from his own

---

[ii] God Himself adopts this method to correct His wayward children, giving sinners "up in the lusts of their hearts" (Rom. 1:24) so they can experience the darkness of their sins and be drawn to repentance.

diocese while the physical structures of the Church were occupied by heretics, many of whom held high ecclesial offices. In St. Bruno's day, most of the cardinals abandoned the true pope. When St. John Fisher stood against the king's takeover of the English Church, he stood alone among the English episcopacy. We too must be willing to stand alone.

Our Lord was unjustly condemned to death by the high priests and the Sanhedrin. Ecclesial leaders have likewise, at times, unjustly condemned saints, like St. Joan of Arc, St. Mary MacKillop, and the fifty-five nuns of the *Encarnacion* who voted for St. Teresa of Avila as prioress. The leaders who excommunicated these holy people — and in St. Joan of Arc's case labeled her a heretic and had her executed — may have acted illegitimately or outside their jurisdiction. Yet in such moments it can be difficult to discern the true children of the Church from the false. For a time, those who did no wrong were undoubtedly troubled by the fear that they were separated from the Church — and perhaps even from God's grace.

Good men and women may likewise be excommunicated in our own day. But we should not be distressed. As St. Augustine wrote:

> Sometimes, too, divine providence will allow even good men to be expelled from the Christian community through some outbreak of turbulence and discord on the part of fleshly-minded people. When they show inexhaustible patience in putting up with such an insult or injury for the sake of the peace of the Church and do not undertake any novelties in the way of schism or heresy, they will teach us all with what heartfelt loyalty and what genuine charity we should serve God.... *The Father who sees in secret* (Matt. 6:4) will in secret award these men their crown. This kind is rarely to be seen, but, all the same, instances of them are not lacking; indeed there are more of them than you could imagine.[277]

Christ gave the bishops the power to bind and loose. But that power must still be wielded in accordance with justice and truth. Those falsely condemned by leaders in the Church can take comfort that, as long as they act with humility, refusing to respond to persecution and corruption by tearing apart the Body of Christ in schism, they are serving God and will be rewarded. There is a day of judgment for everyone — sheep and shepherd alike. But especially shepherds.

Justified in the End

Those persecuted from within must trust Divine Providence, who will, one day, straighten the crooked paths. Yet our saints teach us that that day may be long coming — Joan of Arc was burned as a heretic, and it took centuries for the Church to recognize the *Pucelle* as a saint. St. Mary MacKillop predicted the persecution of the Josephites wouldn't end until after her death, and so it was. Sts. Thomas More and John Fisher were executed, while the persecution of Catholics in England would continue for centuries.

Similarly, the excommunication of the nuns at *Encarnacion* was lifted, but St. Teresa and her companion, St. John of the Cross, still faced persecution for becoming Discalced their entire lives. We can add St. Alphonsus Liguori to the list, who had only Divine Mercy to rely on at his deathbed, fearing he had ruined the Redemptorists, a project from God.

In all these examples, God allowed His saints to suffer persecution, and even a degree of apparent separation, from the Church. Yet in every case, His saints were vindicated. The Church that rejected her persecuted saints now honors them.

Co-redemption with Christ

Catholics in the twenty-first century intuitively understand these teachings from the saints. We know that obedience is necessary, but we have learned the hard lesson that it must not be given blindly. We have seen the outrageous and demoralizing unmasking of pedophilic priests. We observe all around us what the Bible calls "fornicators" — those who commit adultery with other gods, seeking to change the fundamental teachings of the Church from within by promoting gay "marriage," abortion, contraception, female ordination, universalism, and a host of other offenses against the Faith.

Faithful Catholics must stand against these errors while loving Mother Church as she exists on earth in a state of pilgrimage. Yet we must also always be mindful of that Church in Heaven reigning triumphantly with Christ, who guarantees that the Church on earth will ultimately never lead us into error, even when her shepherds engage in scandalous behavior. It is our love for what the Church is — really, truly, and metaphysically the unblemished Bride of Christ — that allows us to recognize all the ways in which human actors within the Church betray her holiness. Sexual abuse, pedophilia, money laundering, heretical sermonizing, abuses of Our Lord on the altar — we see and are pained by it all. Sometimes we wonder how anything so thoroughly injured can possibly be healed. But with God, all things are possible. We choose to remain in the Church out of obedience to Christ and His prayer for the unity of His Church.[iii]

Schism is born of pride, so we choose to obey. We cannot start our own church, which would be to somehow create another Body of Christ. Yet we recognize we cannot always follow the wicked shepherds God sometimes permits to govern His Church. In rare circumstances, as St. Augustine, St. Thomas Aquinas, and countless others have asserted, we may even be required to fraternally correct our shepherds in order to be loyal to the Good Shepherd.

[iii] In His prayer for the Church at the Last Supper in John 17 — His last message to His disciples before His trial, Crucifixion, and death — Jesus asks His Father that His followers would "be one, even as we are," five separate times. There is no acceptance of "denominations" in Christ's hope for the Church.

Yes, at times our judgment falters. We disobey when we know we know we should submit. We can speak harshly when we know we should be gentle. We invert the lessons of the saints, becoming quick to defend ourselves and our wounded pride, but slow to defend the Faith. We trust ourselves and our own power to bring about a "just" solution in the here and now, when we know we should rely on God's Providence, ever mindful that "the anger of man does not work the righteousness of God" (James 1:20). But when we do fall, we must get back up, resolving again to embrace obedience and love — including, like many of the saints, that perfect obedience and love that reaches beyond what is strictly necessary.

We must bear the Cross, all the while remembering that the Cross is not the end but the means. Remember: God made us with a purpose for times such as these — as individuals within our particular families and nations, in His Church, and facing these seemingly insurmountable crises. He raised up each of the saints in this book to overcome the trials of their own times. We remember and venerate them for responding to His graces, striving for perfection, and accepting His call. Now, God wants us to do the same. We must be the saints of our time.

When we shoulder our cross not with an ungenerous heart of resignation but with an overflowing heart of love, we "complete what is lacking in Christ's afflictions" (Col. 1:24), taking part in His redemptive sacrifice that saves the world. We will share the sweet interior happiness of Padre Pio in his life of pain. We will have the holy joy of the imprisoned St. John of the Cross. We will possess the irrepressible good humor of St. Thomas More on his ascent to the gibbet.

Perhaps most satisfying of all, we will know that the impact of our works will echo in eternity. Persecution is not the end of our good work, but the means of our sanctification. In return for temporary suffering, Our Lord has bounteously offered us an eternal reward. Was Paul's power diminished by his arrest in Jerusalem?

Athanasius's by his exiles? Bruno's by his removal from the Curia? Joan's by her absence from the battlefield? Fisher's or More's by their martyrdoms? Teresa's or John's in being reviled? Liguori's in his rejection? MacKillop's in her haggling with the hierarchy? Pio's in his "imprisonment"? Sheen's in his "exile" to Rochester? Quite the contrary. These trials merited them eternal life with God, before whom they now intercede on our behalf.

Many saints looked like failures during their lifetimes. We can feel the same way. Yet the Cross is Christ's throne of victory before the only witness who truly matters: God. He did not fail, and neither did His saints. Their work has life-giving power. Like the grain of wheat that fell to the ground and died (John 12:24), they preferred God's will and Christ's suffering to their own wills, egos, and comforts. And thus, their sacrifices bore abundant fruit. Through their heavenly intercession before the face of God, whom they now see with undimmed splendor, they continue to bear fruit in our lives today for the redemption of the world.

Like our beloved saints, that vision of God is the end of our sufferings on earth. That is the glory Our Lord has prepared for us. That is our hope amidst our persecution from within.

Endnotes

Introduction: When Shepherds Turn on the Flock

1   Donald R. McClarey, "Pope Paul VI and the Smoke of Satan," *The American Catholic*, December 4, 2011, http://web.archive. org/web/20140717024323/http://the-american-catholic. com:80/2011/12/04/pope-paul-vi-and-the-smoke-of-satan/.

2   Fr. Teiji Yasuda, O.S.V., *Akita: The Tears and Message of Mary*, trans. John M. Haffert (Asbury, N.J.: 101 Foundation, 1989), 78, https://maryourhelp. org/e-books/marian-apparitions/Our-lady-of-Akita.pdf.

3   Thomas Aquinas, *Summa Theologica* III, q. 82, art. 9.

4   Fulton J. Sheen, *Treasure in Clay: The Autobiography of Fulton J. Sheen* (New York: Image Books/Doubleday, 2008), 328–329.

Chapter 1: Our Lord Jesus Christ — The King of Betrayed Saints

5   St. Augustine, *Sermon 224*, in St. Augustine, *Sermons on the Liturgical Seasons*, trans. Sister Mary Sarah Muldowney, R.S.M., (Washington, DC: Catholic University of America Press, 1959), 185.

Chapter 2: St. Paul the Persecutor and Persecuted

6   *Ignatius Catholic Study Bible*, RSV, Second Catholic Edition (San Francisco: Ignatius Press, 2005), 220.

7   Ibid., 243, see note on verse 21:17.

8   Ibid., 333, see note on verse 2:12.

9   St. John Chrysostom, *Homily 46 on the Acts of the Apostles*, trans. J. Walker, J. Sheppard and H. Browne, and revised by George B. Stevens, in *Nicene*

and *Post-Nicene Fathers*, First Series, vol. 11, ed. Philip Schaff (Buffalo, NY: Christian Literature, 1889), rev. and ed. for New Advent by Kevin Knight, https://www.newadvent.org/fathers/210146.htm.

10   *Ignatius Catholic Study Bible*, 234, see note on verse 16; St. John Chrysostom, Homily 46.

CHAPTER 3: THE PERSECUTION AND EXILES OF ST. ATHANASIUS

11   Socrates, *Church History*, bk. 1, chap. 5, trans. A. C. Zenos, in *Nicene and Post-Nicene Fathers*, Second Series, vol. 2, ed. Philip Schaff and Henry Wace (Buffalo, NY: Christian Literature, 1890), rev. and ed. for New Advent by Kevin Knight, https://www.newadvent.org/fathers/26011.htm.

12   Socrates, *Church History*, bk. 1, chap. 6.

13   First Council of Nicaea, "Synodal Letter," trans. Henry Percival, in *Nicene and Post-Nicene Fathers*, Second Series, vol. 4, ed. Philip Schaff and Henry Wace (Buffalo, NY: Christian Literature, 1900), rev. and ed. for New Advent by Kevin Knight, https://www.newadvent.org/fathers/3801.htm.

14   First Council of Nicaea, "The Nicene Creed," New Advent, https://www.newadvent.org/fathers/3801.htm.

15   St. Athanasius, *Letter 10*, §7, trans. R. Payne-Smith, in *Nicene and Post-Nicene Fathers*, Second Series, vol. 2, ed. Philip Schaff and Henry Wace (Buffalo, NY: Christian Literature, 1892), rev. and ed. for New Advent by Kevin Knight, https://www.newadvent.org/fathers/2806010.htm.

16   St. Athanasius, *Encyclical Letter*, §§5–6, trans. M. Atkinson and Archibald Robertson, in *Nicene and Post-Nicene Fathers*, Second Series, vol. 4, ed. Philip Schaff and Henry Wace (Buffalo, NY: Christian Literature, 1892), rev. and ed. for New Advent by Kevin Knight, https://www.newadvent.org/fathers/2807.htm.

17   St. Athanasius, *Letter 47*, trans. Archibald Robertson, in *Nicene and Post-Nicene Fathers*, Second Series, vol. 4, https://www.newadvent.org/fathers/2806047.htm.

18   St. Athanasius, *Apologia de Fuga*, §24, trans. M. Atkinson and Archibald Robertson, in *Nicene and Post-Nicene Fathers*, Second Series, vol. 4, https://www.newadvent.org/fathers/2814.htm.

19   St. Athanasius, *Ad Episcopus Aegypti et Libyae* (To the bishops of Egypt and Libya), §22, trans. M. Atkinson and Archibald Robertson, in *Nicene and Post-Nicene Fathers*, Second Series, vol. 4, https://www.newadvent.org/fathers/2812.htm.

20   St. Athanasius, *History of the Arians*, pt. 5, chap. 41, trans. M. Atkinson and Archibald Robertson, in *Nicene and Post-Nicene Fathers*, Second Series, vol. 4, https://www.newadvent.org/fathers/28155.htm.

21   Ibid., pt. 8, chap. 74.

22   Ibid., pt. 8, chap. 77.

23   Ibid., pt. 8, chap. 70.

24   Ibid., pt. 8, chap. 75.

25   Ibid., pt. 8, chap. 80.

26   St. Athanasius, *Discourse 1 Against the Arians*, §8, trans. John Henry New-man and Archibald Robertson, in *Nicene and Post-Nicene Fathers*, Second Series, vol. 4, https://www.newadvent.org/fathers/28161.htm.

27   St. Jerome, *The Dialogue Against the Luciferians*, §19, trans. W. H. Fremantle, G. Lewis, and W. G. Martley, in *Nicene and Post-Nicene Fathers*, Second Series, vol. 6, ed. Philip Schaff and Henry Wace (Buffalo, NY: Christian Literature, 1893), rev. and ed. for New Advent by Kevin Knight, https://www.newadvent.org/fathers/3005.htm.

28   St. Athanasius, *De Synodis*, §14, trans. John Henry Newman and Archibald Robertson, in *Nicene and Post-Nicene Fathers*, Second Series, vol. 4, https://www.newadvent.org/fathers/2817.htm.

29   Sozomen, *Ecclesiastical History*, bk 6, §12, trans. Chester D. Hartranft, in *Nicene and Post-Nicene Fathers*, Second Series, vol. 2, ed. Philip Schaff and Henry Wace (Buffalo, NY: Christian Literature, 1890), rev. and ed. for New Advent by Kevin Knight, https://www.newadvent.org/fathers/26026.htm; Socrates, *Church History*, bk. 4, §12.

30   St. Athanasius, *Discourse 2 Against the Arians*, §§67–68, trans. John Henry Newman and Archibald Robertson, in *Nicene and Post-Nicene Fathers*, Second Series, vol. 4, https://www.newadvent.org/fathers/28162.htm.

31   St. Athanasius, *Ad Episcopus Aegypti et Libyae*, §21.

32   St. Gregory Nazianzen, *Oration 21*, §§26, 33, trans. Charles Gordon Browne and James Edward Swallow, in *Nicene and Post-Nicene Fathers*, Second Series, vol. 7, ed. Philip Schaff and Henry Wace (Buffalo, NY: Christian Literature, 1894), rev. and ed. for New Advent by Kevin Knight, https://www.newadvent.org/fathers/310221.htm.

33   Ibid., §31.

34   Ibid., §37.

Chapter 4: The Persecution of St. Bruno

35   Roberto de Mattei, "St. Bruno's Filial Resistance to Pope Paschal II," March 4, 2015, Rorate Caeli, https://rorate-caeli.blogspot.com/2015/03/de-mattei-st-brunos-filial-resistance.html.

36   "Butler's Lives of the Saints — Saint Bruno, Bishop of Segni, Confessor," CatholicSaints.Info, accessed September 25, 2022, https://catholicsaints.info/butlers-lives-of-the-saints-saint-bruno-bishop-of-segni-confessor/.

37   "Bruno of Segni: A Pamphlet on Simoniacs (Late Eleventh Century),"
      Internet Medieval Sourcebook, Fordham University, https://sourcebooks.
      fordham.edu/source/11brunosegni-simony.asp.

38   "Gregory VII: Lay Investitures Forbidden 1080," Internet Medieval Source-
      book, Fordham University, https://sourcebooks.fordham.edu/source/g7-
      reform2.asp.

39   "Gregory VII: Simony and Celibacy 1074," Internet Medieval Sourcebook,
      Fordham University, https://sourcebooks.fordham.edu/source/g7-re-
      form1.asp.

40   Thomas Oestereich, "Pope St. Gregory VII," *Catholic Encyclopedia*, vol.
      6 (New York: Robert Appleton, 1909), https://www.newadvent.org/
      cathen/06791c.htm.

41   "Pope Gregory VII (c.1015-r.1073-c.1085): Letters on the Conflict with Em-
      peror Henry IV, 1075–1078," Letter no. 76, Internet Medieval Sourcebook,
      Fordham University, https://sourcebooks.fordham.edu/source/1075Gregor
      yVIIlettersandconflict1.asp. See also Oestereich, "Pope St. Gregory VII."

42   For the previous century's controversy, see George Sauvage, "Berengarius
      of Tours," *Catholic Encyclopedia*, vol. 2 (New York: Robert Appleton, 1907),
      https://www.newadvent.org/cathen/02487a.htm.

43   Sauvage, "Berengarius of Tours."

44   Bernhard Gigalski, *Bruno, Bischof von Segni, Abt von Monte-Cassino (1049-
      1123): sein Leben und seine Schriften: ein Beitrag zur Kirchengeschichte im
      Zeitalter des Investiturstreites und zur theologischen Litteraturgeschichte des Mit-
      telalters* (Muenster, Germany: Verlag von Heinrich Schöningh, 1898), 31.

45   Ibid., 30–34.

46   Ibid., 34

47   "Clement III, Antipope," Encyclopedia.com June 30, 2023, https://www.
      encyclopedia.com/religion/encyclopedias-almanacs-transcripts-and-maps/
      clement-iii-antipope.

48   Jodoc Adolphe Birkhauser, "St. Bruno," *Catholic Encyclopedia*, vol. 3
      (New York: Robert Appleton, 1908), https://www.newadvent.org/
      cathen/03014a.htm.

49   "Biographical Dictionary, Pope Victor III, Consistory Celebrated in 1086,"
      The Cardinals of the Holy Roman Church, Florida International University,
      https://cardinals.fiu.edu/bios1086.htm.

50   Ibid.

51   Giglaski, *Bruno*, 51.

52   "Butler's Lives of the Saints — Saint Bruno, Bishop of Segni, Confessor."

53   Giglaski, *Bruno*, 74.

54   Klemens Löffler, "Conflict of Investitures," *Catholic Encyclopedia*, vol.
      8 (New York: Robert Appleton, 1910), https://www.newadvent.org/

cathen/08084c.htm; see also James Loughlin, "Pope Paschal II," *Catholic Encyclopedia*, vol. 11 (New York: Robert Appleton, 1911), https://www.newadvent.org/cathen/11514b.htm.

55   Mattei, "St. Bruno's Filial Resistance."

56   Ibid.

57   *S. Brunonis Opera Omnia* (Works of St. Bruno), Patrologia Latina, vol. 165.

58   Ibid.

59   Ibid.

60   *Epistola III*, "Inimici mei," *Ad Paschalem Summum Pontificem*, Patrologia Latina, vol. 165, 1139.

61   Carlton J. H. Hayes, "Paschal II," *Encyclopedia Brittanica*, vol. 20 (1911), https://en.wikisource.org/wiki/1911_Encyclop%C3%A6dia_Britannica/Paschal_(popes).

62   Canon 12, specifically. See Peter the Deacon, *Chronicon monasterii Casinensis* (Monte Cassino Chronicle), 783, as cited in Gigalski, *Bruno*.

63   *Chronicon monasterii Casinensis*, 783–784, as quoted in Gigalski, *Bruno*.

64   *Epistola IV*, Patrologia Latina, vol. 165, 1141.

65   "Biographical Dictionary, Pope Victor III, Consistory Celebrated in 1086."

66   Gigalski, *Bruno*, 104.

67   Gigalski, *Bruno*, 105.

68   Bruno of Segni, "A Pamphlet on Simoniacs," no. 13, *inter alia*.

69   James MacCaffrey, "Pope Callistus II," *Catholic Encyclopedia*, vol. 3, https://www.newadvent.org/cathen/03185a.htm.

Chapter 5: The Persecution, Excommunication, and Execution of St. Joan of Arc

70   Unless otherwise indicated, all quotations and other details in this chapter rely on Craig Taylor, trans., *Joan of Arc: La Pucelle* (Manchester, UK: Manchester University Press, 2006). Quotations are taken from pages 86, 95, 138, 142, 146–148, 152–154, 157, 159–161, 163, 165, 168, 197–199, 201–202, 205–206, 213–217, 221–222, 224, 239, 262–263, and 348–352.

71   Pope Benedict XV, *Divine Disponente* (May 16, 1920), https://www.vatican.va/content/benedict-xv/la/bulls/documents/hf_ben-xv_bulls_19200516_divina-disponente.html. An excerpt of the bull in English is at https://www.angelus.online/angelus-online-may/june-2020/divina-disponente.

Chapter 6: The Persecution and Execution of St. John Fisher and St. Thomas More

72   James Monti, *The King's Good Servant, But God's First: The Life and Writings of St. Thomas More* (San Francisco: Ignatius Press, 1997), 299.

73   Unless otherwise indicated, the quotations and details in the rest of this chapter rely on E.E. Reynolds and Ryan Grant, eds., *St. John Fisher: Reformer, Humanist, Martyr* (Post Falls, ID: Mediatrix Press, 2015). Quotes come from pages 210, 213, 214, 216–217, 228, 231-233, 239–242, 258, 265, 270, 277, 293, 305, 330, 324, 351–352, 364–365, 370–374, 378–380, 385, and 393–394.

74   Mary Basset, *St. Thomas More's History of the Passion [The Sadness of Christ]* (London: Burns & Oates & Washbourne, 1941), 101–102.

75   Ibid.,113–114.

76   St. John Fisher, *A Spiritual Consolation and Other Treatises*, ed. D. O'Connor (London: Art & Book, 1903), 18.

77   Ibid., 55.

78   William Roper, *Life of St. Thomas More, Knt.* (London: Burns & Oates, 1905), 86, 91–93.

79   Monti, *King's Good Servant*, 454.

80   Ibid., 455.

CHAPTER 7: THE PERSECUTION OF ST. JOHN OF THE CROSS AND ST. TERESA OF AVILA

81   Discalced Carmelites of Boston and Santa Clara, *Carmel: Its History, Spirit, and Saints* (New York: P. J. Kenedy, 1927), 11.

82   Ibid.

83   Bernard Hamilton, *The Latin Church in the Crusader States* (London: Variorum, 1980).

84   "Celebrating St. Albert of Jerusalem," The Carmelites Australia and Timor-Leste, https://www.carmelites.org.au/item/1025-celebrating-st-albert-of-jerusalem.

85   "St. Albert," The 140 Saints of the Colonnade, St. Peter's Basilica.Info, http://www.stpetersbasilica.info/Exterior/Colonnades/Saints/St%20Albert-6/St%20Albert.htm.

86   "Europe," Carmelites, https://ocarm.org/en/europe.

87   "Carmelite Rule," The Carmelites Australia and Timor-Leste, https://www.carmelites.org.au/about-the-carmelites/rule.

88   Paul de la Croix, "Carmelite Spirituality," EWTN, https://www.ewtn.com/catholicism/library/carmelite-spirituality-12567.

89   "Carmelites," *Catholic Encyclopedia*, vol. 3, 360, as reproduced at https://en.wikisource.org/wiki/Page:Catholic_Encyclopedia,_volume_3.djvu/412.

90   Leopold Gluckert, O.Carm., "Blessed John Soreth," Carmelite Institute of North America, https://carmeliteinstitute.net/blessed-john-soreth-1394-1471/. For more on the Soreth reforms, see page 20 of Patrick Thomas McMahon,

O.Carm., *Carmelite Spirituality*, https://flowerofcarmellcc.weebly.com/up-loads/1/4/0/7/14079488/carmelite_spirituality_mcmahon.pdf.

91   Mark O'Keefe, O.S.B., *In Context: Teresa of Avila, John of the Cross, and Their World* (Washington, D.C.: Institute of Carmelite Studies, 2020), 88.

92   Ibid., 87.

93   Ibid., 31.

94   Ibid., 103. Unless otherwise indicated, quotations and information pre-sented in the rest of this chapter concerning St. Teresa's life derive from her *Vida*, chaps. 5, 7, 9, 20, 28, 29, and 32–34. References to the *Fundaciones* will be cited as *Foundations*.

95   *Foundations*, chap. 1, p. 1.

96   O'Keefe, *In Context*, 42, 107.

97   O'Keefe, *In Context*, 109.

98   O'Keefe, *In Context*, 62–63.

99   *Foundations*, 52.

100   "St. Teresa of Avila," EWTN, https://www.ewtn.com/catholicism/saints/teresa-of-avila-780.

101   *The Canons and Decrees of the Council of Trent*, trans. Theodore Alois Buckley, CapDox (Capuchin Franciscan Friars Australia), https://www.capdox.capuchin.org.au/reform-resources-16th-century/sources/the-canons-and-decrees-of-the-council-of-trent/.

102   Ibid.

103   David Lewis, "St. Teresa of Avila," EWTN, https://www.ewtn.com/catholicism/library/st-teresa-of-avila-5894.

104   William Thomas Walsh, *St. Teresa of Avila* (1943; repr., Charlotte, NC: TAN Books, 1992), 234.

105   Ibid., 233–234, 241.

106   Helen Hester Colville, *Saint Theresa of Spain* (New York: E. P. Dutton, 1909).

107   *Foundations*, chap. 1, first paragraph.

108   O'Keefe, *In Context*, 92, 107.

109   Walsh, *St. Teresa*, 302.

110   *Foundations*, 8.

111   Ibid., 10.

112   Walsh, *St. Teresa*, 328.

113   Ibid., 387.

114   *Foundations*, chap. 20.

115   Walsh, *St. Teresa*, 388.

116   Ibid., 389–390.

117   Ibid., 392.

118   "An Outline of the Life of St. Teresa," in *The Life of Teresa of Jesus: The Auto-biography of Teresa of Ávila*, trans. and ed. E. Allison Peers, digitally scanned,

1995, and available at Carmelite Monks, https://www.carmelitemonks.org/Vocation/teresa_life.pdf.

119 November 18, 1572. See footnote 8, p. 273, chap. 2 (Spiritual Marriage) of The Seventh Mansions, in *The Interior Castle*, trans. The Benedictines of Stanbrook, 3rd. ed (London: Thomas Baker, 1921), https://www.sacred-texts.com/chr/tic/tic00.htm.

120 Walsh, *St. Teresa*, 394–396.

121 Ibid., 396, 435.

122 *Foundations*, chap. 20.

123 See *Foundations*, 123.

124 *Foundations*, 123.

125 Walsh, *St. Teresa*, 439–442, 446.

126 Ibid., 443-447.

127 Ibid., 447.

128 See O'Keefe, *In Context*, 160.

129 O'Keefe, *In Context*, 164–165

130 Walsh, *St. Teresa*, footnote on 448.

131 Ibid., footnote on 449.

132 Ibid., 208.

133 Unless otherwise indicated, all quotations and details in this section are from Walsh, *St. Teresa*, 462–473, 503.

134 Father Gabriel Barry, O.C.D., "The Reform," Secular Order Discalced Carmelites, https://www.helpfellowship.org/OCDS%20Lessons/Lesson%2016.htm.

135 See Letter to the Archbishop of Evora (no. 10, January 1578), in *The Letters of St. Teresa*, trans. John Dalton (London: Thomas Baker, 1902), https://digital.library.upenn.edu/women/teresa/letters/letters.html.

136 See Letter to Rubeo (no. 18), in *The Letters of St. Teresa*.

137 Walsh, *St. Teresa*, 516.

138 Ibid.

139 Fr. Paschasius Heriz, O.C.D., *Saint John of the Cross* (Washington, D.C., 1919), 85. Unless otherwise indicated, quotations and details in the remainder of this section are from Paschasius, 85–106.

140 Walsh, *St. Teresa*, 543–544.

141 Ibid., 547–548.

142 Ibid., 548–549.

143 Ibid., 551.

144 Ibid., 551–552.

145 Paschasius, *Saint John*, 129.

146 Walsh, *St. Teresa*, 579.

147 Ibid., 580; *Vida*, 20.

148   "A Circular Letter from the Superiors General (2014)" Carmelites, https://ocarm.org/en/item/3608.

149   Paschasius, *Saint John*, 173. This is the source for the rest of this section; 179–199.

150   Kieran Kavanaugh, O.C.D., General Introduction, *The Collected Works of St. John of the Cross*, trans. Kieran Kavanaugh, O.C.D., and Otilio Rodriguez, O.C.D. (Washington, DC: ICS, 2017 [1991]), 25.

151   Paschasius, *Saint John*, 190, *inter alia*.

152   "Carmelites, Discalced," Encyclopedia.com, https://www.encyclopedia.com/religion/encyclopedias-almanacs-transcripts-and-maps/carmelites-discalced.

153   "The Memorable Canonization of 1622," Carmelites, March 9, 2022, https://www.ocarm.org/en/item/5718-the-canonization-of-st-teresa-of-avila-in-1622-was-like-none-before.

154   "Saint Teresa of Ávila Doctor of the Church," Carmelites, March 9, 2022, https://ocarm.org/en/item/5717-teresa-of-avila-doctor-of-the-church.

155   "Teresa de Jesus, doutora da Igreja," Irmas Carmelitas, https://www.irmascarmelitas.com.br/index.php?pr=conteudo&mn_codigo=15&ct_codigo=164.

156   "St. John of the Cross, Priest and Doctor of the Church," Carmelites, https://www.ocarm.org/en/item/230-st-john-of-the-cross-priest-and-doctor-of-the-church.

157   "History of the Carmelite Order," Carmelites Australia and Timore-Leste, https://www.carmelites.org.au/about-the-carmelites/history-of-the-carmelite-order.

Chapter 8: The Persecution of St. Alphonsus Liguori

158   Frederick M. Jones, C.S.S.R., *Alphonsus de Liguori: Saint of Bourbon Naples, 1696–1787, Founder of the Redemptorists* (Liguori, MO: Liguori, 1999), 471–472.

159   Mother Austin Carroll, *The Life of St. Alphonsus Liguori, Bishop, Confessor, and Doctor of the Church* (New York: P. O'Shea, 1882), 4.

160   Fr. Paolo O. Pirlo, S.H.M.I., "St. Alphonsus Liguori," in *My First Book of Saints* (Parañaque City, Philippines: Sons of Holy Mary Immaculate — Quality Catholic, 1997), 166–167.

161   Tom Rochford, S.J., "Saint Francis Jerome," Jesuits, https://www.jesuits.global/saint-blessed/saint-francis-jerome/.

162   Martin Luther, *The Bondage of the Will*, pt. 1, in *The Annotated Luther*, vol. 2, ed. Kirsi I. Stjerna (Minneapolis: Fortress Press, 2015), 181.

163   Letter to Jean Dehorgny in Rome (September 10, 1648 [sent from
      Paris, June 25, 1648]), Globethics, https://repository.globethics.net/
      handle/20.500.12424/574231.

164   Number 23, "Errors of the Jansenists," Condemned in a decree by the Holy
      Office, December 7, 1690, in Henry Denzinger, *Sources of Catholic Dogma*, 30th
      ed., trans. Roy Deferrari (Fitzwilliam, NH: Loreto, n.d.), 339.

165   Fr. John A. Hardon, S.J., "The Sacred Heart and the Eucharist," Fr. John A
      Hardon, S.J. Archives, http://www.therealpresence.org/archives/Sacred_
      Heart/Sacred_Heart_001.htm.

166   Ibid.

167   Number 26, "Errors of the Jansenists," in Denzinger, *Sources of Catholic
      Dogma*.

168   Jones, *Alphonsus de Liguori*, 267, 272. For the Church's teaching, see Bl. Pius
      IX, *Ineffabilis Deus* (December 8, 1854), Papal Encyclicals Online, https://
      www.papalencyclicals.net/pius09/p9ineff.htm.

169   F. A. Forbes, *Life of Pius X* (New York: P. F. Kenedy, 1918), 85.

170   Jessica M. Murdoch, "The New Jansenism," *First Things*, Feburary 21, 2017,
      https://www.firstthings.com/web-exclusives/2017/02/the-new-jansenism.

171   Francis, *Amoris Laetitia* (March 19, 2016), nos. 301–302.

172   Jones, *Alphonsus de Liguori*, 266. Unless otherwise indicated, quotations
      and other details in the remainder of this chapter come from Jones, 75, 269,
      447–449, 451, 456, 459, 460, 463–465, 479–486, 494. 498, 525, 530–533;
      or from Carroll, *Life of St. Alphonsus Liguori*, 73, 106–107, 196, 414,
      492–493, 501–502, 504–505, 513–518, 526, 538–539, 550, 567, 608, 971.

173   Jeff Grabmeier, "When Europeans Were Slaves: Research Suggests White
      Slavery Was Much More Common Than Previously Believe," Ohio State
      News, https://news.osu.edu/when-europeans-were-slaves--research-sug-
      gests-white-slavery-was-much-more-common-than-previously-believed/.

174   Carroll, *Life of St. Alphonsus Liguori*, 558.

175   Harold Castle, "St. Alphonsus Liguori," *Catholic Encyclopedia*, vol. 1
      (New York: Robert Appleton, 1907), https://www.newadvent.org/
      cathen/01334a.htm.

176   Carroll, *Life of St. Alphonsus Liguori*, 558.

177   Ibid., 598.

178   Ibid., 607.

179   Castle, "St. Alphonsus Liguori."

180   The Redemptorists, Baltimore Province, https://redemptorists.net/.

Chapter 9: The Persecution and Excommunication of St. Mary MacKillop

181 Unless otherwise indicated, all quotations and other information in this chapter rely on Fr. Osmund Thorpe, *Mary MacKillop*, 3rd ed. (North Sydney, NSW: The Generalate, Sisters of St. Joseph of the Sacred Heart, 1994); and Lesley O'Brien, *Mary MacKillop Unveiled* (North Blackburn, Victoria: CollinsDove, 1994).

182 Christian Bergmann, "The History Behind Mary MacKillop's Excommunication," Catholic Archdiocese of Melbourne, August 5, 2021, https://melbournecatholic.org/news/the-history-behind-mary-mackillops-excommunication.

183 Ibid.

184 Ibid.

185 Ibid.

186 "MacKillop Banished after Uncovering Sex Abuse," ABC News, October 6, 2010, https://www.abc.net.au/news/2010-09-25/mackillop-banished-after-uncovering-sex-abuse/2273940.

187 Sr. Maria Casey, C.S.J., "Canonisation of St. Mary MacKillop," Sisters of Saint Joseph of the Sacred Heart, October 17, 2020, https://www.sosj.org.au/canonisation-of-st-mary-mackillop/.

188 "Australians in Rome Cheer Canonization of 'Outback Saint' Mary MacKillop," Catholic News Agency, October 17, 2010, https://www.catholicnewsagency.com/news/21184/australians-in-rome-cheer-canonization-of-outback-saint-mary-mackillop.

Chapter 10: The Persecution of St. Padre Pio

189 Padre Pio, *Words of Light* (Brewster, MA: Paraclete Press, 1991), 17.

190 Bernard C. Ruffin, *Padre Pio: The True Story*, rev. and exp. 3rd ed. (Huntington, IN: Our Sunday Visitor, 2018), 23.

191 Cleonice Morcaldi, *La Mia Vita Vicino A Padre Pio: Diario Intimo Spirituale* (Rome: Edizioni Dehoniane, n.d.), 88

192 Padre Pio da Pietrelcina, *Epistolario*, vol. 2, *Corrispondenza con I Dirrettori Spirituali, 1910–1922* (San Giovanni Rotondo [FG], Italy: Convento Santa Maria delle Grazie, 1995), 95, https://docplayer.it/23260886-Padre-pio-da-pietrelcina-epistolario-primo-corrispondenza-con-la-nobildonna-raffae-lina-cerase.html.

193 Ruffin, *Padre Pio*, 32, 81–84, 98.

194 Padre Pio, *Epistolario*, vol. 1, 759–760.

195 Padre Pio, *Words of Light*, 88–89

196 Ibid., 96–97.

197 Padre Pio, *Epistolario*, vol. 1, 103.

198 Ibid., 640.

199 Gennaro Preziuso, *The Life of Padre Pio: Between the Altar and the Confes-sional*, trans. and ed. Jordan Aumann (New York: Alba House, 2000), 109.

200 Padre Pio, *Epistolario*, vol. 1, 136

201 Ibid., 640,

202 Ruffin, *Padre Pio*, 139.

203 Francesco Castelli, *Padre Pio e il Sant'Uffizio, 1918–1939: fatti, protagonisti, documenti inedita* (Rome: Studium, 2011), 47.

204 Ibid., 181.

205 "Saint Pio of Pietrelcina," *Malta Independent*, September 22, 2008, https://www.independent.com.mt/articles/2007-09-22/newspaper-opinions/Saint-Pio-Of-Pietrelcina-197093.

206 Ruffin, *Padre Pio*, 183–184.

207 Francesco Castelli, *Padre Pio Under Investigation: The Secret Vatican Files* (San Francisco: Ignatius Press, 2011), 116–117.

208 Ruffin, *Padre Pio*, 184–186.

209 Ibid., 187.

210 Castelli, *Padre Pio Under Investigation*, 15.

211 Ibid., 90.

212 Ibid., 28.

213 Ibid., 69, 153, 174, 229, 239.

214 Castelli, *Padre Pio e il Sant'Uffizio*, 116.

215 Ruffin, *Padre Pio*, 213–214.

216 Ibid., 398, 413.

217 Ibid., 214.

218 Padre Pio da Pietrelcina, *Epistolario*, vol. 4: *Corrispondenza con Diverse Catego-rie di Persone* (San Giovanni Rotondo (FG), Italy: Convento Santa Maria delle Grazie, 1998), 218, https://docplayer.it/10595650-Padre-pio-da-pietrelcina-epistolario-quarto-corrispondenza-con-diverse-categorie-di-persone.html.

219 Renzo Allegri, *Padre Pio: A Man of Hope*, trans. Gary Seromik (Cincinnati: Franciscan Media, 2019); see also Ruffin, *Padre Pio*, 219.

220 Guiseppe Pagnossin, *Il Calvario de Padre Pio*, vol. 1 (Padua: Tipografia M. Suman, 1978), 252, 260.

221 Castelli, *Padre Pio e il Sant'Uffizio*, 127.

222 Pagnossin, *Il Calvario*, 225.

223 Padre Pio da Pietrelcina, *Epistolario*, vol. 4, 424.

224 Ruffin, *Padre Pio*, 246.

225 Ibid., 248–249.

226 Padre Pio da Pietrelcina, *Epistolario*, vol. 4, 35–36.

227 Ruffin, *Padre Pio*, 250.

228 Ibid., 205–257.

229 Castelli, *Padre Pio e il Sant'Uffizio*, 161.

230   Pagnossin, *Il Calvario*, 605.

231   Ruffin, *Padre Pio*, 261.

232   Padre Pio da Pietrelcina, *Epistolario*, vol. 4, 311, 313.

233   Ruffin, *Padre Pio*, 266–267.

234   Ibid., 401–402.

235   Ibid., 403–406.

236   Ibid., 430.

237   Padre Pio, *Words of Light*, 20.

238   Ruffin, *Padre Pio*, 412–413.

239   Pagnossin, *Il Calvario*, vol. 2, 99.

240   Ibid, 416–418.

241   Ibid., 421.

242   Ibid., 422–423.

243   Fr. Gabriele Amorth, *Padre Pio: Stories and Memories of My Mentor and Friend* (San Francisco: Ignatius Press, 2021), 109.

244   Padre Pio da Pietrelcina, *Epistolario*, vol. 4, 314–315.

245   Amorth, *Padre Pio*, 111.

246   Ibid., 110.

247   Ruffin, *Padre Pio*, 430.

248   Amorth, *Padre Pio*, 112.

249   Ibid., 136.

250   "Padre Pio's Mass," EWTN, https://www.ewtn.com/catholicism/library/padre-pios-mass-13830; Amorth, *Padre Pio*, 73–75; Ruffin, *Padre Pio*, 295, 332–333; Morcaldi, *La Mia Vita Vicino A Padre Pio*, 32.

251   Padre Pio da Pietrelcina, *Epistolario*, vol. 4, 264–265.

252   Ruffin, *Padre Pio*, 188.

253   Amorth, *Padre Pio*, 55.

254   Padre Pio, *Words of Light*, 79, 83.

CHAPTER 11: THE PERSECUTION OF VEN. FULTON SHEEN

255   Fulton J. Sheen, *Treasure in Clay: The Autobiography of Fulton J. Sheen* (New York: Image/Doubleday, 2008), 328. Unless otherwise indicated, all quotations and details in this chapter rely on this source or Thomas C Reeves, *America's Bishop: The Life and Times of Fulton J. Sheen* (New York: Encounter Books, 2001).

256   Michael O'Neill, " 'They Might Be Saints' — Archbishop Fulton J. Sheen," *National Catholic Register*, January 13, 2022, https://www.ncregister.com/blog/archbishop-sheen-they-might-be-saints.

257   "Life is Worth Living," Internet Movie Database, https://www.imdb.com/title/tt0211820/.

258   "Bishop Fulton Sheen, April 14, 1952," *Time* Covers, http://content.time.com/time/covers/0,16641,19520414,00.html.

259   Marie Brenner, "Fast and Luce," May 28, 2014 (from March 1988 issue), https://www.vanityfair.com/news/1988/03/clare-boothe-luce-profile.

260   "People: July 22, 1966," *Time*, https://content.time.com/time/subscriber/article/0,33009,836088,00.html.

261   "Watch Life Is Worth Living," Fulton J. Sheen Company, https://www.bishopsheen.com/pages/watch-life-is-worth-living.

262   Joseph N. Hanneman, "Fulton Sheen's Intense Life of Holiness Worthy of Sainthood, Biographer Writes," Catholic World Report, March 13, 2015, https://www.catholicworldreport.com/2015/03/13/fulton-sheens-intense-life-of-holiness-worthy-of-sainthood-biographer-writes/.

263   "Vatican Theologians Approve Fulton Sheen Miracle," Catholic University of America, June 18, 2014, https://communications.catholic.edu/news/2014/06/Sheen-miracle-2.html.

264   Tim Drake, "Archbishop Fulton J. Sheen Declared 'Venerable,'" *National Catholic Register*, June 29, 2012, https://www.ncregister.com/news/archbishop-fulton-j-sheen-declared-venerable.

Conclusion: To Follow Bad Shepherds

265   Aquinas, *Summa Theologica* II–II, q. 104.

266   Ibid., art. 5.

267   St. Augustine, *De Verb. Dom.*, viii, as cited in Aquinas, *Summa Theologica* II–II, q. 104, art. 5.

268   Aquinas, *Summa Theologica* II–II, q. 104, art. 5.

269   Francis De Sales, *Introduction to the Devout Life* (San Francisco: Ignatius Press/Lighthouse Catholic Media, 2015), 97.

270   *Catechism of the Catholic Church,* Glossary, p. 895.

271   Aquinas, *Summa Theologica* II–II, q. 33, art. 4.

272   Pope Innocent III, *Between God & Man: Six Sermons on the Priestly Office*, trans. Corinne J. Vause and Frank C. Gardiner (Washington, D.C.: The Catholic University of America Press, 2004), 21–22.

273   St. Robert Bellarmine, *On the Roman Pontiff*, trans. Ryan Grant (Post Falls, ID: Mediatrix Press, 2016), 310.

274   St. Francis de Sales, *The Catholic Controversy*, trans. Rev. Henry Benedict Macksey, O.S.B. (Charlotte, NC: TAN Books, 1989), 225–226.

275   John C. Olin, ed., *The Catholic Reformation: Savonarola to Ignatius Loyola* (New York: Fordham University Press, 1992), 125.

276   Padre Pio da Pietrelcina, *Epistolario*, vol. 4, 311, 313.

277   St. Augustine, *True Religion*, trans. Edmund Hill, O.P., in *On Christian Belief*, ed. Boniface Ramsey (Hyde Park, NY: New City Press, 2005), 36–37.

About the Authors

ALEC TORRES IS A former speechwriter for President Donald Trump and House Speaker Kevin McCarthy and has ghostwritten for cabinet secretaries, ambassadors, national media personalities, and business leaders. He is the co-founder of Allograph, a strategic writing, communications, and design firm. Today, Alec lives with his wife, children, and dogs in Texas.

JOSHUA CHARLES IS A former White House speechwriter for Vice President Mike Pence, a number-one *New York Times* best-selling author, a historian, a columnist, a writer, a public speaker, and a ghostwriter for Fortune 500 CEOs, political leaders, and more. He is a scholar at the Faith and Liberty Discovery Center in Philadelphia, a PragerU lecturer, and the Pope Leo XIII Fellow of Catholic Teaching on Capitalism, Socialism, and Communism at St. Thomas University in Miami, Florida. He lives in California.

Sophia Institute

SOPHIA INSTITUTE IS A nonprofit institution that seeks to nurture the spiritual, moral, and cultural life of souls and to spread the gospel of Christ in conformity with the authentic teachings of the Roman Catholic Church.

Sophia Institute Press fulfills this mission by offering translations, reprints, and new publications that afford readers a rich source of the enduring wisdom of mankind.

Sophia Institute also operates the popular online resource CatholicExchange.com. *Catholic Exchange* provides world news from a Catholic perspective as well as daily devotionals and articles that will help readers to grow in holiness and live a life consistent with the teachings of the Church.

In 2013, Sophia Institute launched Sophia Institute for Teachers to renew and rebuild Catholic culture through service to Catholic education. With the goal of nurturing the spiritual, moral, and cultural life of souls, and an abiding respect for the role and work of teachers, we strive to provide materials and programs that are at once enlightening to the mind and ennobling to the heart; faithful and complete, as well as useful and practical.

Sophia Institute gratefully recognizes the Solidarity Association for preserving and encouraging the growth of our apostolate over the course of many years. Without their generous and timely support, this book would not be in your hands.

www.SophiaInstitute.com
www.CatholicExchange.com
www.SophiaInstituteforTeachers.org

Sophia Institute Press is a registered trademark of Sophia Institute.
Sophia Institute is a tax-exempt institution as defined by the
Internal Revenue Code, Section 501(c)(3). Tax ID 22-2548708.